Story

YOUR PERSONAL COMPUTER CAN MAKE YOU RICH IN STOCKS AND COMMODITIES

CURTIS M. ARNOLD

WEISS RESEARCH, INC.
2000 Palm Beach Lakes Boulevard • Suite 200
West Palm Beach, Florida 33409

Acknowledgments

I would like to thank my editor and publisher, Martin D. Weiss, without whose encouragement and support this book would not have been possible. Dan Derby deserves credit for coding the programs, structuring the necessary files and writing the program documentation. Martina Schwenk and Leslie Underwood—along with the entire Weiss Reserach staff—were invaluable not only for their work on the illustrations and word processing but also for coordinating the numerous details of publication.

Copyright © 1984 by Weiss Research, Inc.

ISBN -09613048-0-4
Library of Congress Catalog Card Number 83-S1 498

Software by Daniel Derby
Book & cover design by LaVonne Hyde

MANUFACTURED IN THE UNITED STATES OF AMERICA

TABLE OF CONTENTS

PROGRAMS

MONETARY INDICATORS

MISCELLANEOUS INDICATORS

UTILITY

INTRODUCTION

 The title of this book promises a lot—that you can amass considerable wealth by applying your computer and the principles you will learn here to the stock and commodity markets.

I don't believe this is an overstatement. With basic market principles and the signals dictated by your computer, you can make profits of over 50% a year which, if accomplished consistently for five years, would transform a $10,000 investment into more than $75,000. If you consider that the markets now offer the potential for even greater rewards when you hit a "big winner," you will realize that the opportunities to "get rich" in stocks or commodities are virtually unlimited.

There has never been a better time than today to make a fortune in the stock and commodity markets. This is because of three factors:

(1) *The variety and number of instruments traded*: You have literally thousands of stocks and hundreds of commodities from which to choose.

(2) *Leverage*: This allows you to control a large amount of stock or a commodity with only a small margin deposit. By using options in the stock market and the awesome leverage available in the commodity markets to trade gold, silver, oil, T-bills, T-bonds, stock indexes and scores of commodities, you can multiply your investment as much as 10 or even 100 fold in one trade alone.

(3) *Volatility*: Markets become volatile when the future is uncertain. Throughout the 1980s, as uncertainty reigns on the economic, political and international fronts, once calm and tranquil markets have been transformed into stormy and volatile arenas with large and very fast

price swings. Volatile markets are most dangerous and risky. But they also offer the greatest opportunities. They are the markets where old fortunes are lost and new fortunes made.

This brings us to our "special advantage"—the computer. We are living in a highly sophisticated information age. And the new fortunes will be made by the "informed" people; while the uninformed will receive the necessary information "too late" and will be left behind. Moreover, when these data are broadcast to them through secondary sources, they will not know how to interpret them; they will have no predefined standards which tell them, at a glance, when and what to buy or sell. Instead, their investment decisions will be subject to the decision-making tools of yesterday—emotions, rumors, tips and brokers' opinions.

You, on the other hand, will be cool and collected, lying in wait for the right opportunity. Your computer will monitor and scan hundreds of markets and, when the time is right, it will give you your signal to act. It won't ask for the opinion of your broker, relatives or friends. It won't debate with you for long hours about some esoteric fine point of economic theory. It will give it to you straight.

Then the ball is in your court. Whether you have the courage to act on these signals is up to you. Sounds easy, right? But it isn't. Many times I have regretfully ignored signals from my computer because of my personal bias toward a particular market and the opinions of fellow analysts. Shut out other opinions! Reduce your ego involvement! Listen to your computer! Your performance in the markets will improve dramatically.

Your computer is neither a gung-ho optimist that always looks for prices to go up (a "bull") nor a fanatic pessimist that lies in wait for the day when prices go down (a "bear"). It has neither a "bullish" nor "bearish" bias.

Therefore, if it gives you a buy signal, you can make money by buying the stock or commodity at a low price and selling it at a higher price. And if it gives you a sell signal, you can make an equal amount of money by *selling short*—in effect, borrowing the stock, selling it at a high price, waiting for it to fall, buying it back at the lower price and collecting the difference.

Because this book combines a knowledge of two fields—investments and computers—there are two areas where learning can take place. Some readers may have a good background in the stock and commodity markets but have never used a computer before. Others may own a computer but have never traded the markets. Still others may have a limited knowledge of both fields. I am attempting to address the needs of all readers by taking you on a straight course from zero knowledge to mastery of the computerized tools that can make you successful in the markets. This book is *not* designed to make you a computer expert or teach you *everything* there is to know about the stock and commodity markets. So I would encourage you to continue learning in both fields.

As in any learning experience, of course, you can follow either a small- or large-budget approach; and this is particularly true about how you use this book. If you have a limited budget, you can get all the data manually from your newspaper as described on page 198, use only the free programs provided in the back of this book and stick with limited-risk, low-cost investments. If you have more money to spend, you may wish to subscribe to the data sources referenced in chapter two, purchase some of the more sophisticated programs available today and take considerably greater risks in the markets. The choice is entirely yours.

1

GETTING STARTED:
HARDWARE, SOFTWARE & DATABASES

1

SELECTING HARDWARE

If you already own a computer you may wish to skip this chapter but you might want to skim it lightly to be sure you have all the necessary hardware (equipment) to do the job. There are many different makes and models of microcomputers on the market; but the key is to select a microcomputer for which a lot of the good software (programs) is being written.

If we were considering a business application such as a computer to run a general ledger, we would not want to buy the hardware before ascertaining that a good general ledger package was available to run on our machine. Likewise, since we seek to run stock and commodity applications, we must select a computer for which this specific software is designed.

There seems to be a good deal of investment software available for the Apple, Radio Shack's TRS-80, and the IBM Personal Computer. You could probably also find investment software for any microcomputer with a CPM operating system. But the Apple, Radio Shack's TRS-80 and IBM Personal Computer are unquestionably dominating the field at this time. You will probably not be limited in your software selection if you own one of these computers. Personally, I own an Apple II Plus and an IBM PC, so much of the software discussed in this book is Apple or IBM dependent. But if you own another type of computer, similar packages are available and are listed in the Appendix. Here's what you will need:

MEMORY: Assuming you are going to be using an Apple II or an IBM PC, you will need at least 48,000 characters or "bytes" of memory capacity (48K), although 64K is now standard on most new models.

MONITOR: This is the CRT (TV-like screen) that sits on top of your computer. Selecting your monitor is a question of personal taste, but I would recommend you stay away from ordinary TV screens in that they usually do not provide the necessary resolution or fine detail needed for producing readable graphs.

DISK DRIVES: Along with your computer and monitor, you will need at least one floppy disk drive (Computrac software requires two drives). Each floppy disk can hold approximately 150,000 characters on a side, and it is on these disks that you will store your data and all your programs. With your computer, monitor and disk drives, you now have your brain, your window to it, and your library.

PRINTER: Next, you will need a graphics printer. It isn't *absolutely* necessary but it sure comes in handy. There is a wide variety of graphics printers on the market to choose from and, accordingly, they vary quite a bit in price depending on their speed, quietness and resolution. Reliability is the most important thing to look for in a printer, so select a model that has a reputation for being a good "workhorse." Your computer dealer can help you select one that is: (a) compatible with your computer, (b) supported by your stock or commodity analysis program and (c) within your price range.

MODEM: At this point, your computer system is completely operational and self-sufficient in that it can process data which you type into it, such as stock or commodity quotes from your daily newspaper. But it would make life a lot easier if your computer had the capability of receiving all these data from a distant "database"—from another much larger computer that holds all the latest information which you could use, as well as all the past histories you wish to analyze. In order for your computer to access the larger computer's database, the two must have the ability to "talk" to each other through a small piece of hardware called a "modem."

When selecting a modem, you will probably hear the term "baud rate." This refers to the speed at which information is transmitted. A 300 BPS (i.e. bits per second) baud rate will be adequate for your purposes. You may also wish to select a modem with an automatic dialing feature. This allows you to program your computer to automatically dial the phone number of the database which you wish to access.

Your computer system is now complete. You have everything you need to access data from other databases, create your own library, process information and create charts and reports. The world is literally at your fingertips! Your completed system should now look something like figure 1-1:

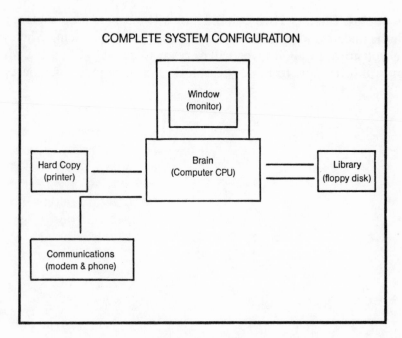

Figure 1-1

With the purchase of your computer, you also receive an "operating system," the Basic language, and various other "utilities." The operating system is the brain that controls your computer. You should become familiar with its functions by learning how to set up or "initialize" disks, create and save files, load the computer and run programs, etc. You may also wish to learn how to write your own programs in one of the easier-to-use computer languages, "Basic." You will find classes offered at both your local computer stores and colleges.

For the purposes of this book, however, you will *not* need to know how to write programs; there is a host of sophisticated "user friendly" software packages commercially available to allow you to analyze the stock and commodity markets. Remember, your computer is a tool—a means to an end. What counts is how you apply that tool. This is where your imagination and creativity come into play. So unless you are a computer buff, don't get bogged down in the complexities of the equipment or programming.

As we close Chapter 1, you should have all your hardware in place and a basic understanding of how to use your operating system. When you feel you are at this point, you will be ready to go on to Chapter 2 where you will learn how to build your stock and commodity databases.

2

BUILDING STOCK AND COMMODITY DATABASES

Accurate and up-to-date information is the basic building block for any computer analysis. But how much do you need? Where do you get it? Once you have it, how do you keep it in an organized, easily accessible form?

First, you must decide whether you wish to follow stocks or commodities, or both. If you follow both, you may need to subscribe to two different databases. Your selection of a database may depend on what part of the country you live in, hours of operation, stock issues or commodity contracts covered and the cost. As new database companies are coming online at an increasing pace, your broker or computer dealer would best be able to direct you to the most appropriate source.

DAILY UPDATES: Your next step will be to keep it up to date. In the evening, after the markets have closed, your computer will dial the database to which you subscribe and collect the day's data for the stocks and commodities that you follow. Your "daily update program" will then store this information or "post it to disk."

RECOMMENDED STOCK-MARKET DATABASE: For my stock-market data, I subscribe to Interactive Data Corporation's IDC-PRICE in Waltham, Massachusetts. This database includes information on more than 43,000 securities and options. Also available is information on mutual funds, market indices and key technical market indicators such as:

• The number of new highs and lows

• The number of issues which advanced, declined and remained unchanged

• Upside/downside volume on a daily and weekly basis

RECOMMENDED COMMODITY DATABASE: For my commodity
collection, I use Commodity Systems, Inc. of Boca Raton, Florida. They
have an extensive database and have price information on practically
every commodity that you would ever want to trade. For each commodity
contract, they transmit the following pieces of information daily.

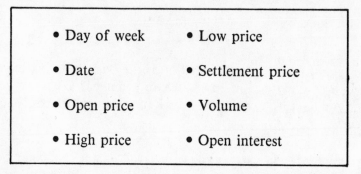

• Day of week	• Low price
• Date	• Settlement price
• Open price	• Volume
• High price	• Open interest

In addition, Commodity Systems, Inc. offers a unique proprietary contract called the **PERPETUAL CONTRACT**—a weighted average of all
contract months of each commodity. If you are not a commodity trader
now, this may sound a little like Greek. Don't be too concerned. But
if you are interested in commodities, I would recommend this contract
because it makes analysis much easier.

The actual procedure of setting up your data collection process is not
difficult. First, depending on the database, you may have to fill out a
form on which you select the specific stock issues or commodity contracts you want and how much historical data you would like to collect
on each one. Other databases keep their data on-line and you can collect just what you want at the time. Their computer knows what you
are doing and bills you accordingly.

You may collect your data via a direct long-distance call, or you can
avoid long-distance charges if you use a local number which then hooks
into the database through Telenet or Tymnet. There is a place for you
to record these telephone numbers in your system. Then, when you in-
struct your computer to "collect data" (you merely select this command
from a "menu" or list of commands on your screen), the program
automatically dials the database and begins the collection process.

HISTORICAL DATA: Next, you must have background information on the stock and commodity prices that you intend to follow. This will allow you to test your theories and trading systems on previous market data. How much historical data you obtain becomes a function of your budget and whether you wish to specialize in just a few stocks and commodities or diversify with a great many. Regardless, two years of daily historical data should be considered a minimum for testing purposes.

There are three ways you can build your historical databases:

(1) You can manually input the information from a book or from daily newspapers. This is obviously the most time consuming and requires thorough double-checking for accuracy. However, it is occasionally necessary if you wish to study a certain variable or stock which is so unusual that it is unavailable from any of the standard databases.

(2) You can order a selected amount of historical data for a stock or commodity and have it sent to you on diskettes by the database company. This is especially handy when you're getting started and have to order long histories for many different commodities or stocks to build your initial database. Make sure, however, the diskettes are compatible with your computer system.

(3) Finally, you can receive the data through the modem. Your 300 baud modem will be painstakingly slow for a massive amount of historical data, but it is the ideal medium for daily updates. However, I do use it for some historical data when I can't wait for a diskette to come in the mail.

In order to limit your cost, you should be deciding as early as possible which stocks or commodities you are going to follow. If you are a beginner, you should talk to a broker and familiarize yourself with some of the basic mechanisms of trading—how to place your orders, trading houses, required margins, etc. Take advantage of the free literature your brokerage house makes available. And, perhaps most important, make sure you are completely aware of the potential risks involved.

Before you go out and buy any hardware or subscribe to any databases, however, you will have to select the right software package to use them.

3

SELECTING SOFTWARE

Unless you are a super-pro at computer programming, you will want to purchase a software package to help you in analyzing the market. In fact, even if you are an expert programmer, you will still want such a package. You could not possibly duplicate—without considerable time and effort— some of the analytical tools that took a team of full-time professionals years to develop. So why reinvent the wheel? Remember, the computer—including both the hardware and software—is merely a "tool" and, for our purposes, a means to an end.

By the time you read this book, software vendors offering analytical programs for trading the markets will be proliferating. Therefore, I recommend you shop around to find the one which best suits your needs and budget (see Appendix B). I can tell you that I currently use Computrac software developed by the Technical Analysis Group in New Orleans, Louisiana.

Computrac

The Computrac package is so flexible and so extensive it is literally mind-boggling. It was designed to be run on the Apple II or Apple II Plus computer and has recently been made compatible with the IBM Personal Computer. The Computrac programs allow you to automatically collect, store, analyze, chart and print out market data for both stocks and commodities. The programs are divided into four major sections or "subsystems," each with their own list of choices or "menu."

The four major subsystems are designated as "utility," "technical analysis," "communications," and "equity subsystem." Regardless of the software package you purchase, even if it is not Computrac, the same functions will exist, although possibly designated by different names. For that reason, we will take the time to review the individual functions so that you may develop an understanding of how a "total system" operates.

THE UTILITY contains all the routines which will allow you to set up and maintain your database. Examples of these routines would be the ability to set up or "initialize" a disk, create a file, review and print out a file on your printer.

TECHNICAL ANALYSIS is a collection of routines allowing you to chart and print the results of trading systems and technical indicators. This is the heart of the system and offers some of the most advanced tools of technical analysis. Some of the "studies" available at this time include spreads, oscillators, demand index, overbought/oversold, relative strength, parabolic, regression, point and figure, moving averages, detrend and momentum—many of which will be explained in later chapters. In addition, a host of "advance/decline" studies are available exclusively for the stock market.

COMMUNICATIONS is the section containing all the programs necessary for the acquisition of commodity data from Commodity Systems, Inc., and stock data from Interactive Data Corporation.

At the time of this writing, Computrac is only compatible with the databases cited in the previous chapter.

THE EQUITY SUBSYSTEM is an integrated bookkeeping system which prints reports showing your current positions and equity, as well as profits and losses. It is very handy for tracking your performance.

In summary, when selecting your software package, it should have the ability to: Communicate with a database and collect data, maintain the database through standard "service routines," analyze the data through the use of technical analysis routines and report your current positions.

PART

2

TECHNICAL ANALYSIS

4

INTRODUCTION TO

TECHNICAL ANALYSIS AND CHARTING

There are essentially two methods of investing or speculating in markets. You can use external or "fundamental" information such as the profit outlook of an individual company, overall economic forecasts or the potential supply and demand of a particular commodity.

Or you can use strictly internal or "technical" information which ignores the fundamentals and focuses instead upon the actual patterns in the price movements and the actual buying and selling in the marketplace. The advantages of the technical analysis are very clear:

(1) Unless you have a very sophisticated and accurate forecasting model (even the largest computer models in the world—at Brookings Institute, Chase Econometrics or the Federal Reserve Board—are notorious for their inaccuracies) or unless you subscribe to the newsletter of a very astute forecaster, by the time you receive the information, most other investors have also received it and have reacted accordingly, pushing the price up or down. In other words, the fundamental information is almost invariably *already* reflected in the market.

(2) There are so many contradictory fundamentals impacting the market at any one time and so many "structural changes" in how these fundamental factors interact that it is often impossible to know how to weigh them. Again, this process of evaluation is all done by the marketplace itself and reflected in the price.

(3) Most important, your computer can readily zero in on technical analysis and make cold and unbiased judgments; whereas fundamental information would normally require much more extensive interpretation on your part.

When you stop and think about this, it will become clear. You can't possibly know more about the value of a company's stock than its own board of directors. Likewise, in the commodity markets, you will never know more about crop conditions or the supply and demand factors at work on a certain commodity than the actual professionals that work in that industry. Fortunately, however, you don't have to.

Hundreds of years of price charts have shown us one basic truth—*prices move in trends*. A trend indicates there exists an inequality between the forces of supply and demand. Such changes in the forces of supply and demand are usually readily identifiable by the action of the market itself as displayed in the prices. Certain patterns or formations which appear on the charts have a meaning and can be interpreted in terms of probable future trend development.

Charts are the working tools of the technical analyst. Until very recently, most charting was done manually. At best, you could subscribe to a chartmaking service (of which there are many excellent ones). They produce daily charts which are mailed to you weekly. You then put in the prices each day until your new chartbook arrives the following week—no problem as long as you are not trying to follow too many stocks and commodities. If you are, however, it could be quite a time consuming job. Now, however, your computer will do all this work for you.

Aside from speed, your computer offers you another advantage in charting—flexibility. When you are dependent upon a chart service, you must see the market from the perspective which they arbitrarily select. Your computer, on the other hand, allows you to control the amount of history you wish to view. You may change the spacing between days. You may look at the data as daily, weekly or monthly. You have the ability to magnify selected portions of the chart. The following examples — representing the same general period for the Dow Jones Industrial Average—show how identical price patterns may be viewed through different perspectives using the graphical capabilities of your computer.

Figure 4-1 is a simple high-low chart packed tightly with *no* space between each day's price.

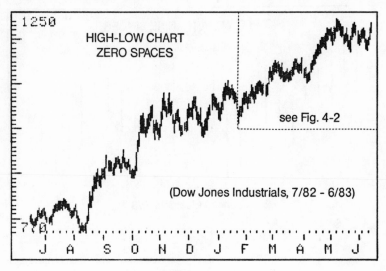

Figure 4-1

But notice in figure 4-2 how the pattern is clarified by adding one space between each day's price, although now only half of the time span fits on the page.

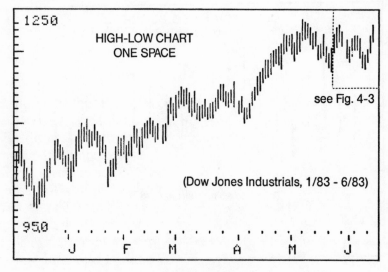

Figure 4-2

Figure 4-3 provides an entirely different perspective as nine spaces are added between each day's price.

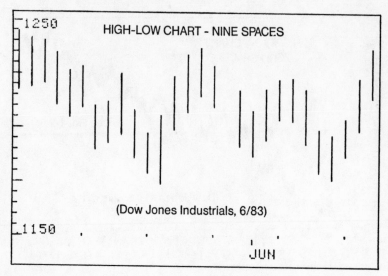

Figure 4-3

Figure 4-4 adds two additional elements of information—the opening and closing price for each day.

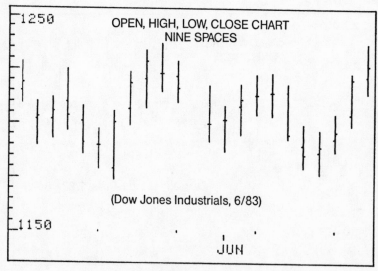

Figure 4-4

Figure 4-5 is a "close only" chart—one continuous line connecting each day's close. It is an extremely valuable analytical tool rarely offered by chart services.

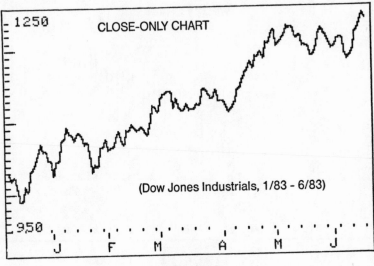

Figure 4-5

In figure 4-6, we adjust our scales so as to make the price pattern appear flatter, still another advantage of your computerized charting.

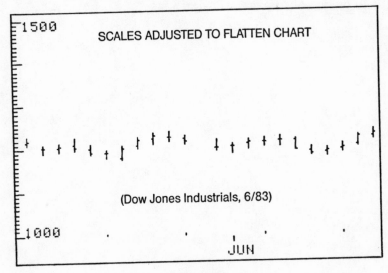

Figure 4-6

You can view a much broader time perspective in figure 4-7 which uses data in weekly—rather than daily—form.

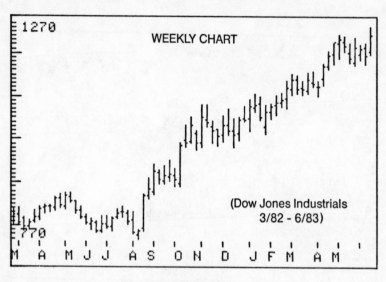

FIGURE 4-7

These are only a few of the myriad of possibilities. The charts themselves, however, are not the goal. Rather, they are simply a handy device for revealing to you—at a glance—critical trends and chart patterns which will help guide your investment decisions.

CHAPTER

5

TRENDS AND TRENDLINES

Prices move in trends because of an imbalance between supply and demand. When the supply of a stock or commodity is greater than the
demand, the trend will be down as there are more sellers than buyers;
when demand exceeds supply, the trend will be up as buyers "bid up"
the price; and if the forces of supply and demand are nearly equal, the
market will move sideways in what is called a "trading range." Eventually, new information will enter the market and the market will begin
to trend again either up or down, depending on whether the new information is taken as positive or negative.

Remember, you can profit in **both** an *uptrend* or a *downtrend* by *buying* or *selling short*—selling borrowed stocks which you hope to buy back
later at a lower price. When you buy, it is said you are "going long"
and you "are long" or "stay long" until you sell out. When you sell
short, the expressions used are "go short," "be short" or "stay short."
A major uptrend is a "bull market" and an opportunity to profit by
being "bullish." A major downtrend is a "bear market" so you will
want to stay "bearish." The key to trend analysis, of course, is to determine *when the pattern will change* so that you can shift in time from
bearish to bullish or vice-versa.

Trends which are very brief are called *minor* trends; those lasting a few
weeks are known as *intermediate* trends; and trends lasting for a period
of months are *major* trends.

TRENDLINES will help you determine what trend is in force. If a market
is moving up, you draw a line connecting each successively higher bottom. As long as the market remains on or above this line, the uptrend
is in force. Conversely, in a downtrend, you would draw a line connec-

21

ting each successively lower top. As long as prices remain on or below
this line, the downtrend is in force:

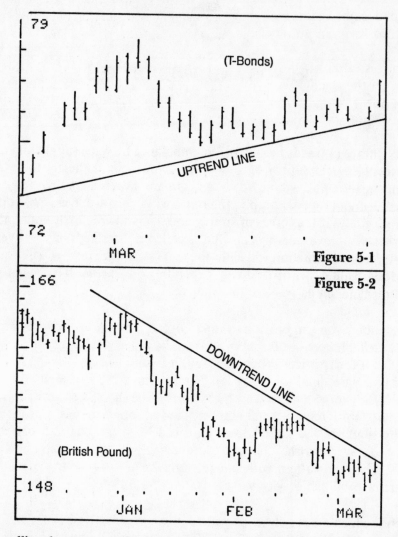

Figure 5-1

Figure 5-2

Trendline theory states that once a trendline is penetrated, the trend which
was previously in force is reversed. Thus, if an uptrend line is penetrated,
it is a signal to sell; and if a downtrend line is penetrated, it is a signal
to buy. But there is still more to know about trendlines.

Let's say your downtrend line has just been decisively broken and you
now believe we are starting a new uptrend. You can't draw a new up-

trend line yet because you only have one bottom. You must wait until prices move higher for about a week, then react downward for a couple of days, and later start moving higher again. This will give you a second, somewhat higher bottom which you can connect to the first bottom to form an uptrend line. So far, so good.

If prices, after moving higher, react downward and form a third bottom on the trendline, the trendline then becomes more valid. We say that prices "tested" the trendline and it "held." The longer this trendline remains intact, the more authority it will have.

You will find that very steep trendlines are not very authoritative in that they will often be broken by a brief sideways movement or "consolidation," after which prices shoot up again. It is the trendlines with the gentler slope—either upward or downward—that usually offer more technical significance.

In sum, factors to consider in weighing the validity of a trendline include: (a) number of bottoms (or tops) that have formed on or near the trendline, (b) the overall duration of the trendline and (c) the steepness of the angle.

Getting back to our example, what if the market accelerates and a third bottom is formed way above our trendline? Now where is the real trend?

We may have to wait until the fourth bottom forms before we know for sure. Until then, it would be a good idea to draw in two trendlines, A and B:

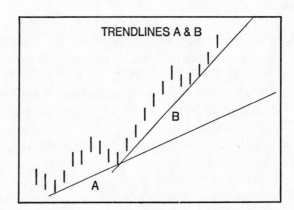

Figure 5-3

FAN LINES. When a market drops sharply, you will of course have a steep downtrend line. Often this trendline will be broken by a sharp rally, at which point a new trendline must be drawn. At a later date, this second trendline might be broken by a rally and a third trendline would need to be drawn. Such lines are known as "fan lines."

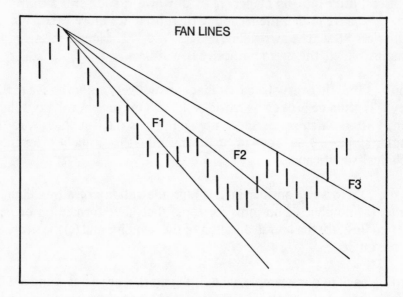

Figure 5-4

The rule is that when the third fan line has been broken, the trend has changed to the upside. In rising markets, this rule can also be applied in reverse.

VALID PENETRATIONS. As stated earlier, a penetration of an up-trend line is a signal to sell; and a penetration of a downtrend line is a signal to buy. But let's not forget that charting is an art and not a science. Therefore, we must appraise the validity of the penetration. Here are a few questions to ask when a penetration occurs:

Was penetration by just a small amount? If so, it remains suspect and we must look at other factors.

Did the price actually *close* below the trendline or was it merely the low of the day which broke the trend, an event which we call penetration on an "intraday basis"? An intraday break often is not sufficient evidence to confirm a change in trend; and even the close itself should be *significantly* below the trendline.

Did *volume* pick up on the day in question? If so, there is a good chance the trendline break was valid. Was the break accompanied by a gap or a reversal pattern? (Gaps and reversal patterns are discussed in Chapters 7 and 9.) If so, this would also lend credence to a change in trend.

Conversely, did the penetration occur as a result of several days of sideways movement? This would look more like a test of the trendline than a penetration of it. Further movement up or down should be awaited before a conclusion is drawn.

"PULLBACKS" or "throwbacks" are very interesting phenomena that often occur after the breaking of a trendline. Here's what happens in this case: An uptrend line is broken. Prices continue lower for a few days. Then they rally back right up to the trendline again. Finally, the market proceeds to move lower. (The reverse would occur upon the breaking of a downtrend line.)

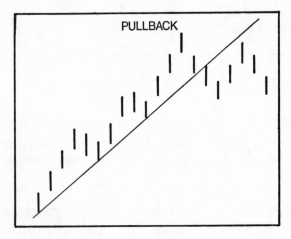

Figure 5-5

In the example illustrated in figure 5-5, you can see that the pullback actually caused prices to go higher than the price at which the trendline was broken. Thus, had you sold short when the trendline was broken, you would have a loss a few days later. One way many professionals handle this situation is to wait for the pullback before selling short. One problem here is that sometimes the pullback never materializes and you wind up selling short at much lower levels or missing the move completely. I usually recommend selling half of your positions on the trendline break and the other half on the pullback.

TREND CHANNELS. In an uptrend, you can construct a trend channel by drawing a line *parallel* to the uptrend line using as your starting point an intermediate top made between two successively higher bottoms:

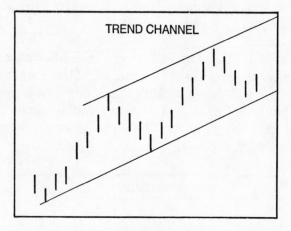

Figure 5-6

RETURN LINE. This second line is often called the "return line" since it marks the area where reaction against the prevailing trend originates. The area between the basic trendline and the return line is the "trend channel."

This return line is less reliable than the basic trendline but is valuable enough to be considered in your trading strategy. One short-term trading strategy applied by professionals in an up market is to buy on or near the basic trendline and take profits on or near the return line. Another variation on this technique is to draw a parallel line equidistant between the basic trendline and return line. Now you have an upper channel or "sell zone," and a lower channel or "buy zone" (Figure 5-7).

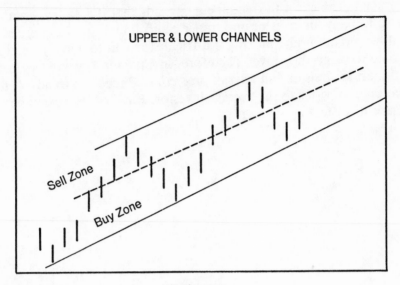

Figure 5-7

A return line can also be used to forewarn of an impending change in trend. Any time prices fail to move up to the area of the return line, you can consider the market is weakening. Use this as a warning and be on the alert for a break of the trendline the next time prices approach it:

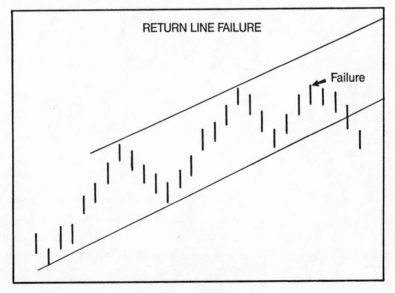

Figure 5-8

The main problem with trendline analysis is that it's too easy and, as a result, many an investor and trader can follow it, pushing prices up or down prematurely, making it difficult for you to make *your* trade in time to catch the move. Therefore, in Chapter 7, we delve deeper into chart analysis to find ways of *predicting* a break in a trend—*before* it becomes obvious to the average investor. But first let's examine one more critical factor—volume.

6

VOLUME

In the stock market, volume refers to the number of shares that change hands on a given day. In commodity markets, it refers to the number of contracts traded. Each transaction is the result of the meeting of demand, on the one hand, with supply on the other. When demand exceeds supply, prices tend to rise. Conversely, when supply exceeds demand, prices tend to fall. Therefore, volume occurring during advances is termed "demand volume"; volume occurring during declines is "supply volume."

We study volume because it can be a measure of supply and demand. There are many ways to visualize the relationship of volume and prices. Some analysts think of volume as a gauge of "market pressure." My own particular "picture" is this: Imagine you have turned on the garden hose and are pointing it skyward. You toss a plastic ball into the stream of water, and it shoots upward. But if you turn down the water pressure, what happens to the ball? It continues upward from its own momentum for a second or two, but then falls back. It can't continue higher until you increase the water pressure. Like the plastic ball, prices need increasing volume to continue higher. When prices move higher, but on diminished volume, they are likely to fall back.

The basic rules of volume analysis are as follows:

1. When prices are rising and volume is increasing, the present trend will continue, i.e., prices will continue to rise.

2. When prices are rising and volume is decreasing, the present trend is not likely to continue, i.e.,the price rise will decelerate and then turn downward.

3. When prices are falling and volume is increasing, the present trend will continue, i.e., prices will continue to fall.

4. When prices are falling and volume is decreasing, the present trend is not likely to continue, i.e., the price decline will decelerate and then prices will turn upward.

5. When volume is not rising or falling, the effect on price is neutral.

How can our computer help us to use this concept in practical applications? Let's assume XYZ stock has been in a trading range for several weeks with an average daily volume of 50,000 shares changing hands. Prices now begin to move higher and the daily volume picks up to 80,000 shares. We are justified in believing that prices will continue higher, fueled by "demand volume." Sure enough, prices do continue to move higher on strong volume over the next three weeks.

Then, in the fourth week, prices tumble and lose 30% of their previous gains. Do we sell the stock or hold? Again, the clue lies in the volume picture. We notice that during the fallback, XYZ stock has been trading only 40,000 shares per day. Therefore using our volume rules, we can surmise that this is only a *temporary* reaction. What might be actually happening in the marketplace? Any number of factors could be contributing to the fall in prices. Early buyers could be taking profits or any new buyers could be waiting for a setback before buying. All of these are natural, healthy reasons for a correction and, therefore, we have no reason to abandon our position at this point...unless we notice that volume is beginning to increase on down days.

As expected, in week 5, prices begin shooting up again on volume averaging 90,000 shares a day. Week 6 continues in the same way. Week 7 brings a reaction in prices, but again on reduced volume of 50,000 shares per day. We hold our stock. Week 8 sees prices rising again to new highs, but volume—oddly enough—is only averaging 60,000 shares per day. This is a clear-cut warning signal: Demand volume is drying up. New demand may still come into the market if favorable news events occur, but if not, prices are in danger. Remember, prices can only go up if fueled by rising demand volume, but if they fail to get that extra boost, they can fall under their own weight. As expected, prices turn down the next few days on heavy volume; we sell our stock.

The XYZ example represents only one possible scenario. What if prices have been in a sideways trading range and then begin to fall on low volume. Would we consider this move false? Not necessarily. Although prices must be accompanied by strong volume to confirm an up move, *down* moves often begin on light volume. Remember, a market can fall under its own weight; and it is important to be aware that *volume usually tends to be lighter when prices are falling than when rising.*

In the XYZ example, the last phase or "leg" of the move was on light volume. But oddly enough, tops may also be formed on *heavy* volume—a "climax" which usually occurs after a market has been moving up for a considerable amount of time.

This is a contradiction which reflects a classical problem which has puzzled technical analysts for many years and there is no complete solution. However, if you closely observe the market action it may help you determine if it is a climax or not. Typically, prices make new highs in the morning on heavy volume, but by afternoon, prices are substantially lower while volume is still heavy, producing a reversal day (see Chapter 7). This is a classic example of "distribution'—a period when previous owners of the stock are dumping their shares and taking profits, while Johnny-Come-Latelies are buying it at the top. The previous owners who have been buying for weeks have more stock to distribute than the Latelies can handle. So, supply overcomes demand, prices crash, and the new buyers are left holding the bag. Stocks are said to be "moving from strong hands to weak hands."

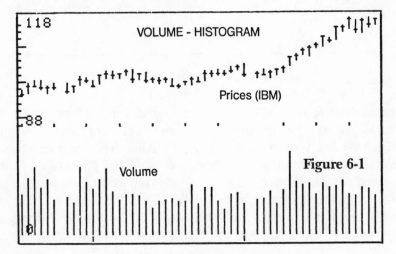

VOLUME - HISTOGRAM

Prices (IBM)

Volume

Figure 6-1

Bottoms often display quite the opposite pattern, occurring on light volume. Volume tends to dry up, indicating a lessening of supply pressure. If prices then move higher on increased volume, it is a good sign that the decline has ended.

How do we graphically represent volume? The traditional way has been in the form of a bar chart directly beneath the price chart. (Figure 6-1).

You have an advantage with your computer in that you can look at volume in many different ways (see Program #4). When looking at the actual volume itself, I prefer to chart it as a continuous line, rather than a bar chart. Notice also, I leave more space between each day's price so I can readily identify the corresponding change in volume for *each* day:

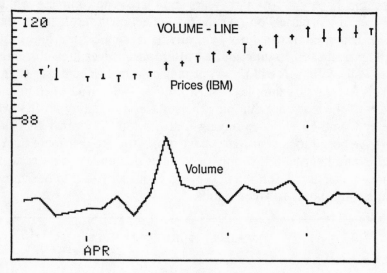

Figure 6-2

Some analysts feel that the absolute change in volume from day to day is not as important as the deviation from the current average volume. Again, by using your computer as an analytical tool, you can be way ahead of those who must rely only on commercially produced charts. Here's what I do: First, I run a 10-day moving average on volume (for more on moving averages, see Chapter 13). Then I run a continuous line of current volume on the same graph. If the current volume line is above the 10-day moving average, I know that the volume is increasing. Conversely, when the current volume is below the 10-day moving average, volume is decreasing:

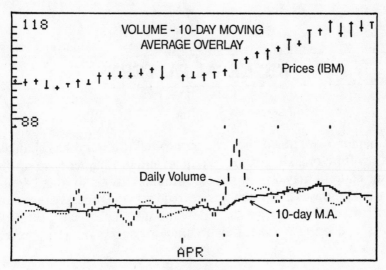

Figure 6-3

In sum, an understanding of volume patterns adds a third dimension to our analysis. Now we're ready to begin to apply these concepts to key patterns which appear on our charts.

CHAPTER

7

REVERSAL PATTERNS

In Chapter 5, we noted that one way to tell if a trend has changed is to watch for a breaking of the trendline; and in Chapter 6 we saw how volume patterns may or may not confirm this change. Further investigation would show us that when a price trend is in the process of reversal—either from up to down or from down to up—a *characteristic pattern* takes shape on the chart and becomes recognizable as a "reversal formation."

THE HEAD AND SHOULDERS TOP formation is one of the most common and also one of the most reliable of all the major reversal patterns.

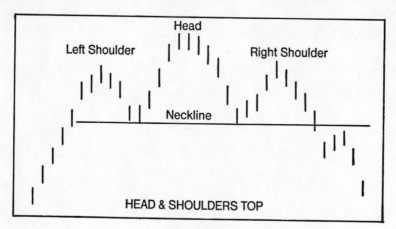

Figure 7-1

It consists of a left shoulder, a head and a right shoulder.

The left shoulder is formed usually at the end of an extensive advance during which volume is quite heavy. At the end of the left shoulder,

34

there is usually a small dip or recession which typically occurs on low volume.

The head then forms with heavy volume on the upside and with lesser volume accompanying the subsequent reaction. At this point, in order to conform to proper form, prices must come down somewhere *near* the low of the left shoulder—somewhat lower perhaps or somewhat higher but, in any case, below the top of the left shoulder.

The right shoulder is then formed by a rally on usually less volume than any previous rallies in this formation.

A neckline can now be drawn across the bottoms of the left shoulder, the head and right shoulder. A breaking of this neckline on a decline from the right shoulder is the final confirmation and completes the Head and Shoulders Top formation. This is, therefore, your signal to sell short.

A word of caution. Very often, after moving lower, prices will pull back to the neckline before continuing their descent. You may wait for this pullback to sell or use it as a point to add to your original short positions.

Most Head and Shoulders are not perfectly symmetrical. One shoulder may appear to droop. Also, the time involved in the development of each shoulder may vary, causing the structure to lose symmetry. The neckline, rather than being horizontal, may be sloping up or down. The only qualification on an up-sloping neckline is that the lowest point on the right shoulder must be appreciably lower than that of the top of the left shoulder.

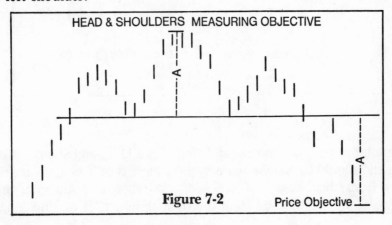

HEAD & SHOULDERS MEASURING OBJECTIVE

Figure 7-2　　　Price Objective

A Head and Shoulders formation can also be extremely useful in estimating the probable extent of the move once the neckline has been penetrated.

Here's what you do: Referring to figure 7-2, measure the distance vertically from the top of the head to the neckline. Then measure the same distance down from the point where prices penetrated the neckline (following the completion of the right shoulder). This gives you the minimum objective of how far prices should decline following the successful completion of the Head and Shoulders Top. To double check your estimate, one guideline to look at is the extent of the previous rise. If the up move preceding the Head and Shoulders Top has been small, the ensuing down move may be small as well. Thus, the extent of the previous advance should be at least as large as the objective you have estimated from the formation.

THE HEAD AND SHOULDERS BOTTOM formation is simply the inverse of a Head and Shoulders Top, and often indicates a trend reversal from down to up. The typical Head and Shoulders Bottom formation is illustrated in figure 7-3.

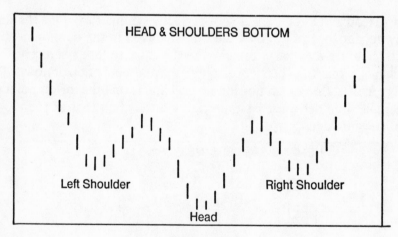

Figure 7-3

The volume pattern is somewhat different in a Head and Shoulders Bottom and should be watched carefully. Volume should pick up as prices rally from the bottom of the head and then increase even more dramatically on the rally from the right shoulder. If the breaking of the neckline is done on low volume we must be suspect of this formation. The breakout could be false, only to be followed by a retest of the lows. A high volume breakout, on the other hand, would give us good reason to believe the Head and Shoulders Bottom formation is genuine.

The only other noticeable difference in the Head and Shoulders Bottom formation is that it may sometimes appear flatter than the Head and Shoulder Top. Often the turns are more rounded. Otherwise, all the rules and measuring objectives can be applied equally well.

DOUBLE TOP FORMATIONS appear as an "M" on a chart as in figure 7-4. They are very "popular." But watch out! Many analysts often mislabel and misinterpret Double Top and Bottom formations. In any uptrend, after a reaction, each new wave up will appear to be "making" a Double Top (see figure 7-5).

But in truth, at this point there is *absolutely no evidence pointing to*

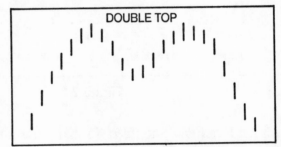

Figure 7-4

a Double Top. Nine times out of ten, the trend will remain in force and prices will simply go on to make new highs. So don't be fooled. You have no confirmation whatsoever of a Double Top until the valley has been broken as in figure 7-6.

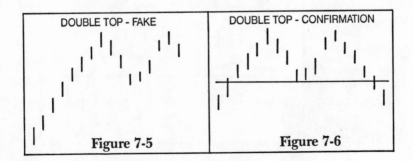

Figure 7-5   **Figure 7-6**

Volume, again, can offer a clue in the formation of this pattern. If the volume on the rise of the second peak is less than on the first peak, you have an initial indication that prices may fail to go above the previous high, turn around and go on to confirm the double Top. High volume accompanying the second rise would minimize that possibility.

Another factor to use in determining the validity of a Double Top formation is the time element. If two tops appear at the same level but quite close together in time, the chances are good that they are merely part of a consolidation area. If, on the other hand, the peaks are separated by a deep and long reaction, this is more likely a true Double Top:

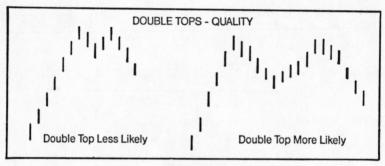

Figure 7-7

As with the Head and Shoulders formation, a pullback to the valley area is very possible. If you wish to measure the objective from the breakout point, you can simply take the distance from peak to valley and subtract from the valley to the "M" as in figure 7-8.

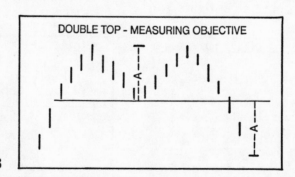

Figure 7-8

DOUBLE BOTTOMS are the inverse of Double Tops and appear on the charts as a W formation:

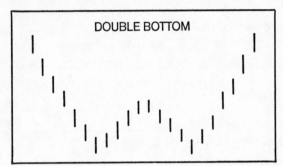

Figure 7-9

All of the rules associated with Double Top formations also apply to Double Bottoms. The volume patterns, of course, are different. A valid Double Bottom should show a marked increase in volume on the rally up from the second bottom.

TRIPLE TOPS are more rare than Double Tops. They appear on a chart similar to the pattern shown in figure 7-10.

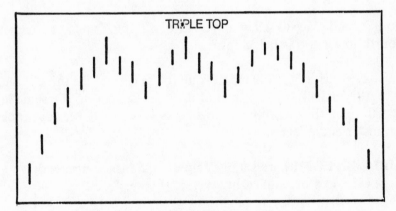

Figure 7-10

Volume is usually less on the second advance, and still less on the third. The highs need not be spaced as far apart as those which constitute a Double Top, and they need not be equally spaced. Also, the intervening valleys need not bottom out at exactly the same level; either the first or the second may be deeper. But the triple top is not confirmed until prices have broken through both valleys.

There are several different trading strategies that can be employed to take advantage of the Triple Top formation. After a Double Top has been confirmed, if prices are rallying again but on light volume, it is a good place to sell short with a stop (exit point) above the highest peak of the Double Top:

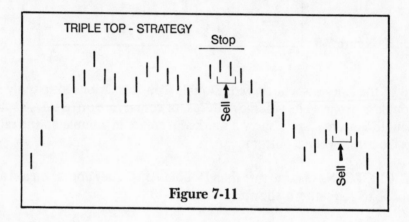

Figure 7-11

Another good place to sell would be after a Triple Top has formed and a fourth lower top is being formed.

If, however, prices continue to rally up to the level of the three previous peaks, they usually go higher; and if prices descend to the same level a fourth time, they usually go lower. It is very rare to see four tops or bottoms at equal levels.

TRIPLE BOTTOMS are simply Triple Tops turned upside down and all the rules can be applied in reverse. (Figure 7-12).

The accompanying volume pattern, however, is different. The third low should be on light volume and the ensuing rally from that bottom should show a considerable pickup in activity.

ROUNDING TOPS AND BOTTOMS. Because Rounding Tops are so rare, we will limit our discussion to Rounding Bottoms, commonly referred to as "Saucer Bottoms."

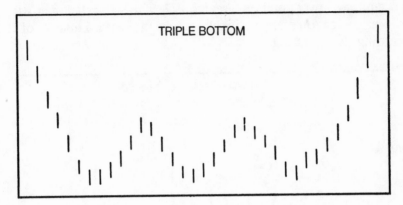

Figure 7-12

The chart pattern in figure 7-13 shows a gradual change in the trend direction, produced by a step-by-step shift in the balance of power between buying and selling. As we begin a Rounded Bottom, we will notice volume decreasing as selling pressure eases. The trend then becomes neutral with very little trading activity occurring. As prices start up, volume increases as well. Finally, price and volume continue to accelerate, with prices often literally blasting out of this pattern.

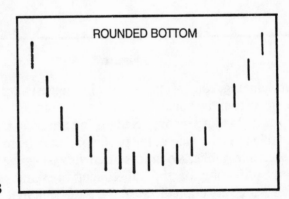

Figure 7-13

BROADENING FORMATIONS, such as the one illustrated in figure 7-14, usually have bearish implications. They appear much more frequently at tops than at bottoms and, for that reason, we will limit our discussion to Broadening Tops. The theory is that *five minor reversals are followed by a substantial decline*. In the classic pattern, reversals #3 and #5 occur at successively higher points than reversal #1; and reversal

#4 occurs at a lower point than reversal #2. This same characteristic pattern was evident on many individual stocks in the third quarter of 1929, preceding the great crash.

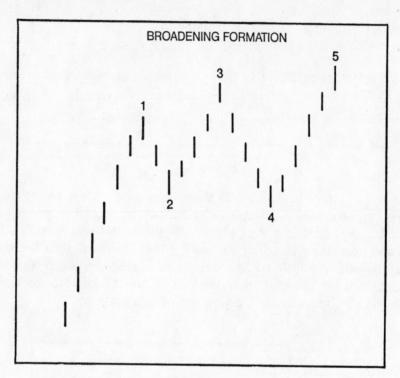

BROADENING FORMATION

Figure 7-14

The Broadening Top formation usually suggests a market that is lacking support from the "smart money" and is out of control. Quite often, well informed selling is completed during the early stages of the formation; and in the later stages, the participation is from the less informed, more excitable public. Volume is often very irregular and offers no clue as to the direction of the subsequent breakout. The price swings themselves are very unpredictable so it is difficult to tell where each swing will end.

Broadening Tops are a difficult formation to trade. However, you can usually be quite sure the trend has turned down after a break of the lower of the two valleys.

WEDGE FORMATIONS. Up until now, the reversal formations we have discussed have all been powerful enough to reverse an intermediate or major trend. The Wedges, on the other hand, usually only reverse a *minor* trend and, as a general rule of thumb, should typically take 3 weeks or so to complete. It is a chart formation in which price fluctuations are confined within converging straight lines. These form a pattern which itself may have a rising or falling slant.

In a **RISING WEDGE,** both boundary lines slant up from left to right but the lower line rises at a steeper angle than the upper line. After breaking the lower line boundary, prices usually decline in earnest:

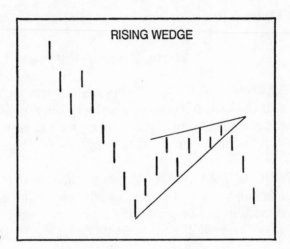

Figure 7-15

Generally, each new price advance, or wave up, is feebler than the last, indicating that investment demand is weakening at the higher price levels. Rising Wedges are usually more reliable when found in a Bear Market. In a Bull Market, what appears to be a Rising Wedge may actually be a continuation pattern known as a "Flag" or "Pennant" (discussed in the next chapter). This is more likely to be true if the Wedge is less than three weeks in length.

In a **FALLING WEDGE,** both boundary lines slant down from right to left but the upper line descends at a steeper angle than the lower line. Differing from the Rising Wedge, once prices move out of a Falling Wedge, they are more apt to drift sidewise and "saucer-out" before beginning to rise. (Figure 7-16).

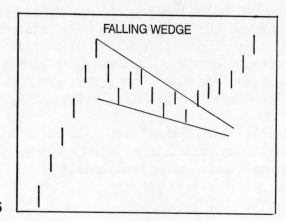

Figure 7-16

Minor Reversal Patterns

A REVERSAL DAY TOP occurs when prices move higher but then close near the lows of the day, usually below their opening and below the mid-point of the day's range. An even stronger reversal is indicated if the close is below the previous day's close. (Figure 7-17).

A REVERSAL DAY BOTTOM occurs when prices move lower but then close near the highs of the day, usually above the opening and above the mid-point of the day's range. An even stronger reversal is indicated if the close is above the previous day's close. (Figure 7-18).

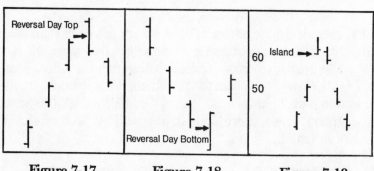

Figure 7-17   Figure 7-18   Figure 7-19

THE ISLAND REVERSAL. Suppose the price of a stock in a rising market closes at its high of 50 and then on the following day, opens at its low of 60, leaving a "gap" of 10 points (see chapter nine). A few days later, the market moves back down and forms another gap in approximately the same 50-60 area. Thus, all the trading above 60 will appear on the chart to be *isolated*, like an island, from all previous and subsequent fluctuations. This is called an "island reversal."

Island Reversals are quite rare, but are an extremely good indicator of a reversal in the trend. Their appearance indicates that an extreme change in sentiment has occurred.

Thus, we have seen various patterns which can often signal a critical change in market direction. In the chapter to follow, you will see various formations which give you precisely the opposite indication. We recommend you compare these chapters carefully and bear in mind the key differences between these formations whenever making a trading decision.

CHAPTER

8

CONSOLIDATION PATTERNS

We have seen how trends are reversed. But at other times, a trend may be interrupted, resulting in sideways movement for a time, before continuing on in its previous direction. Such sideways movements may even result in a break of the trendline. These formations are known as "consolidation" or "continuation patterns." The ability to differentiate between reversal patterns and continuation patterns is vital.

TRIANGLES have occasionally been known to reverse a trend. But usually they act as a period of consolidation from which prices continue on in the same direction. Triangles form as a result of indecision on the part of both buyers and sellers. During this time, market participants tend to withdraw to the sidelines, resulting in narrower market fluctuations and diminishing volume. A breakout of the triangle usually occurs as the result of some news affecting the market. And this breakout, if legitimate, is accompanied by a sharp increase in volume.

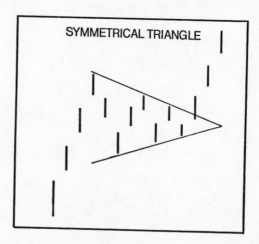

Figure 8-1

THE SYMMETRICAL TRIANGLE , sometimes known as a "coil," is the most common type. It is formed by a succession of price fluctuations, each of which is smaller than its predecessor, resulting in a pattern bounded by a downslanting line and an upslanting line. (Figure 8-1).

A Symmetrical Triangle, by definition, must have at least four reversal points. From that point onward, the breakout may occur at any time in the triangle, even before reaching its apex. More powerful moves are found when prices break out decisively at a point somewhere between half and three-quarters of the distance between the left side of the triangle and the apex.

Symmetrical Triangles are not as reliable as the Head and Shoulders formations, and really work out only about two-thirds of the time because they are subject to false breakouts called "End Runs" or "Shakeouts":

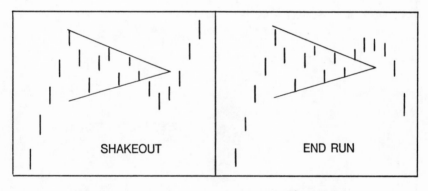

Figure 8-2	**Figure 8-3**

There is no way to avoid getting caught in such false moves—unless you recognize their characteristic volume patterns. A breakout to the upside should be on high volume. If volume is light, be suspect of a possible false move and "End Run."

Downside breakouts are a different matter. Prices often break out on low volume with a pickup in volume not occurring for a few days. Oddly enough, a high-volume breakout on the downside is often the signal of a "Shakeout."

RIGHT-ANGLE TRIANGLES, both Ascending and Descending, are better predictors of the future direction of prices than Symmetrical Triangles. In theory, prices will break toward the flat side—upward in an Ascending Triangle and downward in a Descending Triangle.

THE ASCENDING RIGHT-ANGLE TRIANGLE is characterized by a top-line boundary that is horizontal and a bottom-line that is sloping upward. (Figure 8-4).

This formation occurs when demand is growing yet continues to meet supply at a fixed price. If demand continues, the supply being distributed at that price will eventually be entirely absorbed by new buyers, and prices will then advance rapidly.

THE DESCENDING RIGHT-ANGLE TRIANGLE will exhibit a horizontal lower boundary and a down-sloping upper boundary:

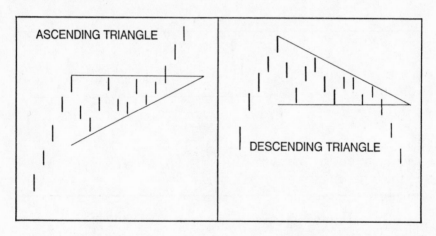

Figure 8-4   Figure 8-5

This formation occurs when there is a certain amount of demand at a fixed price yet supply continues to come into the market. Eventually, the demand is exhausted and prices break out of the triangle on the downside.

Triangles, both Symmetrical and Right-Angle, can be used for some measuring though they are not as reliable as the Head-and-Shoulders measuring formula. Assuming, for example, a breakout on the upside, you simply draw a line parallel to the lower side of the triangle and expect prices to rally up to that line:

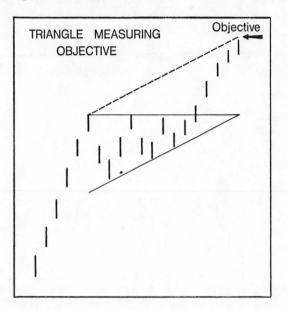

TRIANGLE MEASURING OBJECTIVE

Objective

Figure 8-6

Also, prices should resume their uptrend at the same approximate angle as the uptrend which preceded the triangle's formation.

THE RECTANGLE formation, sometimes known as a "line," forms as a result of a battle between two groups of approximately equal strength. Although offering little forecasting ability as to which direction the breakout should occur, once prices begin to move out of the formation, it can be very useful in setting objectives. (Figure 8-7).

Volume characteristics are similar to triangles in that volume tends to diminish as the Rectangle lengthens. Breakouts have less tendency to be false than with the Symmetrical Triangles. However, breakouts are more likely to be followed by a pullback.

All in all, there is a somewhat greater tendency for Rectangles to be consolidation rather than reversal patterns. When a Rectangle is a reversal pattern, it is much more likely to occur at a major or intermediate bottom rather than at a top.

A minimum measuring objective can be derived from adding the width of the Rectangle to the point of breakout. Normally, wide-swinging Rectangles will offer more dynamic moves than the narrower ones. A move out of a narrow Rectangle will often hesitate at its minimum objective before moving on:

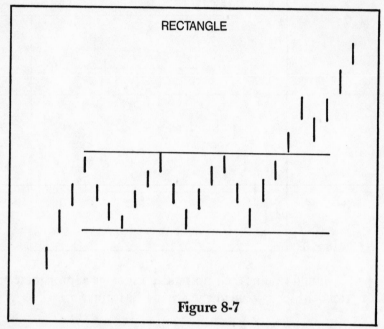

RECTANGLE

Figure 8-7

FLAGS AND PENNANTS are true consolidation patterns and are very reliable indicators both in terms of direction and measuring. In an up

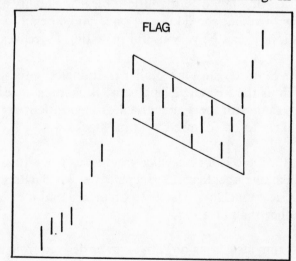

FLAG

Figure 8-8

market, flags usually form after a dynamic, nearly straight move up on heavy volume. Prices react on lower volume and a series of minor fluctuations eventually form a downward-sloping, compact parallelogram. (Figure 8-8).

The pennant is very similar to the flag except that it is bounded by converging rather than parallel lines:

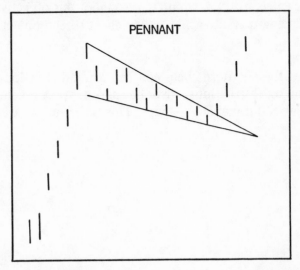

Figure 8-9

Flags and pennants, in order to be considered valid should conform to three rules—(1) they should occur after a very sharp up or down move;

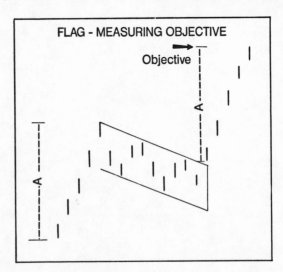

Figure 8-10

(2) volume should decline throughout the duration of the pattern; and (3) prices should break out of the pattern within a matter of a few weeks.

The measuring formula for flags and pennants is identical. You simply add the height of the "pole," formed in the move preceding the formation, to the breakout point of the flag. (Figure 8-10).

In practice, price may tend to overshoot this objective somewhat in an advancing market, while falling short of the objective in a declining market.

All of these patterns help confirm a trend. But looking more closely at market fluctuations, we notice another phenomenon which can also give us additional clues—gaps. This is the subject of our next chapter.

9

GAPS

Gaps represent an area on the chart where no trading takes place. For example, if a stock reaches a high of, say, 50 on Monday, but then opens at 60 on Tuesday, moving straight up from the opening, no trading occurs in the 50-60 area. This no-trading zone appears on the chart as a hole or a "gap." Thus, in an uptrending market, a gap is produced when the highest price of any one day is lower than the lowest price of the following day, or the reverse in a downtrending market.

Gaps can be valuable in spotting the beginning of a move, measuring the extent of a move or confirming the end of a move. There are four different types of gaps: "Common gaps," "breakaway gaps," "measuring gaps," and "exhaustion gaps." Since each has its own distinctive implications, it is important to be able to distinguish between them.

COMMON GAPS—also known as "temporary gaps," "pattern gaps" or "area gaps"—tend to occur in a sideways trading range or price congestion area. Usually, the price moves back up or down subsequently as the market returns to the gap area in order to "fill the gap." If this does occur, the gap offers little in the way of forecasting significance.

It may be noted, however, that common gaps are more apt to develop in consolidation rather than in reversal formations. In other words, the appearance of many gaps within consolidation patterns (such as a Rectangle or Symmetrical Triangle) is a signal that the breakout should be in the same direction as that of the preceding trend. (Figure 9-1).

THE BREAKAWAY GAP occurs as prices break away from an area of congestion. Typically, prices will break away from an Ascending or Descending Triangle with a gap.

This gap implies that the change in sentiment has been strong and that the ensuing move will be powerful. Often the market does not return to "fill the gap," particularly if volume is heavy after the gap has formed. If volume is not heavy, there is a reasonable chance the gap will be filled before prices resume their trend. (Figure 9-2).

THE MEASURING GAP typically occurs in the middle of a price move and can be used to measure how much farther a move will go. Rather than being associated with a congestion area, it is more likely to occur in the course of a rapid, straight-line advance or decline, usually pat approximately the halfway point. (Figure 9-3).

THE EXHAUSTION GAP signals the end of a move. Like Measuring gaps, Exhaustion gaps are associated with rapid, extensive advances or declines. The problem, of course, is: how do you know whether it's a Measuring gap or an Exhaustion gap? One clue may be found in the volume. An Exhaustion gap is often accompanied by particularly high volume. Another method for detecting an Exhaustion Gap is with a Reversal Day. (Figure 9-4).

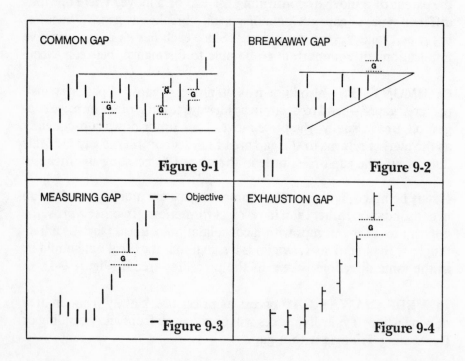

Now, combining the concepts of the past several chapters, we have numerous tools for deciding when a market could be turning. The next question which arises is: How far will it go? Chapter 10 begins to provide some answers.

CHAPTER

10

RETRACEMENT THEORY

No market moves steadily down or steadily up. Instead, each movement in the primary direction is followed by a reaction, which can, in turn, be followed by another thrust.

Each thrust, measured from bottom to top or top to bottom, is known as the "swing" or "move." Each reaction or rally retraces part of the move and, therefore, is known as a "retracement." When the reaction is greater than the move, we must consider that the trend has changed, at least, for the near term. Retracement theory sets predetermined target levels for these moves and lends itself readily to computer applications.

Of course, our first problem is to determine the primary trend. But once we are reasonably assured that the market is in a downtrend or an uptrend, the key is to know how far a move is likely to be retraced before the market resumes that trend. Knowing that, we could better judge an appropriate point to enter the market on a reaction. Aside from correctly judging the primary trend, correctly timing entries on reactions is probably the most important aspect of trading.

What is a "normal" retracement? This question has been debated for years. The general consensus is that a normal retracement recaptures between one-third and two-thirds of the previous move. Another school of thought says 40-60%. Most agree that the 50% retracement is the most likely.

W. D. Gann went as far as to divide each move into eighths and thirds, giving us 1/8, 1/4, 3/8, 1/3, 1/2, 5/8, 2/3, 3/4 and 7/8 as all possible retracement levels. Of these, the most important to him were the 1/2, 5/8, 3/4 and 7/8 levels. Meanwhile, students of Elliott Wave Theory consider the Fibonacci retracement levels of .382 and .618 to be the most critical. My own work shows special significance attached to these numbers, especially the .618; and often I've seen a market react exactly to this level before moving on.

Therefore, on your charts, it would be a good idea to keep track of some of the significant retracement levels such as in figure 10-1.

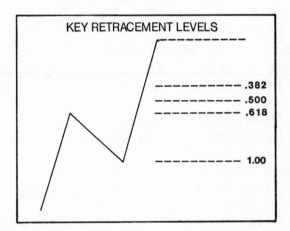

Figure 10-1

Keep in mind that each "move" is part of a larger move that has its own individual probable retracement levels. Consequently, you may want to go back and look at the current entire pattern in an even broader, longer-term perspective, viewing it as merely a retracement within the context of an even larger move. Since this can quickly get pretty messy on the chart, I suggest you use my simple "Retrace" program that will allow you to print out the retracement levels in report form (see Appendix A). You will often find key retracement levels of different moves coinciding with one another, lending more credibility to your forecast that the market will indeed find support at that level.

When using the "Retrace" program, you need only enter the price made at the top and bottom of the move. It will then tell you at any price level between these two points, how much of the move has been retraced.

11

SUPPORT AND RESISTANCE

In addition to retracement theory, what are some other ways of judging when a reaction or a rally is coming to an end and when the primary trend should resume? Support and resistance will give you some clues.

A SUPPORT LEVEL is a price level at which sufficient demand exists to at least temporarily halt a downward movement in prices.

A RESISTANCE LEVEL is a price at which sufficient supply exists to at least temporarily halt an upward movement.

In an uptrend, each former top—once surpassed—becomes a support level. In a downtrend, each former bottom—once penetrated—becomes a resistance level:

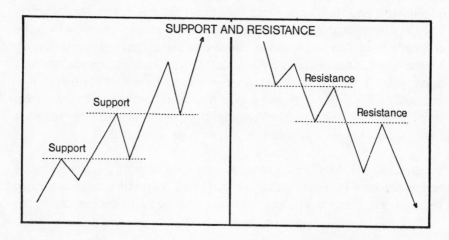

SUPPORT AND RESISTANCE

Figure 11-1   Figure 11-2

A congestion pattern forms an even more formidable support or resistance barrier since more actual trading took place at that price level:

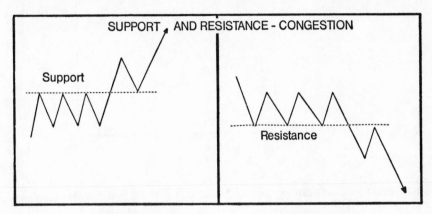

Figure 11-3   **Figure 11-4**

One more rule to remember: When a support level is broken, it becomes resistance, and when a resistance level is broken, it becomes support. How does this happen?

Let's take the hypothetical situation illustrated in figure 11-5. A group of buyers has been waiting on the sidelines and watching a stock decline from 80 to 60. At this price, they believe the stock is cheap so they buy. The stock begins to rise and eventually reaches 70. But they are confident the stock will go much higher. Unfortunately, the stock begins to decline and eventually falls to 50. At this point, the investors begin to feel they have made a mistake and vow to dump the stock if they can at least get their money back. Luckily, the stock begins to rally and as it reaches 60, these investors sell their shares, turning the stock price down once again.

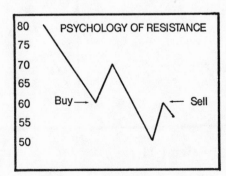

Figure 11-5

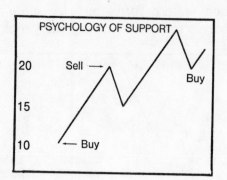

Figure 11-6

Months pass. Our same group of investors finds a hot new stock—ABC Company. (Refer to figure 11-6.) They buy it at 10 and, after a few months, the stock has risen to 20. This time they don't repeat the same mistake they made earlier. Instead, they sell the stock and pocket a huge profit. Two weeks later, the stock has dropped to 15 and they congratulate themselves for having taken their profits at 20. But a month later, the price of ABC has risen to 25. Now they don't feel so smart. "Maybe we should have held on longer for even more profit," is their refrain. They decide that if they get another chance to buy the stock again at 20, they will. This is one example of how previous tops can act as support.

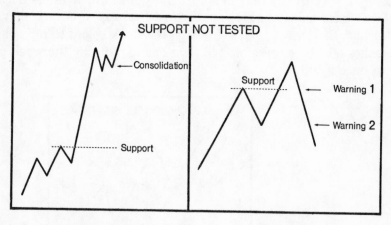

Figure 11-7   **Figure 11-8**

In figure 11-1, we showed a typical zigzag type of market, i.e., where each reaction found support at the previous top. Referring to figures 11-7 and 11-8, there are two other possibilities that can come up. A market may surge wildly, in which case we would not expect a reaction to take prices back to the previous top. Instead, on reaction, prices are likely to form a consolidation or reversal pattern somewhat above the price level of the previous top.

Another possibility is that prices break below their previous top, giving you your first warning signal of a change in direction, with a stronger warning occurring if prices break below their previous bottom.

Before leaving the subject of support and resistance, we should state one final rule: Once a support or resistance level has been attacked, it is weakened. It may resist a second attack, but the third attack will usually break through.

CHAPTER

12

MOMENTUM

Momentum is simply the rate of change—the *speed* or *slope* at which a stock or commodity ascends or declines. It is calculated by taking the difference between prices separated by a fixed interval of time. For example, today's 5-day momentum value would be today's price minus the price recorded 5 days ago; yesterday's would be yesterday's price minus that of 5 days before yesterday and so on. Expressed mathematically:

$$M(5)_T = \text{Price of today - price of 5 days ago}$$
$$\text{or } M(5)_T = P_T - P_{T-5}$$

Let's take a hypothetical example:

DAY	PRICE	5-DAY MOMENTUM
1	500	---
2	508	---
3	510	---
4	515	---
5	510	---
6	495	-5
7	508	0
8	526	16
9	528	13
10	540	30

One basic way to use a momentum indicator is to buy when it becomes positive and sell when it turns negative. Logically, you are buying when the market is picking up momentum and selling when that momentum is lost. The problem is that, by definition, you're entering the market *after* it has made its turn. But even if you miss the beginning of the move, you should catch most of it, if indeed the market is turning. Later, this should also allow you to exit the market with a profit before prices actually start moving against you in earnest:

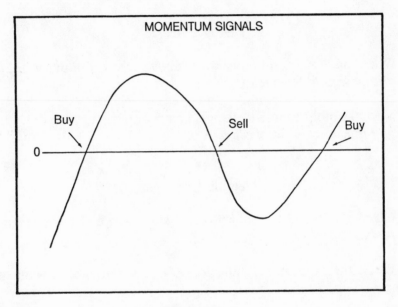

MOMENTUM SIGNALS

Figure 12-1

CYCLES AND MOMENTUM. One school of thought contends that in order for a momentum indicator to be valid, it must be based on *cycle length*. If it is, it will measure the rate of change of prices within a cycle.

Cycles are found by measuring from one bottom to the next. Cycles are sometimes consistent and easy to spot while at other times they are very difficult to find. Let us assume we have checked on the recent history of a market and have found that it consistently makes a bottom every 20 days or so. The rule states that our calculation of momentum should be set at one-half the days in the cycle, or in this case, 10 days.

This concept can be taken even further by following *three* momentum indicators at the same time–the 10-day momentum *plus* one at 1/4 of the cycle (5 days) and one at the full cycle (20 days). Thus, you will be plotting a 5-day, 10-day and 20-day momentum simultaneously on the same graph. (For more on cycles, see Chapters 23, 24 and 25.)

Up to this point, we can summarize the theory of momentum indicators as follows:

Rising Prices:

1. When the momentum indicator is above zero and moving up, *upward momentum is increasing.*

2. When the momentum indicator is above zero and moving down, *upward momentum is decreasing.*

Declining Prices:

3. When the momentum indicator is below zero and moving down, **downward momentum is increasing.**

4. When the momentum indicator is below zero and moving up, *downward momentum is decreasing.*

OSCILLATORS. A completely different approach to the use of momentum indicators attempts to anticipate the end of a move when momentum is either "too high" or "too low." These conditions, respectively, are known as "overbought" and "oversold." The idea is that, in an overbought condition, nearly all investors who have had any intention of buying this particular stock or commodity have probably *already* committed all or most of the money they intend to commit for the time being; while in an oversold condition, they have *already* done most of the their selling. The general rule is to sell when the momentum indicator shows an overbought reading and buy when an oversold condition is indicated. (Figure 12-2).

Momentum may be zero, positive or negative. If a market is at the same price after 5 days, the 5-day momentum will be zero. If it is higher, the momentum is positive; and if lower, negative. The key question is this:

Is there a maximum positive or negative value for momentum? In commodity markets the answer is *yes.* There is usually a specified, mandatory limit as to how much a price is allowed to move each day. So, in this case, the maximum 5-day momentum would generally be that daily limit multiplied by 5.

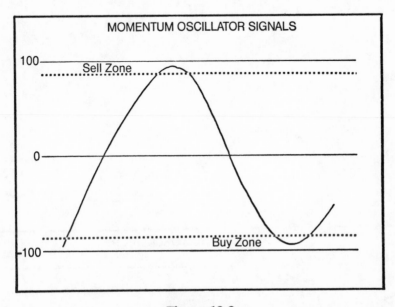

Figure 12-2

A momentum indicator used in this way is referred to as an "oscillator." The momentum indicator we have been discussing, however, is not an oscillator in its present form. It must first be "normalized," which means that all values must be converted to a range between +1 and -1, or +100% and -100%. To accomplish this, we divide the momentum value by the maximum obtainable momentum value. For example, in the T-bill market, the limit for one day is 60 points. Using a 5-day momentum would give us a maximum obtainable momentum of 300. Thus, a momentum value of 150 would translate into an oscillator value of +0.5 or +50%.

Figures 12-3, 12-4 and 12-5 show a 5-day momentum, a 5-day momentum oscillator, and combined 5, 10 and 20-day momentum oscillators.

Bear in mind that any limit we set—whether based upon actual market

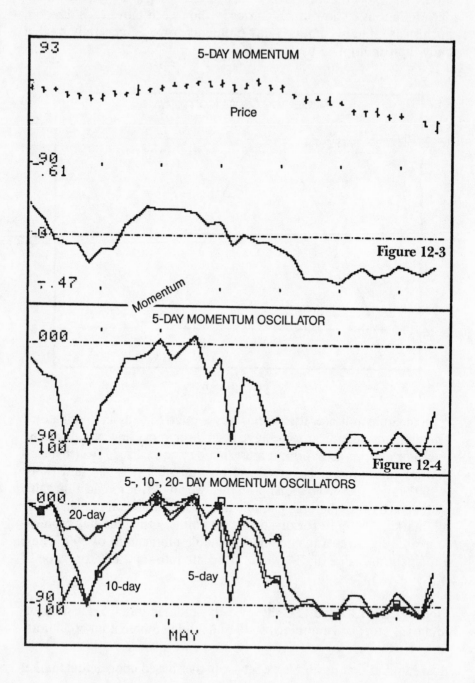

Figure 12-3

Figure 12-4

limits or not—is an arbitrary guideline to give you a general idea of the overbought or oversold condition. A more valid way to set limits is to run the momentum indicator for approximately one year of history and use the indicator's highs and lows of that period as your maximum and minimum.

It is very easy, with a computer, to develop a trading system using overbought/oversold oscillators. These would be the logical steps to follow:

1. Select how many days to use for momentum.

2. Decide on one or more oscillators.

3. Define the maximum ranges—what will constitute an overbought or oversold condition.

4. Construct trading rules.

Some examples of different trading rules might be:

1. Sell when the 5-day oscillator goes above 0.9 or 90%.

2. Sell when the 5-day oscillator stays above 90% for 2 days.

3. Sell when both the 5-day and 10-day oscillators are above 90%.

In short, momentum indicators can be used to trade with the trend when they cross the zero line or against the trend when they hit a peak. Be aware that when you are either selling into an overbought condition or buying into a oversold condition, you are categorically bucking the short-term trend. You are betting on what your oscillators claim is a high probability of a technical reaction occurring. Accordingly, this type of method is best suited to very short-term trading. In developing a trading system based on momentum, I would prefer to trade *with* the trend. Overbought/oversold oscillators do, however, provide indispensable technical information to the analyst—I wouldn't be without them.

13

MOVING AVERAGES

Moving averages are used to determine when a trend has changed direction and are the basis of many trend-following systems. In a simple three-day moving average, for example, we add the three most recent days and divide by three. Thus, if today is Wednesday, the moving average for today would be the average price of Monday, Tuesday and Wednesday. Then, on Thursday, we would drop off Monday's price and take the average of Tuesday, Wednesday and Thursday; and so on. The formula for a simple 3-day moving average (M3) would be:

$$M3 = \frac{P_T + P_{T-1} + P_{T-2}}{3}$$

Where P_T equals today's close; P_{T-1} equals yesterday's close; and P_{T-2} equals the close of the day before yesterday. Table 13-1 shows a hypothetical example:

TABLE 13-1. BUILDING A 3-DAY MOVING AVERAGE

Day	Price	3-day moving average
1	5	--
2	6	--
3	7	6
4	9	7.33
5	11	9

The simple moving average gives equal weight to each price in the sample.

A WEIGHTED MOVING AVERAGE on the other hand, can be used to give more significance to the most recent price, the earliest price or the middle price in the group. Another popular type of weighting factor is known as *exponential smoothing* which will be calculated for you automatically with program #12.

Prepackaged software is readily available to compute both simple and exponentially-smoothed moving averages. In addition, such software usually lets you set the number of days (or weeks or months as the case may be) in the moving average. As the number of days in the moving average increases, the moving average becomes smoother, less responsive to short-term fluctuations and, thus, slower to respond to changes in trend. The advantage is that you will experience fewer false starts; and the primary disadvantage is that much of the price move will have already taken place by the time the slow moving average has signaled a change. Your computer research in this area will tell you which moving average shows optimum results for each stock or commodity you wish to trade. This is the first step toward developing a moving average system.

Moving Average Systems

A moving average system is a set of trading rules that are applied to moving averages. On the same chart you may be interested in:

(a) the relationship between price and moving average, or

(b) the relationship between two or more moving averages themselves.

The most basic way to use a moving average is to simply interpret a change of direction in a single moving average as a signal to buy or sell. (Figure 13-1).

However, this is perhaps *too* simple. A more common approach would be to study the relationship between actual price and a single moving average. In the stock market, when a stock price is above its 200-day moving average, it is considered a bullish sign. (Shorter-term signals

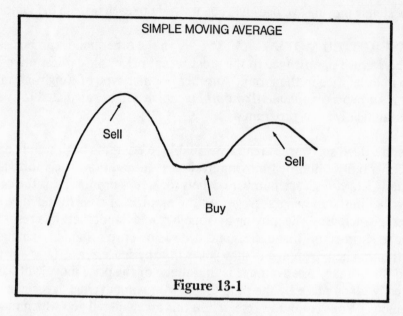

Figure 13-1

would be generated using a 10- or 20-day moving average.) The basic strategy would be as follows: Buy when prices cross *above* the moving average. Sell when prices cross *below* the moving average. Typically, you may wish to use closing prices only:

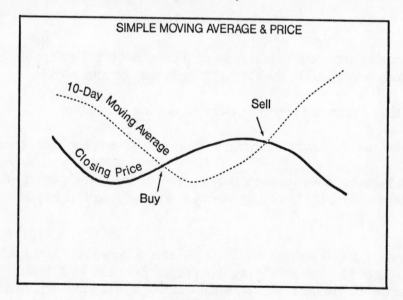

Figure 13-2

THE TWO CROSSOVER MODEL is the next step up in level of complexity, making use of two simple moving averages. A typical example would be a 14-day moving average combined with a 50-day moving average. (This particular combination was found to be very effective in the gold market in a study done by Merrill Lynch.) The rule would be: Buy when the 14-day moving average crosses above the 50-day moving average; sell when it crosses below the 50-day moving average.

A modified version of this system would take into account the actual prices as well. The rules might then be:

(1) Buy when the actual price crosses above *both* moving averages and exit the market when the price crosses below *either* moving average.

(2) Sell short when the actual price crosses below *both* moving averages and exit the market when the price crosses *above either moving average*.

Finally, three or more moving averages may be combined to make a system. Such qualifications usually result in fewer trades and trades of a shorter duration. Moreover, it is probably too complex. Remember, making a system more complex does not necessarily make it a better one.

THE 200-DAY MOVING AVERAGE OF THE DOW illustrated in figure 13-3, is an excellent long-term indicator, and as such may be better utilized by the investor rather than the trader. Its signals, once generated, are seldom wrong over the longer term. If, after both the Dow and the 200-Day Moving Average have been declining for some time, the Dow should move up and cross the Moving Average, it indicates that a new bull market has begun. Later, confirmation of this initial signal occurs when the 200-Day Moving Average itself turns up.

During the first stage of the bull market, both the Dow and the Moving Average move up in concert. Eventually, the Dow suffers its first serious setback which may or may not send prices below the Moving Average. But this does not necessarily signal an end to the bull market. If the market correction is severe, the Moving Average may turn down as well. Again, this does not necessarily mean the bull market has ended. Instead, the Moving Average will usually turn back and go on to new highs.

It is only *after* this *second* leg up in the 200-Day Moving Average that

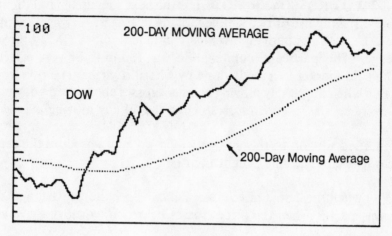

Figure 13-3

you should begin to look for market deterioration and sell signals—an initial crossing *below* the Moving Average by the Dow and then, a decline in the Moving Average itself.

All these moving averages ignore volume. Attempts to evaluate both *price* and volume simultaneously are discussed in the next chapter.

14

ON-BALANCE VOLUME

Earlier, just as studying volume on a day-to-day basis helped us to determine the power of a particular price move, so does On-Balance Volume (OBV) help us to detect patterns of accumulation and distribution (see Program #5).

JOSEPH GRANVILLE calculates it this way: If today's closing price is higher than yesterday's, we add today's volume to a cumulative total. If the closing price is lower, today's volume is subtracted from the total. On days when prices remain unchanged, the cumulative volume also remains unchanged. Here is an example to illustrate the technique:

TABLE 14-1. CALCULATING ON-BALANCE VOLUME

DAY	PRICE	VOLUME	ON-BALANCE VOLUME
1	10	7,000	7,000
2	12	5,000	12,000
3	15	8,000	20,000
4	15	4,000	20,000
5	14	5,000	15,000
6	12	3,000	12,000

On-Balance Volume can be equally effective with individual stocks, the stock averages, or individual commodities. Accumulation is indicated by rising OBV; distribution by falling OBV. Since the starting point is arbitrary, the absolute level of the on-balance volume is of no significance. We are only interested in the contour of its curve when it is compared with the contour of the price curve—either graphically or in tabulated form.

For example, let's say prices are moving sideways. Is this an accumulation which will lead to a continuation of the trend? Or is it a distribution which implies that prices will turn around and move in the opposite direction? The OBV can often tell us the true state of affairs. As a rule, the OBV parallels the price. It is only when there is a *divergence* between the OBV and the price that we can tell if accumulation or distribution is occurring. For example, if prices have been moving sideways in a trading range while OBV has been increasing, we would conclude that accumulation was occurring. The rising OBV resulted from more stock being purchased on up days than was sold on down days:

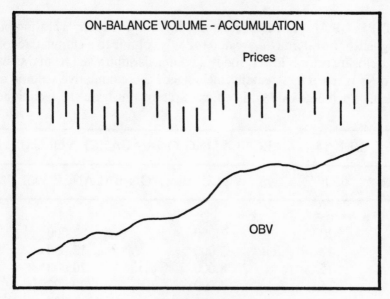

Figure 14-1

Distribution is indicated if prices are moving sideways and the OBV is falling. We could conclude a major top is forming and prices should drop quickly. (Figure 14-2).

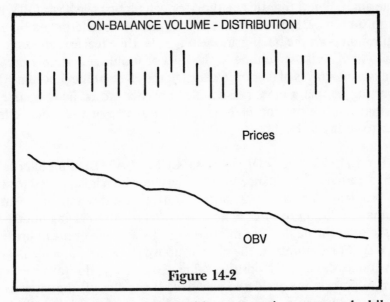

Figure 14-2

What if prices, instead of moving sideways, are in an uptrend while the OBV is moving sideways? Again, we would have a *divergence* between price and OBV. This divergence would indicate that the price rise is not being accompanied by strong volume and that this market is weak and could easily reverse:

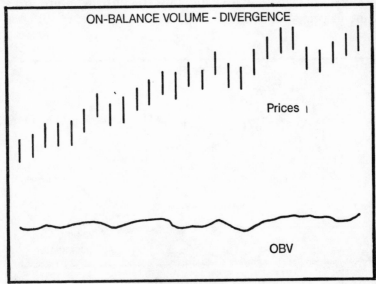

Figure 14-3

Some analysts feel that this method for calculating the basic OBV may be too simplistic. Since each day's price change is determined by transactions on *both* the buying and selling side, they feel it is an exaggeration to assign *all* the volume to the plus or minus side simply because the close one day is higher or lower than the close of the preceding day. Others argue that a more reasonable approach would be to ignore the previous day's close and determine if prices rise or fall from today's open to today's close.

MARK CHAIKEN'S VOLUME ACCUMULATOR is an alternative to the Granville On-Balance Volume System which is supposed to solve this problem. It provides a more sensitive intraday measurement of volume in relation to price action. He does this by placing added emphasis upon the day's close in relation to its average or *mean* price for that day. For example, if the close is above the mean, a percentage of the volume is assigned a positive value. Conversely, if it falls below the mean, a portion is considered negative. If the close is the same as the high, all volume is treated as positive. Likewise, if the close is the same as the low, all volume is treated as negative.

An accumulative line is drawn and, like in Granville's OBV, the trader is advised to look for divergences between this line and the price trend. For example, if the cumulative line fails to confirm an upward trend, a decline in price may be indicated.

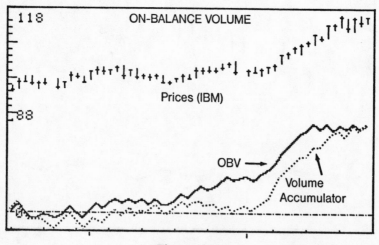

Figure 14-4

Although the Volume Accumulator and Granville's OBV will often agree, this is not always the case. Comparing figure 14-4, you will notice the difference in these two indicators when applied to the same data.

Still, with all its faults, OBV is a very useful tool for spotting accumulation and distribution. For a much more comprehensive study of OBV, traders can refer to Granville's *New Strategy Of Daily Stock Market Trading For Maximum Profit.*

With the array of tools you have mastered regarding price and volume analysis, you have now taken the first important steps towards your goal of consistently winning in the markets. Most of the techniques you have learned can be applied equally well to any market—individual stocks, the Dow Jones averages, gold, silver, soybeans, the German mark, T-bonds—you name it. But when you attempt to analyze the stock market you will need additional tools designed specifically for that purpose.

First, I will give you the necessary background on the composition of the various stock averages in order for you to better understand the relationships between them. I will then explain Dow Theory–the most traditional of trading systems–and explore its applications. Next, I will delve into a whole new set of technical indicators designed to judge the strength or weakness of the market as a whole. Finally, I will examine the options market and some of the specialized computer programs available in that area.

3

STOCK MARKET

CHAPTER

15

"THE AVERAGES" & DOW THEORY

How is the stock market doing? Sounds like a simple question. But in fact it is an extremely provocative one—one which you will find more difficult to answer with a brief reply the more you learn about the market. Usually the person who poses the question wants to hear "good," "bad," or "indifferent." But for you and I who study the stock market, it's not that simple. A one-word answer tells us nothing about chart patterns, volume, divergences, nonconfirmations of the various averages, the various industry sectors, etc. It doesn't even address the fundamental problem: What is the stock market?

The stock market is really the sum total of *each and every* stock that is traded. The problem is we usually don't measure it that way. Instead we use a variety of market "averages" which reflect far more limited samples of stocks considered representative of the total.

THE DOW JONES INDUSTRIAL AVERAGE is the most popular and tracks the price of 30 large industrial companies, but was never intended by its inventor, Charles H. Dow, to be analyzed or tracked to the exclusion of the other Dow Jones averages—20 transportations, 15 utilities and 65 composite stocks. Nevertheless, it is the Industrials which are the most widely followed of the four and the one usually referred to in summaries of daily stock-market activity.

The broader market averages—the Standard and Poors 500 Stock Index (S&P 500), the New York Stock Exchange Index (NYSE), and sometimes the Value Line Index—are often preferred by market professionals and technical analysts because they are more representative of the overall market than the 30 Dow Jones Industrials.

THE S&P INDEX represents 500 heavily capitalized, bluechip companies.

THE NEW YORK STOCK EXCHANGE INDEX, created in 1966 as a result of criticism that the Dow is not a true reflector of the market, comprises *all* stocks listed on the New York Stock Exchange and is thus the broadest measure of that market.

THE VALUE LINE, is comprised of 1700 stocks listed on various exchanges and is unique in that it is the only "unweighted" average of those discussed here. This means that each stock, regardless of its price, is weighted equally in determining the index value. Thus, by watching this index in relationship to the S&P, for example, you can judge how the secondary, less capitalized companies are doing in relation to the "bluechips."

Dow Theory is not a fancy little formula for which you can buy software. Instead, it is a comprehensive "theory" of stock market behavior. It is, in effect, one of the first major "technical" studies ever attempted on the stock market, and though occasionally criticized, still must be considered to be a valuable tool due to its long record of success in stock-market prognostication.

In 1897, two market averages were compiled. The "Rails," which included 20 railroad companies, have since been broadened to include the airlines and renamed the "Transports." The Industrial Average, representing most other types of business and made up originally of only 12 issues, was increased later to 20 in 1916 and 30 in 1928. In 1929, all stocks of public utility companies were dropped from the Industrial Average and a new Utility Average of 20 issues was set up, and reduced to 15 in 1936. Finally, the three have been averaged together to make the Dow Jones 65 - Stock Composite Index. Traditional Dow Theory pays no attention to the utility or composite averages; its interpretations are based exclusively on the Rails (transports) and Industrials.

There is much to suggest that Charles H. Dow did not think of his theory as a device for forecasting the stock market, but rather as a barometer of general business trends. The basic principles of the theory were outlined by him in editorials he wrote for the *Wall Street Journal*. Upon his death in 1902, his successor as editor of the newspaper, William P. Hamilton, took up Dow's principles and, in the course of 27 years of writing on the market, formulated them into the Dow Theory as we know it today. As you read the basic tenets of the Dow Theory below, you will soon see the origin of basic terminology and theory used in modern-day technical analysis.

1. THE AVERAGES DISCOUNT EVERYTHING THAT CAN BE KNOWN. Because the averages reflect the combined market activities of thousands of investors, including those possessing the best foresight and information, the averages in their day-to-day fluctuations discount everything known, everything foreseeable, and every condition which can affect the supply or demand for stocks. Unpredictable happenings such as earthquakes may not be reflected in the averages, but they are soon appraised after they occur. Because of this discounting function, the behavior of the averages affords the first clue as to the future of stock prices.

2. THE THREE TRENDS. The three trends that are continually unfolding are the Primary (Major Trend), Secondary (Intermediate Trend), and Day-to-Day (Minor Trend). These trends are sometimes likened to the ocean's tide, waves and ripples.

3. THE PRIMARY TRENDS. These broad movements usually last for more than a year and may run for several years, resulting in general appreciation or depreciation in value of more than 20%. So long as each successive rally reaches a higher level than the one before it and each secondary reaction stops at a higher level than the previous reaction, the Primary Trend is up and we are in a *bull market*. Conversely, when each intermediate decline carries prices to successively lower levels and each intervening rally fails to exceed the top of the previous rally, the Primary Trend is down and we are in a *bear market*.

4. THE SECONDARY TRENDS are reactions occurring in a bull market and *rallies* occurring in a bear market. Normally, they last from a few weeks to a few months and retrace from one-third to two-thirds of the gain or loss registered by the preceding swing in the Primary Trend.

5. THE MINOR TRENDS. The Secondary Trend is composed of Minor Trends or day-to-day fluctuations which are considered unimportant to the Dow theorist. They usually last less than six days but may last up to three weeks.

6. THE BULL MARKET. The Primary Trend usually consists of three phases. The first phase is known as "accumulation" and occurs when business conditions are still poor and the public is generally discouraged with the stock market. The second phase is usually a fairly steady advance on increasing activity as business conditions and corporate earnings begin to improve. The third phase is characterized by highly publicized "good news." Price gains are often spectacular and the public becomes heavily involved.

7. THE BEAR MARKET. Primary down trends are also usually characterized by three phases. The first phase, known as distribution, is when farsighted investors sell their shares to the less informed public. The second phase is the panic phase. In this phase buying decreases, selling becomes more urgent, and the downward trend of prices accelerates on mounting volume. After the panic phase, there may be a fairly long secondary recovery or a sidewise movement. Finally, the business news begins to deteriorate and prices resume their decline though less rapidly than before. The bear market ends when everything possible in the way of bad news has been discounted.

8. PRINCIPLE OF CONFIRMATION. No valid signal of a change in trend can be generated by either the industrials or rails (transports) independent of the other. In other words, if one average makes a new high over its previous peak but the other average falls short of exceeding its previous peak, a nonconfirmation has occurred. The move must be considered suspect until both averages confirm by exceeding their previous peaks.

9. VOLUME. In bull markets volume tends to increase on rallies and decrease on declines. But, in Dow Theory, *conclusive* signals as to the market's trend can only be produced by price movement. Volume only affords collateral evidence which may aid interpretation of otherwise doubtful situations.

10. LINES. A Line refers to a sidewise movement in one or both of the averages, which lasts from a few weeks to a few months, in the course of which price fluctuates within a range of approximately 5%. A Line can substitute for a Secondary Trend. A breakout from the Line area is usually significant. It cannot be known in advance which way the breakout will occur, but more often than not, it is in the direction of the trend.

11. CLOSING PRICES. Dow Theory pays no attention to any extreme highs or lows which may be registered intraday, but takes into account only the closing figures.

12. A TREND IN EFFECT CONTINUES UNTIL REVERSED. This final tenet simply means that once a new primary trend is definitely signaled by the action of the two averages, the odds that it will continue, despite any near-term reactions, are at their greatest. But as the Primary Trend carries on, the odds in favor of its further extension grow smaller.

16

BREADTH OF MARKET INDICATORS

THE ADVANCE-DECLINE LINE is the most common measure of market breadth and is considered to be one of the most important technical indicators of the condition of the stock market. It is derived by taking the difference between the number of advancing issues and the number of declining issues each day. This daily figure is then added or subtracted each day to a cumulative number in order to determine the advance-decline line.

The purpose is to tell you if the market *as a whole* is gaining strength or losing strength—a measure which will often signal a major change in the direction of the market before any of the averages. As an example, when the Dow is advancing, yet the advance-decline line is falling, it means that even though the Dow is up, a majority of the *other* stocks is declining—a warning that the "technical condition" of the market is deteriorating and that the bull market is in "poor health."

Conversely, if the Dow is falling, yet the advance-decline line is rising, it implies that even though the Dow stocks are declining, a majority of other stocks are beginning to advance—a good signal that the market is technically strong and may turn upward shortly.

The theory behind the advance-decline line can best be understood by the "bathtub" analogy. Picture the market as a bathtub and the water level as represented by the advance-decline line. Advancing stocks raise the water level and declining stocks lower the water level. Market strength or weakness is determined by that water level.

The "smart money" is always the first to get out when the water level of the market stops rising and starts to come down, even though the

Dow may still be in an uptrend. This smart money is the first "water" to flow out the drain. Likewise, the "dumb money" is the last water to leave the tub -- when the flow is speeded up, panic selling takes place and the lowest prices are reached in one last precipitous drop.

At that time, the bear market has ended and a new bull market is about to begin. Just as the smart money was the first to leave the bathtub when it was full, it is also the smart money which will be the first to flow back when it is empty.

The smart money then becomes the bottom layer of water, the foundation upon which the new bull market will be built, and on which all the other layers of water will rest. Thus, smart money is the first in and first out; while dumb money, sitting up on the surface, is last in, last out.

Simple enough so far. But a little more study reveals that we must also consider *which phase* of the bull or bear market we are in and whether we are attempting to predict a market top or market bottom.

The first phase of a bull market is characterized by a rising advance-decline line as the smart money enters the market.

In the second phase, the advance-decline line also trends higher but usually tops out late in the second phase or early in the third phase as the smart money begins to get out.

In the third phase, it should clearly complete its rise, signalling the end of the bull market. The advance-decline line then trends lower throughout the first two phases of the new bear market and most, if not all, of the third phase.

We find that the advance-decline line indicator is much better at picking market tops than market bottoms. Market tops are always forewarned by a declining advance-decline line. During bear market bottoms, however, the advance-decline line often turns up at the same time as the Dow and sometimes even later with a certain lag. Notice in figure 16-1 how the advance-decline line gave no warning that the market was about to bottom in August 1982.

Here's a recap of the possible advance/decline situations. (Remember to take into consideration what phase the market appears to be in. Also, never rely solely on one indicator alone.)

TABLE 16-1. ADVANCE/DECLINE INDICATOR

DOW	ADVANCE/DECLINE LINE	PROGNOSIS
Rising prices	Falling	Lower
Approaching or at previous top	Considerably below corresponding top	Lower prices
Approaching or at previous top	Considerably above corresponding top	Still higher prices
Falling	Rising*	Higher prices
Approaching or at previous bottom	Considerably above previous bottom	Higher prices
Approaching or at previous bottom	Considerably below previous bottom	Still lower prices

*Time lag possible here. Should be used more as a confirming than a forecasting tool.

The advance-decline line in its "raw" form is shown in Figure 16-1. It is simply a cumulative sum of advances minus declines (see Program #9).

Some analysts prefer the smoothing effects of a moving average, with a 10-day moving average commonly used. (see Figure 16-2.)

THE UNCHANGED ISSUES INDEX is also a valuable tool. Sometimes it is useful to watch not only the numbers of stocks that advance and decline but also the number that remain unchanged. In theory, when a higher than normal percentage of stocks remain unchanged in price, the market is likely making a top. The index is calculated each day by dividing the number of issues which are unchanged in price by the total number of stocks traded. The percentage derived from the calculation will usually fluctuate in a range between 5% and 25%. Readings near the low end of the range are considered bullish, while readings near the high end are bearish (see Program #10).

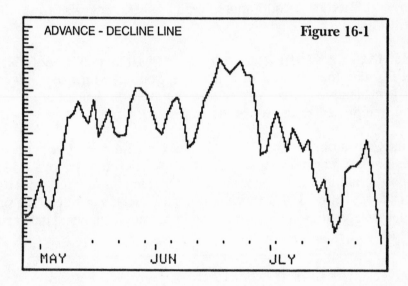

ADVANCE - DECLINE LINE   Figure 16-1

MAY   JUN   JLY

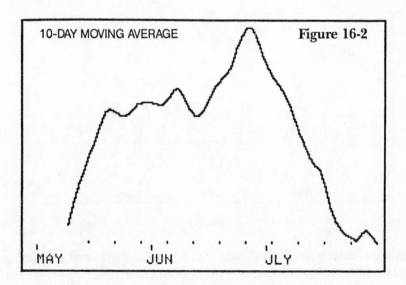

10-DAY MOVING AVERAGE   Figure 16-2

MAY   JUN   JLY

Advanced Indicators

Over the years, many analysts have developed sophisticated breadth indices by *combining* volume with advance-decline data. The remainder of this chapter explores eight unique market breadth indices, each developed by a different analyst. The material is quite technical and is included here as a reference for those who might want to explore the concept of market breadth more deeply. Others may wish to skip to the next chapter.

THE HAURLAN INDEX developed by Dave Holt, publisher of *Trade Levels,* takes the advance /decline concept one step further. This index is made up of three different moving averages which flash short-term, intermediate, and long-term buy or sell signals.

In the Haurlan Index, the short-term index is a 3-day weighted moving average of advances over declines. When the index moves above + 100, a short-term buy signal is generated, which remains in effect until the index drops below -150 at which time a sell signal is generated. The sell signal then remains in effect until the index moves above + 100 again and so on:

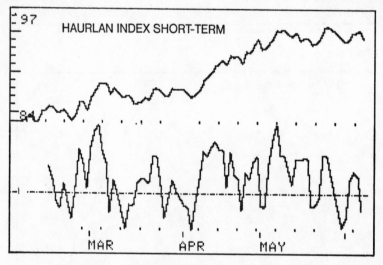

Figure 16-3

The Haurlan Intermediate Term Index is a 20-day weighted moving average, interpreted the same way you would interpret any price chart.

Buy and sell signals are determined by the crossing of trend lines or support/resistance levels:

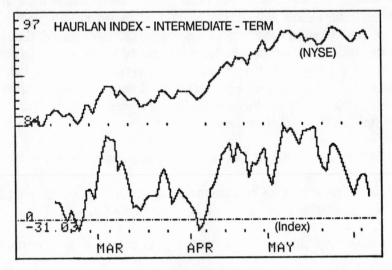

Figure 16-4

The Long-term Index—a 200-day weighted moving average of net advances over declines—is used to measure the primary trend of the market and not to determine precisely timed buy and sell points:

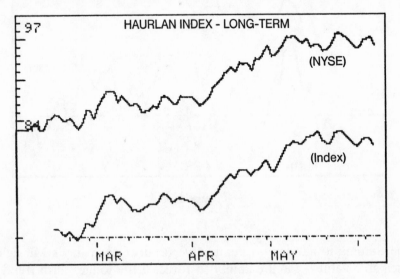

Figure 16-5

THE McCLELLAN OSCILLATOR and SUMMATION INDEX developed in the late ''60s by Sherman and Marian McClellan, represent another approach to the advance/decline concept. They are a short- to intermediate-term indicator of market behavior, pointing out overbought and oversold conditions. They use the same advance-decline line, but take the difference between the equivalent of a weighted 20-day moving average and a weighted 40-day moving average. This then behaves like an oscillator, fluctuating between a maximum and minimum range, forming chart patterns which are useful in forecasting market turns and the duration of market moves.

The McClellan Oscillator has two important characteristics:

1. The oscillator reaches an extreme value, measuring overbought and oversold conditions, *before* important turning points.

2. The oscillator then passes through zero at or very soon *after* the turning points:

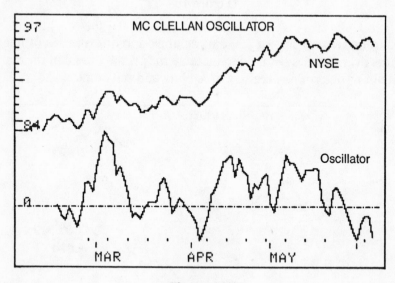

Figure 16-6

The Summation Index—a cumulative total of each day's McClellan Oscillator value—has the ability to forecast the longer term trend of the market. (Figure 16-7).

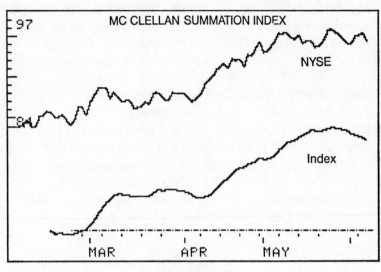

Figure 16-7

Figure 16-8 shows the position of the Summation Index at the August 1982 market bottom. Notice how it failed to go lower than in June.

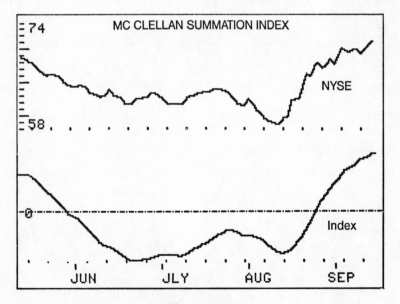

Figure 16-8

A 50-page booklet, *Patterns for Profit*, detailing how to use and interpret both the McClellan Oscillator and Summation Index is available from Trade Levels, Inc., 21241 Ventura Boulevard, Suite 269, Woodland Hills, CA 91364.

THE ARMS INDEX is among those that take the breadth of market studies one step further by adding *volume* to the equation. It measures the relative strength of volume entering advancing stocks against the strength of volume entering declining stocks, and is calculated as follows: Divide the number of advancing stocks by the number of declining stocks. Then divide the upside volume by the downside volume. Finally, divide the first answer by the second result. Expressed in a formula:

$$X = (A/D) / (UV/DV)$$
where X = Arms Index
$$A = \text{advancing stocks}$$
$$D = \text{declining stocks}$$
$$UV = \text{upside volume}$$
$$DV = \text{downside volume}$$

This gives you the short-term index. Readings below 1.0 are bullish; readings above 1.0 are bearish. Extreme readings of 1.50 or higher are very bearish; and of .50 or lower very bullish. "Climax readings" would be at 2.00 and .30.

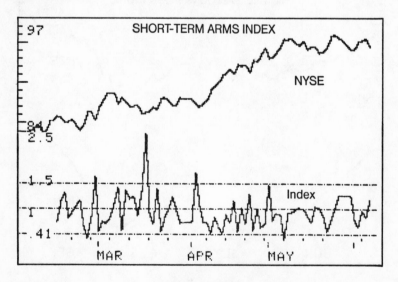

Figure 16-9

A short-to-medium term trading signal can be obtained by plotting a 5-day moving average of the short-term index. Here, a sell signal is generated when the index rises above 1.00; a buy signal produced when it falls below 1.00.

An intermediate to long-term trading signal can be generated by using a 10 day moving average of the index and, as such, it may be viewed as an overbought/oversold indicator. A longer term signal can be pro-

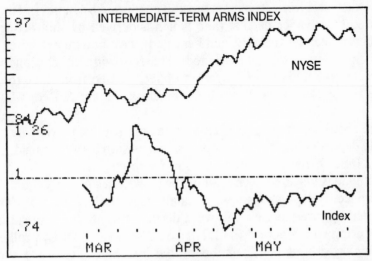

Figure 16-10

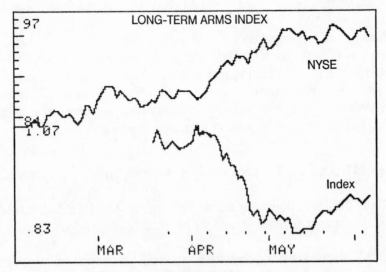

Figure 16-11

duced by using a 10-day/25-day moving average crossover of the index. On the resulting graphs (see figures 16-9,16-10 and 16-11) you can also use trendline and support/resistance theory. (More information on this system can be found in Gerald Appel's *Winning Stock Selection Systems*, published by Signalert Corporation, Great Neck, New York.)

THE HUGHES BREADTH INDICATOR is the result of some of the most exhaustive work on market breadth conducted by James F. Hughes. He used an advance-decline ratio which is derived by subtracting the number of declines from the number of advances and then dividing that number by the total issues traded. The following conclusions were abstracted from his *Weekly Market Letter*, written from 1960 to 1964 while at the New York firm of Auchincloss, Parker & Redpath.

Hughes believed that sustained major advances in the market are completely dependent upon a harmonious relationship between breadth and price. Indeed, he found good reason to be concerned whenever the breadth index began to decline while the Dow Jones Averages continued to advance. His research showed that all major declines since 1919 were preceded by three to ten weeks of a declining trend in the breadth index, during which period the DJIA could stage at least two rallies to new highs without confirmation by the indicator. Following such a divergence, the DJIA would generally decline to levels *below* the price level it had reached at the time the breadth index reached *its* high.

Such major divergences do not generally occur in markets which are in trading ranges. Rather, they are associated with periods of high speculative activity following sustained advances. Therefore, although relatively rare, when they do occur, major breadth/price divergences carry with them a high technical probability that the subsequent decline will end with a multiple price collapse or "selling climax."

A SELLING CLIMAX occurs under the following circumstances:

(a) Daily declines should represent 70% or more of total issues traded and daily advances of 15% or less of total issues traded.

(b) Until the market has a day or two of visible technical recovery, consecutive climax days are counted as only *one* selling climax.

(c) Following one selling climax, if a rally fails to gain 50% of the ground lost during the decline, the decline should resume. If a second climax appears, the rally objective is raised to two-thirds of the decline. And, following a triple selling climax, technical probabilities highly favor a twenty percent rally from the lows. Until you have an indication of at least three selling climaxes, there is no justification for buying. But, as a general rule, whenever five temporary selling climaxes are crowded into thirty-five days or less, the investor can purchase stocks for a move up of intermediate proportions.

As we saw earlier in the chapter, the failure of our breadth indicators to confirm a new high in the Dow implied lower prices. But it does not necessarily mean that a *major* decline is imminent. Such nonconfirmation has frequently preceded relatively *minor* intermediate trading swings. However, it can be very helpful because as long as the breadth is continuing to make new highs, even if the Dow is not, a bear market is highly unlikely; and, any reaction which develops without a divergence must be regarded as only an intermediate interruption of an uptrend, (This is supported by documentation which goes back as far as 1934).

A BUYING CLIMAX, although not defined by Hughes, can be characterized with criteria which are similar to those of the selling climax: Advancing issues representing 70% or more of total issues and declining issues 15% or less. Since a buying climax takes place generally near intermediate bottoms—not the ultimate tops—and is often followed by new highs, its significance is not as great as a selling climax.

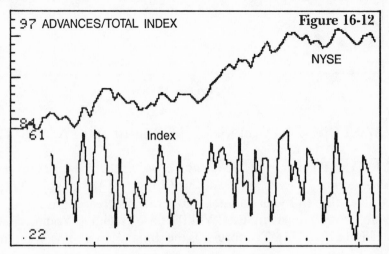

Figure 16-12

I have programmed my computer to look for selling climaxes and find it to be quite accurate in spotting short-term oversold conditions that are likely to result in a bounceback the next day. (Figure 16-12).

RICHARD RUSSELL, publisher of *Dow Theory Letters*, is well known for his work on breadth. Like Hughes, he also uses the advance/decline ratio which he computes by subtracting the number of declining issues and dividing the result by the total issues traded (A - D)/T. Like Hughes, Russell rates this indicator highly, writing that: "In general, I have found the AD ratio to be the dominant indicator or the more reliable indicator of the primary trend of the market. Thus highs on breadth unconfirmed by highs on the Industrial Average generally occur only within a primary bull market. Conversely, new lows on the Industrial Average generally occur within the framework of primary bear markets":

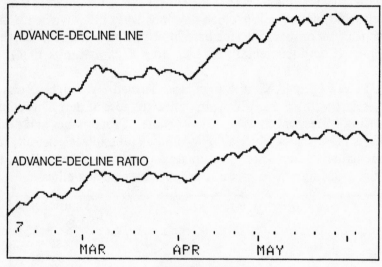

Figure 16-13

The **A/D LINE** is not significantly different from the A/D RATIO.

PAUL DYSART, editor of *Trendway Economic Services*, uses the basic advance-decline line which he calls his Composite Basic Issues Traded Index. He takes this idea one step further in his creation of a Positive Volume Issues Traded Index (PVITI) and a Negative Volume Issues Traded Index (NVITI). The former is the summation of advances minus declines *only on days when total volume of trading increases over that of the previous day*. The latter is defined similarly on days when volume of trading *decreased* from the previous day, and it is this one which Dysart feels is the most valuable since it measures the way the market regains its equilibrium after the effect of increased volume days:

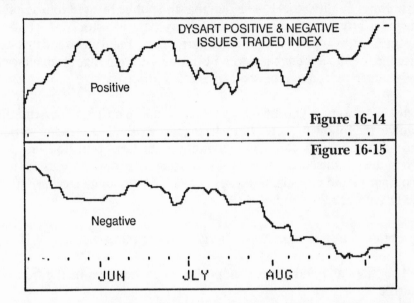

DYSART POSITIVE & NEGATIVE
ISSUES TRADED INDEX

Positive

Figure 16-14

Figure 16-15

Negative

JUN   JLY   AUG

HAMILTON BOLTON, the late editor of the *Bolton-Tremblay Bank Credit Analyst*, was one of the few analysts who calculated an advance-decline index using the *unchanged* issues as a basic component. He used the square root of the difference between the ratio of advances to unchanged and the ratio of declining to unchanged (BOLTON INDEX = square root of A/U - D/U). His reasons for the square root was that it eliminated a strong downward bias.

In dynamic up and down phases of the market, Bolton's index is impacted by (1) heavy excesses of advances over declines or vice versa, and (2) a shrinking, unchanged component in the denominator. In top areas, however, and in slow bottom areas, unchanged issues tend to expand, reducing the index. Such action helps indicate a turn in trend and supports the contention of underlying strength or weakness.

WALTER HEIBY, in his exhaustive book on market breadth, *Stock Market Profits Through Dynamic Synthesis*, concludes that the usual breadth-of-market studies are not complete and do not always hold true. He points to the 1963-64 period when the number of advancing issues each day was a continual disappointment, leading many analysts to expect a major decline which never materialized; and he suggests that the breadth indicators in those years reflected high institutional demand for Dow Jones quality stocks. The fact that the public refused to make the advance a broader one should not have swayed the investor from a bullish posture. Heiby's point has become particularly relevant in today's environment of uncertainty and with institutions accounting for an increasingly larger percentage of stock market trading.

Heiby's answer, which he calls the "Dynamic Synthesis," essentially involves the following steps: First, he takes the last 50-day trading period and splits the chart into four horizontal quartiles—top, bottom, and two in the middle. Second, he looks for four criteria which must be met to obtain a valid buy signal which he calls the "Advance-Decline Quartile Divergence Syndrome."

To obtain a buy signal, four criteria must be met:

1. The Standard and Poor Composite Index must be in the bottom quartile.

2. The Advancing Issues Index must be in the top quartile.

3. The Advancing Issues Index must be greater than the Declining Issues Index.

4. The unchanged Issues must not be in the top quartile.

Similarly, to obtain a sell signal, five criteria must be met:

1. The Standard and Poor Composite Index must be in the top quartile.

2. The Advancing Issues Index must be in the bottom quartile.

3. The Declining Issues Index must be in the top quartile.

4. The Advancing Issues Index must be less than the Declining Issues Index.

5. The Unchanged Issues Index must not be in the lowest quartile.

Finally, after one or another of these sets of criteria have been met, he looks at other indicators such as short sales, odd-lot sales, and odd-lot purchase volume. To my knowledge, Heiby's work has never been programmed and, therefore, might prove to be a very interesting area of investigation for you and your computer. His book is available through the Institute of Dynamic Synthesis in Chicago. Also, many of the other formulas discussed here are available in the Computrac software package (see Appendix B).

17

LEADERSHIP AND QUALITY

During a stock-market rise, determining the quality of stocks leading the advance often can lend an important clue as to what phase it is in. In general, bull markets begin with the high quality blue chips. Then, after a correction, somewhat lower priced stocks are thought to be bargains and rapidly gain investor attention. By the third and final phase of the market advance, the cheaper, more speculative issues—often found on the over-the-counter market or the American Exchange—now make the most rapid gains. This is usually an indication that the bull market is nearing its end.

THE MOST ACTIVE ISSUES is one of the best ways to monitor market leadership. The 15 Most Active Issues (published daily) and the 20 Most Active Issues (published weekly) list which stocks are being most actively bought and sold according to the number of shares traded. Therefore, the lists generally reflect the concentration of big money flows.

How do we determine a quality stock? Price is the best measure; and for the purpose of analysis, we can arbitrarily set the $40 mark as the key threshold: If the majority of the Most Actives has a price of greater than $40 per share, we would consider the advance to be led by *quality* stocks. On the other hand, if the majority of the Most Actives are below $40 per share, with some in the $10-25 price range, we would consider the advance to be primarily speculative, leading us to expect a possible stock-market decline.

When attempting to catch short-term swings, you plot the percentage of the 15 Most Actives that showed a gain for that day. As an example, if 10 issues rise, 2 decline and 3 issues remain unchanged, you would plot 10/15 or 67%. Then you take a 10-day moving average of those percentages.

When the indicator reaches the 60-70% region and starts to turn down, the market will usually be overbought and due for at least a short-term correction. However, if the indicator exceeds 70%, an entirely different signal is flashed and a powerful advance can be expected.

Likewise, when the indicator descends to 30-35% and begins to turn up, the market will be oversold and due for at least a short-term rally. During bear markets, readings of 30% are more usual. (Figure 17-1).

Generally we find that divergences between the trend of the indicator and the trend of the market can also be used to help call turning points. If the indicator is rising while prices are falling, expect the market to turn up. Conversely, if the indicator is falling while the market is rising, expect the market to turn down (see Program #7).

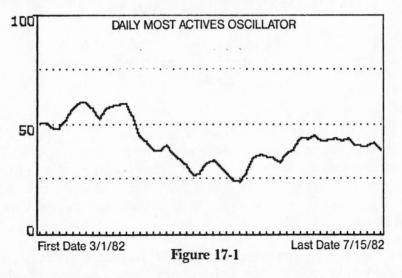

Figure 17-1

Another shorter term indicator using the 15 Most Active Issues is employed by *Indicator Digest* (451 Grand Ave., Palisades Park, NJ 07650). To compute the indicator, simply subtract declining issues from advancing issues. For example, if 10 rose, 4 declined and 1 remained unchanged, the net for the day is 6. If 5 rose, 8 declined and 2 remained unchanged, the net would be -3.

Maintain a 30-day cumulative total of the latest 30 days'' reading. As illustrated in figure 17-2, a buy signal is generated when the 30-day total rises to +9; a sell signal is generated when the 30-day total falls to below -9; and readings between +9 and -9 are neutral, meaning that the previous signal remains in effect (see Program #5).

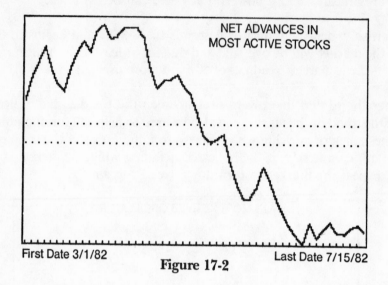

First Date 3/1/82

Figure 17-2

Last Date 7/15/82

NEW HIGHS AND NEW LOWS. This indicator, like the advance-decline line, is also a breadth-of-the-market indicator and can be used in much the same way. "New highs" are defined as the number of issues that have made new highs during the latest 52-week period; whereas "new lows" designate the number of issues that have made new lows during that period.

For instance, if the number of new highs is expanding, it can be considered a bullish sign. If the number of new highs is contracting, while the number of new lows is expanding, it may be considered bearish. The problem is that this interpretation is a bit oversimplified; you really must also consider other factors or it can lead you astray. You must be aware of what phase the market is in and whether divergence exists between your high/low indicator and the market itself.

Let's assume that the Dow Jones has been entrenched in a bear market for two years and your indicator is showing zero stocks at new highs and 650 stocks at new lows. A month later the Dow Jones has plummeted another 50 points, but now the indicator shows 5 stocks at new highs and only 500 stocks at new lows. This is exactly what we are looking for—a major nonconfirmation. It means that 150 stocks have rallied from their lows – an extremely significant event, signalling the end of the bear market. But the context in which all this has occurred is the key. Since the bear market has been in force for two years and since the entire stock-market cycle is typically 4 - 4 1/2 years, we are overdue for a turnaround. If the bear market had recently begun, we would not attach much significance to a similar pattern. Figure 17-3 shows the pattern of new highs and new lows during the critical summer of 1982 prior to the record-smashing rally which soon ensued.

Now, assume a new bull market has begun. At first, the new lows still outnumber the new highs. But we are concerned only with the trend—the fact that each day there are *more* new highs and *fewer* new lows. After four months, the Dow Jones has risen 150 points and our high/low indicator looks healthy. We now have 550 new highs and zero new lows.

One month later, the Dow Jones is 50 points higher but the high/low indicator shows only 400 new highs and 10 new lows. Should we be concerned? Is this the end of the bull market? Maybe not. If, in fact, we are correct in identifying the last major bottom and we are truly in a new bull market, it could be too early for it to be terminating. Rather than a new bear market, our high/low indicator is probably signalling a correction.

It is normal after the first major advance in a bull market for the number of new highs to decrease somewhat—usually as the Dow Jones is entering its first corrective phase. However, if the Dow continues to advance despite a declining number of new highs, it often indicates that a more severe correction is in the making.

To complete the cycle, assume we are 2 - 2 1/2 years into the bull market. We're on the lookout for a turnaround and we detect a serious divergence between the Dow Jones and the high/low indicator: The Dow Jones is still moving higher while the number of new highs is declining. This time, the nonconfirmation can be taken more seriously. Although the peaking out of the number of new highs usually occurs months in advance of the final high in the Dow, this is a good time to begin an orderly liquidation process.

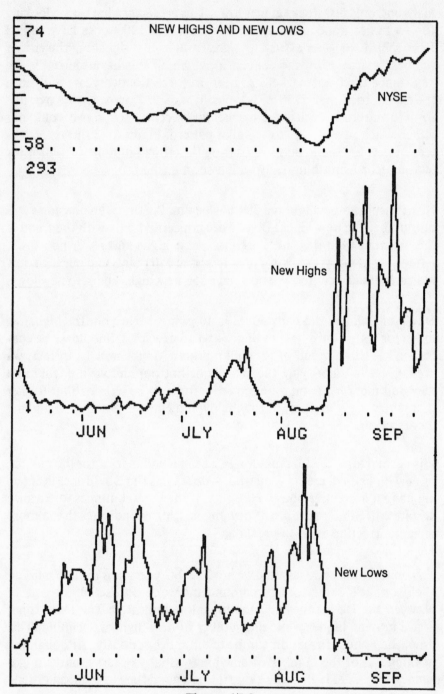

Figure 17-3

Thus, the high/low indicator can be a valuable tool—*if used properly and in conjunction with other indicators.*

But before we leave this chapter, we hasten to add one word of warning. Stock-market cycles have tended to parallel the business cycle in length, with an average lead time of roughly nine months—moving up well in advance of a recovery or boom (which tended to last 2 1/2 - 3 years) and down in advance of a recession (which lasted 1 - 1 1/2 years.) In the 1980s, however, the timing of the business cycles has been reversed with shortened recoveries and long, extensive recessions. If the stock market follows a similar pattern, the bull market could end much earlier than would normally be anticipated.

CHAPTER

18

MARKET SENTIMENT INDICATORS

Market sentiment indicators are those which attempt to gauge the mood of market participants—generally classified as either "sophisticated" or "unsophisticated.'

Sophisticated market players are professionals who make their living from stock-market trading. The specialists, for example, concentrate on only one or two issues and trade on the floor of the Exchange for their own account. In order to give each stock better liquidity and to make a more orderly market for the general public, they are required to buy in the absence of other competing bids and to sell in the absence of other competing offers.

Another group, the Exchange members, are those who have purchased a "seat" on the Exchange. This allows them to trade on the floor without paying commissions.

Although there are, of course, many notable exceptions, as a whole, the general public is most often thought to be unsophisticated and, more often than not, wrong in the world of stock-market trading. Therefore, their activity is also watched very closely for a clue as to where the market may be headed.

Professionals consider market sentiment indicators to be among their most valuable tools. The indicators in this chapter will enable you to determine the "mood" of each of the three groups of market participants discussed; and four programs are provided in the Appendix which will allow you to monitor their actions.

The **SHORT INTEREST RATIO**, published monthly in *Barron's*, is designed to spot when the public becomes overly pessimistic. It is calculated by dividing the total number of short sales outstanding on the NYSE by the average daily trading volume on the exchange that month. If the short interest ratio is above 1.75, it is considered a bullish signal. A reading of slightly above 2.0 (a short interest of twice the average daily volume) was recorded in June of 1982, two months ahead of the dynamic rally that followed in August. Another time the ratio had reached 2.0 was in July 1970, also a very good time to buy stocks.

On the opposite side of the spectrum, the indicator has, on occasion, been used to signal excessive public optimism when the ratio has dropped below 1.0. But such bearish signals have turned out to be very unreliable on several occasions. Therefore, *I suggest you use the short interest ratio primarily as a buy signal.*

ODD-LOT PURCHASES OR SHORT SALES refer to all transactions that involve less than 100 shares of stock. Since these purchases and sales are usually transacted by the less sophisticated market players, these figures, published daily in most newspapers, can often play a role in market timing.

The odd-lot short-sale ratio (see Program #11 in Appendix) is computed by dividing odd-lot short sales by total short sales each week. A moving average may then be used to smooth the data.

The basic theory is that a trend toward increased odd-lot selling is bullish; a trend toward decreased odd-lot selling is bearish. You may also look at the other side of the coin. A trend toward increased odd-lot buying is bearish; a trend toward decreased odd-lot buying is bullish.

It has been found that odd-lotters often tend to panic and sell at the wrong times, with odd-lot short selling reaching a peak just as the market bottoms and still a second peak often reached as the market retests its bottom.

SPECIALIST SHORT SALES—by members of the New York Stock Exchange—is a good indicator of the "smart money movements." Since the specialist's purpose is to make an orderly market, he is restricted in trading activity by certain rules. Still, he is considered to be one of the most astute traders in the game, a fact which can be well documented by past performance. Therefore, when heavy specialist short selling is evident, it is usually a good time to be bearish on the market. Conversely, when specialist short selling is light, it often is a good time to be buying stocks. This is not to say that specialists are always right. But, should you notice that specialist short selling is decreasing at the same time as odd-lot short selling is increasing, one indicator is confirming the other, adding credence to the signal.

The Specialist Short Sale Ratio may be computed weekly by dividing the total number of short sales on the NYSE each week into the number of shares sold short by specialists (see Program #11). These data can also be found in *Barron's*, but there is a two week time lag before the figures are released to the public.

A buy signal can be generated by a single weekly reading below 33%, or a series of four weekly readings averaging below 35%. *A sell signal* is indicated when a single weekly reading exceeds 58% or the average of the latest four weekly readings exceeds 55%. As with the Short Interest Ratio, buy signals tend to be more accurate than sell signals.

MEMBER SHORT SALES also tends to be a good "smart money indicator." Low short selling on the part of the members is considered bullish; heavy short selling is considered bearish. These data are carried weekly and can also be found in *Barron's*.

The Member Short-Sale Ratio is calculated by dividing (a) the number of shares sold short by members of the NYSE by (b) the total number of shares sold short that week (see Program #11). (Or if you want to look at the other side of the coin, you can divide (a) the number of shares sold short by *non*-members of the exchange by (b) total. The result is the "Public Short-Sale Ratio" which, of course, is simply the reciprocal of the Member Short-Sale Ratio.)

It has been found that a reading below 65% in the Member Short-Sale Ratio is usually an excellent buy signal for an intermediate or major move. A study showing this historical relationship was conducted by Norman G. Fosback, in *Stock Market Logic* (The Institute for Economic Research, 3471 N. Federal Highway, Ft. Lauderdale, FL 33306). Here are the results:

TABLE 18-1. MEMBER SHORT SALES AND
THREE-MONTH MARKET PERFORMANCE (1941-75)

Member Short Sales (average of last ten weeks)	S & P 500 Index (3 months later)	Probability of Rising Prices
over 80%	-1.1%	48%
75 - 80%	+0.5%	54%
70 - 75%	+3.3%	68%
65 - 70%	+4.5%	75%
0 - 65%	+5.9%	88%
35-year average	+1.9%	62%

When the 10-week moving average of Member Short Sales was less than 65%, the market's average gain 3 months later was 5.9%; six months later it was 16.5%; and one year later, 24.39%. This indicator also tends to produce better buy signals than sell signals. However, a sale is indicated when the ratio approaches 88%.

MEMBER TRADING, another indicator of member activity, is derived by subtracting the number of shares sold by members of the NYSE from the number purchased. Net buying, designated by a rising line, carries bullish implications. Conversely, a falling line indicates the Members have been selling and should be viewed bearishly. These data are also availably weekly in *Barron's*.

ART MERRILL (Merrill Analysis Inc., Box 228, Chappaqua, NY 10514) has shown that this indicator—using an exponential moving average rather than the raw data—is among the most significant of intermediate and major trend indicators (see Program #12). Another approach would be to maintain an exponential moving average of the net weekly cumulative total of member purchases minus sales. You can then chart the difference between the latest week's readings and the exponential moving average you are maintaining. Your indicator will rise as member trading becomes more positive and falls when it turns negative.

ADVISORY SENTIMENT is often best used as an indicator of contrary opinion. It is common knowledge that stock-market investment advisors tend, for the most part, to be trend followers. They tend to turn bullish quite quickly after market prices start rising and to stay bullish during the bull market. Therefore, with some notable exceptions, they cannot be relied upon for calling a market top. Conversely, when the market has been declining, advisors tend to get overly pessimistic, often right at what turns out to be a major bottom. In sum, they seem to do very poorly at the beginning and end of a bear market.

The degree of advisors' optimism and pessimism can best be determined by the "Sentiment Index" which is maintained by *Investors Intelligence* (2 East Avenue, Larchmont, NY 10538). Abe Cohen—the publisher who tallies the percentage of advisory services that are bullish and bearish—has found that bear markets generally touch bottom when 60% or more of advisory services turn outright bearish; but in bull markets, widespread bullish sentiment does not necessarily end the rise.

CUSTOMER'S MARGIN DEBT refers to the amount of money owed to New York Stock Exchange member firms by customers who have borrowed money to finance their stock purchases. This figure, calculated on the last trading day of each month by the NYSE, is not released to the public until two or three weeks later. The figure can be found in *Barron's* or obtained directly by writing to the New York Stock Exchange, 11 Wall Street, New York, NY 10005.

Margin-account traders have traditionally been considered among the more sophisticated stock-market investors. Watching their borrowing patterns reveals when they are buying or selling stocks. When margin debt is rapidly expanding, it indicates that this group is buying heavily; when margin debt is decreasing, it can be reasoned that they are liquidating on balance.

The trend of Customer's Margin Debt has proven to be an excellent long-term market indicator. Program #21 plots a line representing Customer's Margin Debt and also a line representing a 12-month moving average of the same. A buy signal is given when the current figure moves above the 12-month moving average. A sell signal is rendered when the current figure drops below the 12-month moving average. This particular timing method, developed by Norman Fosback, has proven to be an excellent indicator of bull and bear markets during the past 35 years. The important tops of 1956, 1959, 1961, 1966, 1968 and 1973 were all accompanied or preceded by turns in Customer's Margin Debt. Similarly, troughs established in 1957, 1960, 1962, 1966, 1970 and 1974 were accompanied by upturns in Customer's Margin Debt.

FREE CREDIT BALANCES refers to the cash left on account with New York Stock Exchange member brokerage firms. This series is also published monthly and can be obtained either from *Barron's* or directly from the New York Stock Exchange.

Unlike Margin Debt figures, Free Credit Balances usually reflect the activity of smaller, unsophisticated investors. The reasoning behind this is that only unsophisticated investors would allow their cash balances to lie idle at brokerage firms earning no interest.

Rising credit balances indicate that the small investors are selling stock and thus can be interpreted bullishly. Falling credit balances mean small investors are buying and should be interpreted bearishly.

As with Customer's Margin Debt, a useful technique is to plot the current series of Free Credit Balances against a twelve-month moving average. A buy signal is generated when the current series crosses above the twelve-month moving average; a sell signal occurs when the current series crosses below the twelve-month moving average (see Program #21).

DOW JONES UTILITY AVERAGE—Because of their sensitivity to interest rates, the utility stocks are often seen as a bellwether for the entire market. Utility stocks are more sensitive to interest rates than other stocks for two reasons: 1) utilities are heavy borrowers and thus their earnings are easily hurt by rising interest rates; and 2) utilities customarily pay a high dividend yield and are often purchased as a substitute for bonds. When interest rates rise, investors are likely to sell their utility stocks—purchased originally for their yield—and rush to higher yielding short-term instruments such as T-bills. Thus, the Dow Jones Utility Average is often considered to be a leading indicator for the major trend of the stock market.

A useful technique is to plot the Dow Jones Utility Average overlayed with a 15-week moving average. When the current readings are above the 15-week moving average, the utility stocks can be classified as being in an uptrend and the stock market also should continue higher. When current readings drop below the 15-week moving average, a sell signal is in order (refer to Program #22).

Market sentiment indicators—like the others considered in this book —are almost exclusively concerned with technical factors which are internal to the market. In the next chapter, however, we give a few examples of how your computer can also track fundamental monetary indicators.

19

MONETARY INDICATORS

NET FREE RESERVES are an important measure of liquidity in the banking system. They represent the excess cash that banks hold over and above their legal required reserves and borrowings from the Federal Reserve (figure 19-1). When banks are flush with funds, the banking system is termed to be in a "net free reserves" position. Under such conditions the banks have the ability to finance business growth and economic expansion.

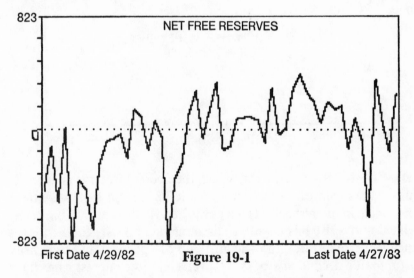

First Date 4/29/82   **Figure 19-1**   Last Date 4/27/83

When net free reserves are negative, the banking system is termed to be in a "net borrowed reserves" position. This means that money is tight and that the necessary funds to fuel a business expansion are not present in the banking system. Such conditions often presage market declines. Conversely, a net free reserves position by the banking system is usually followed by a rising stock market. Even more reliability can be given to the forecast when free reserves are expanding (see Program #13).

MONEY SUPPLY. Another measure of liquidity is the money supply itself. At Weiss Research, our econometric model of the economy shows that the percent change of money-supply growth is a good indicator of future stock-market movements (figure 19-2). Specifically, the percent change in M-1 growth over a 13-week period has a lagged positive correlation with the Standard and Poors 500 Index with the maximum effect of the money supply change being exhibited some four weeks into the future (see Program #14).

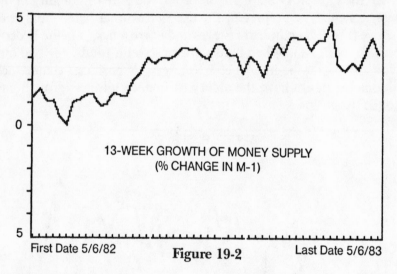

13-WEEK GROWTH OF MONEY SUPPLY
(% CHANGE IN M-1)

First Date 5/6/82   **Figure 19-2**   Last Date 5/6/83

The **DISCOUNT RATE**, the rate which the Federal Reserve charges its member banks, can often have a dramatic impact on stocks. After a major decline in interest rates (such as the Fed funds rate or T-bill rates) has ended and a rise has begun, a discount-rate hike by the Fed gives the incipient rise in rates an official stamp of approval and can easily set off a major decline in stocks. Conversely, after interest rates have risen dramatically and have begun to decline somewhat, a cut in the discount rate by the Fed is, in effect, their way of telling the market that they intend to pump money into the economy and push rates down, triggering a major stock-market rally.

Thus, as a general rule, a cut in the discount rate can be viewed as bullish for the stock market and an increase in the rate would be considered a negative. Our model has shown the maximum impact on the stock market to be three weeks after a discount-rate change. After a very long interest-rate decline, however, a discount-rate cut can often be viewed as a climactic move. This is especially true if the Fed is trying to artificially lower interest rates by cutting the discount rate well *below* the Federal funds rate—the rate at which banks borrow from each other. The reverse is true after a major rise. In either case, you should be on the lookout for a turnaround in interest rates and, subsequently, in stocks (see Program #15).

FEDERAL FUNDS RATE refers to the rate that banks charge one another for overnight loans and is the most reliable tool for anticipating discount-rate changes. Banks in general have two sources available for borrowing: (1) from the Federal Reserve at the discount rate and (2) from other banks at the "fed funds rate." As a rule, banks prefer to borrow in the overnight "fed funds" market. But when the fed funds rate moves substantially higher than the discount rate, it will generally encourage them to seek more money from the Fed. This can be accurately viewed as having negative connotations for the stock market in that a discount rate hike could be triggered when the Fed Funds rate rises above the discount rate by one percentage point (100 basis points) or more as shown in figure 19-3 (see Program #16).

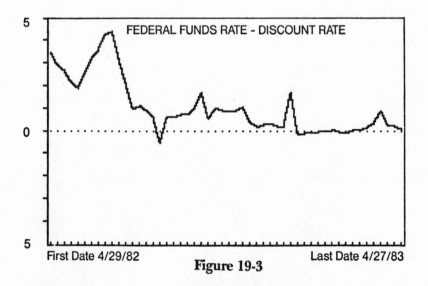

Figure 19-3

These monetary indicators and the various other technical tools described here should help you to determine the general direction of the markets over the medium-term. But in order to further fine-tune your timing, the short-term market indicators may also come in handy as you will see in the next chapter.

20

SHORT-TERM MARKET INDICATORS

With market volatility greater than ever before and with greater leverage available than in most past periods, short-term indicators have become more important in order to give you advance warning of sudden turns.

The **SHORT-TERM TRADING INDEX,** also know as TRIN, evaluates buying and selling pressure. Specifically, it measures the amount of volume going into advancing stocks versus the amount of volume going into declining issues and TRIN can be monitored on a daily or intraday basis. The formula is:

$$\text{TRIN} = \frac{(\text{\# of advancing issues/\# of declining issues})}{(\text{upside volume/downside volume})}$$

As an example, assume that on one day on the New York Stock Exchange we have:

	Issues (number)	Volume (millions of shares)
Advancing	800	50
Declining	600	25

The TRIN that day would be equal to:

$$\text{TRIN} = \frac{(800/600)}{(50/25)} = \frac{1.33}{.2} = .67$$

119

In this case, buying pressure was stronger than selling pressure as comparatively more volume was going into advancing issues. It is generally accepted that a TRIN of between .65 and .90 is a bullish sign for the short term, while a reading of below .65 is considered *very* bullish. Readings of .90 to 1.10 are regarded as neutral, while TRIN above 1.10 carries bearish connotations.

TRIN can be very helpful in timing your purchases and sales, allowing you to get the very best possible executions of your trades. This can sometimes be crucial, especially when dealing in the options market. For example, if I am planning to sell and TRIN is bullish, I am likely to place my "ask" (sell order) slightly above the current "bid." On the other hand, if TRIN is bearish, I usually place my orders to sell immediately or "at the market" as it is unlikely I will receive a better price by waiting.

Still another way to use TRIN is as a short-term confirmation or non-confirmation of the market averages. In other words, if the market declines one day while TRIN is registering a bullish reading, the chances are that the market decline will not continue. Such divergence over two or three days can often forewarn of a market bottom. Confirmation, on the other hand, would be implied when the market moves up and the TRIN is bullish. In such a case, we would expect still higher prices—at least in the near term.

The Short-Term Trading Index is also sometimes employed as an overbought/oversold indicator by using its 10-day moving average:

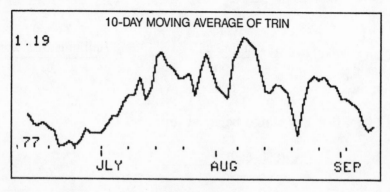

Figure 20-1

If the 10-day moving average of TRIN is below .75, the market is considered to be overbought. If, in addition, the previous one-day reading exceeds 1.20, an immediate correction can be expected.

Conversely, if the 10-day moving average of TRIN is above 1.20, the market is considered to be oversold; and if, in addition, the previous one-day reading is below .65, an immediate corrective rally is called for (see Program #23).

THE TICK indicator is another very commonly cited short-term barometer used intraday since it is updated every few minutes. It refers to the net upticks at that point in time, and can be best described as a snapshot taken of the market which "freezes" the action on the New York Stock Exchange. Each stock whose last trade is completed at a higher price than the previous trade is considered an "uptick." Each stock whose last trade is completed at a lower price is counted as a "downtick." The Tick indicator simply equals all upticks minus all downticks. If traders are bidding prices up, it will be recorded as a higher tick reading. Any reading above + 100 is considered bullish, anything between - 100 and + 100 is neutral, and below -100 is bearish. Thus, the Tick is probably the most sensitive of all market indicators; and by watching *both* the Tick and TRIN you can develop a very good feel for the immediate market direction, timing your purchases and sales accordingly.

CHAPTER

21

INDUSTRY GROUPS

Most stocks can be classified according to groups—General Motors, Ford and Chrysler in the automobile group; ASA and HOMESTAKE in the goldmining group, etc. Since most companies within a group tend to move in unison, monitoring their performance can be helpful in various ways: By charting the performance of each group, you can quickly see which ones are leading an advance and which are lagging behind. If you intend to buy particular stocks, the information can make the selection process much easier. Needless to say, it is usually better to buy those issues which are members of an industry group which is leading the market move.

RELATIVE STRENGTH tracks industry groups in comparison to the market as a whole. The performance of each group is compared individually to the performance of the New York Stock Exchange Composite Index over a selected period of time, allowing you to analyze whether it is outperforming or underperforming the general market. A ranking can then be assigned to each industry group in terms of its relative strength.

I have developed three programs which will allow you to monitor the performance of the industry groups, using *Barron's* "Industry Stock Groups" for your data.

The first program (#17) prints a chart for a specified industry group showing its performance over the most recent one-year period. This allows you to easily monitor the trend of the group itself as illustrated by the example in figure 21-1.

The second program (#18) plots the group's performance *relative* to the New York Stock Exchange Composite Index during the same period.

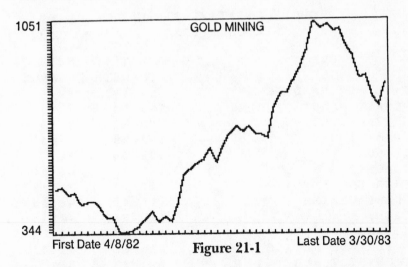

First Date 4/8/82 **Figure 21-1** Last Date 3/30/83

This output can add greatly to your information. For example, while the results of Program #17 may show the index of a particular group gaining in price, the results of Program #18 might show the group to actually be lagging behind the market as a whole. On the other hand, the particular group may be seen to be in a downtrend, while examination of the relative strength chart shows that the group is still performing relatively better than the market as a whole.

Finally, when you are looking for short-sale targets, this indicator will alert you to which industries are the weakest.

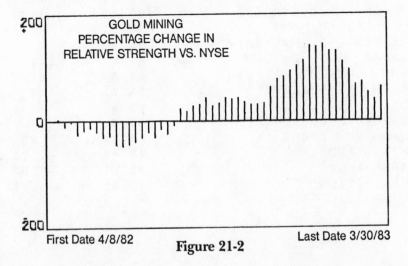

First Date 4/8/82 **Figure 21-2** Last Date 3/30/83

GROUP RELATIVE STRENGTH
PERIOD 1 YEAR

STOCK GROUP	RELATIVE STRENGTH	NET CHANGE
RETAIL MERCHANDISE	183.19	.08
AIRCRAFT MANUFACTURING	155.33	1.83
AIR TRANSPORT	143.65	8.23
GOLD MINING	139.28	9.68
PACKING	133.58	2.7
AUTOMOBILES	127.23	-3.47
OFFICE EQUIPMENT	123.01	1.76
GROCERY CHAINS	119.41	-6.15
RUBBER	119.36	-.01
TEXTILES	117.77	-2.35
NON-FERROUS METALS	115.63	2.45
MOTION PICTURES	112.93	5.7
DOW-JONES TRANSPORTATION	112.32	-.08
ELECTRICAL EQUIPMENT	110.99	-1.54
LIQUOR	107.58	-1.85
MACHINE TOOLS	104.63	4.29
INSTALLMENT FINANCING	103.89	-.05
CHEMICALS	103.82	-1.54
BLDG MATERIALS & EQUIPMENT	102.89	-2.38
DOW-JONES COMPOSITE	102.22	-.55
DOW-JONES INDUSTRIALS	101.89	-.94
DRUGS	101.14	-.12
AUTOMOBILE EQUIPMENT	100.53	-.04
PAPER	97.29	-1.09
FOODS AND BEVERAGES	97.18	-1.61
TOBACCO	96.32	.35
CLOSED-END INVESTMENTS	93.63	.01
BANKS	92.33	1.1
DOW-JONES UTILITIES	84.87	.02
MACHINERY(HEAVY)	84.37	.14
OIL	81.3	-2.58
RAILROAD EQUIPMENT	80.95	.24
FARM EQUIPMENT	79.28	-.98
STEEL AND IRON	78.62	-1.78
INSURANCE	75.45	-1.07
TELEVISION	46.01	-1.22

Figure 21-3

Figure 21-2 is an example of the results of Program #18. Since it is in the form of an oscillator, the industry index may oscillate above or below the center line which represents the New York Stock Exchange Composite Index. (Program #19 is automated so as to print charts of all 36 industry groups in a sequence.)

The third program (#20) ranks each industry in terms of relative strength. A rating of 100.00 would mean that the industry performance matched exactly that of the New York Stock Exchange Composite Index during the given period. A net-change figure is also produced denoting the change from last week's reading. Whereas the charts from Program #19 give a historical perspective, the report generated from Program #20 gives a relative strength "snapshot" showing at a glance the strongest industry groups in the *present*. The period may be set for either three months, six months or one year. (Figure 21-3).

With these programs, your computer will direct you to the sectors which are most likely to generate the most investment profits in the shortest period of time. In the chapter which follows, we discuss a popular investment medium which can enhance your leverage with limited risk.

22

STOCK OPTIONS

Some of you who are reading this book may already have a good understanding of stock options and how to use puts and calls in your trading. Others, who might have computer skills, may not have been exposed elsewhere to the elements of option trading. Therefore, in fairness to those unfamiliar with the nomenclature, I will take the next few pages to introduce the reader to the basics. Again, if you are learned in this area, feel free to skip ahead to option strategies at the end of this chapter.

Stock options can be attractive as they offer investors a potentially large profit from a relatively small investment with a known and predetermined risk. The option buyer knows in advance that the most he can lose is the price he has paid for the option. There are two basic types of stock options—*puts and calls*. Let's start with calls.

A CALL is the right to buy 100 shares of a certain stock at a stated price within a given period of time. Common stocks on which options are traded at the Chicago Board Options Exchange (CBOE) include such well known companies as Dow Chemical, IBM, General Motors, Eastman Kodak, etc. In all, it is possible to buy or sell (write) options on approximately 85 different common stocks on the CBOE. The buyer of the option pays to the "writer" (seller) of the option a sum of money which is kept by the writer whether the option is executed or not. This is known as the "premium."

Let's take, as an example, an "April 50 call" on ABC Company. This entitles the buyer to purchase 100 shares of ABC Company at $50 a share any time between now and April.

In the case of CBOE options, each option is normally for 100 shares of a specific, widely held, actively traded security. In the example above, ABC stock is known as the "underlying security." The $50 price at which the option buyer may elect to exercise the option is known as the "exercise price" or "striking price."

"The expiration date" is the last day on which the buyer is entitled to exercise his option to purchase or sell the stock. CBOE options expire quarterly on either a January/April/July/October cycle, or quarterly cycles beginning in February or March. All options actually expire on the Saturday following the third Friday of the expiration date.

A PUT gives you the right to sell short a particular stock at a fixed price. Thus, an ABC Company April 50 put entitles the buyer to sell short 100 shares of ABC Company common stocks at $50 a share any time during the life of the option.

COST OF OPTIONS. How much does it cost to buy an option? The premium varies with each stock and can be affected by several factors:

(1) *The time factor*. Options are termed "wasting" assets. If an option cannot be exercised at a profit by its expiration date, it becomes worthless. Thus, as the expiration date is approached, the option's time value decreases. All else being equal, the more time remaining until the expiration date, the higher the premium will be. For example, an October option for a particular stock normally commands a higher premium than an otherwise identical July option because the buyer of the October option has an additional three months for the underlying stock to move in the direction expected.

(2) *The current market price of the stock in relation to the strike price of the option*. Assume that in January an investor purchases a July 50 call of ABC Company when the price of the stock is also at $50. In such a case, the investor is only paying "for the time value" of the option. But, if by March the price of the stock has risen to $60, a new investor would have to pay a higher premium for the same call than the original investor. With the stock price at $60, the July 50 call is now called an "in-the-money" option because the market price of the stock is greater than the strike price of the call. If exercised immediately, it should yield a profit of roughly $10. Conversely, if the price of the stock

were now $45 instead of $60, the July 50 call would be referred to as "out of the money" since the price of the stock is below the strike price.

(3) *Supply and demand*. Let's assume that numerous investors expect the price of the stock to rise and rush to buy calls rather than the actual stock. This automatically causes the premium to increase in value. Therefore, the price of the option is also a reflection of supply and demand for the options themselves. If the stock has been going up, there will probably be an increased demand for call options on the stock, thus making the premiums more expensive. Remember too, in such a market there is less interest in selling or writing calls by those who own the underlying stock. On the other hand, when the price of the stock is rising, put options are in less demand and are therefore comparatively less expensive.

(4) *The volatility of the underlying stock*. If a particular stock traditionally fluctuates a good deal, its option is likely to command a higher premium than the option for a stock that normally trades in a narrow price range. One common measure of a market's volatility is referred to as its "Beta." Beta is a measure of the average percentage change in the price of a stock relative to the percentage change of a market index. Thus, options on stocks with a higher beta tend to cost more. It is often for this reason that, as a general rule, premiums do not necessarily increase or decrease point for point with the price of the underlying stock. A one point change in the stock price can often result in less than a one point change in the option premium. However, once an option reaches "parity," the premium is likely to move point for point with the stock. (For a call, parity occurs when the exercise price plus the premium equals the market price of the stock. For a put, parity occurs when the exercise price minus the premium equals the market price of the stock.)

Option Strategies

The options market is made up of two different types of players. The first type uses the options market to reduce risk. This type—the investor or "hedger"—usually owns the underlying security; and to insure a known rate of return on his investments, writes (sells) a call against his stock. By doing so, he relinquishes the right to profit from any advance in the value of the stock during the term of the option, in return for the money he will receive from selling the call. If he feels strongly that the price of the stock may decline over the near term, he may purchase a put.

The second type—the speculator—does not usually own the underlying security and thus is termed "naked" when he buys puts or calls. He hopes to profit from a good percentage move in the value of a stock during a short period of time. Making this type of determination is much more difficult than it seems. The odds are stacked heavily against this player.

Option strategies can be extremely complex and, for the most part, are beyond the scope of this book. One good book on the subject is Max Onsbacher's *The New Options Market*, Walker & Company, 720 Fifth Avenue, New York, NY. It would also be a good idea to purchase an "Option Valuation Program," many of which are based on the "Black-Scholes Model" and are available for your personal computer. These programs attempt to evaluate a "fair price" for a given option based on the underlying stock's price and volatility.

Here are a few "general rules" that I use in my option trading:

1) First, make a decision on the underlying stock before looking at its options.

2) Be sure the stock has a high volatility factor (Beta).

3) Select an option that offers good liquidity—in other words with a volume of at least 500 or so per day.

4) Select an option that is fairly priced.

5) As a rule, select an option that is not too much "out of the money" nor too much "in the money." Usually an option that is "at the money" or slightly "out of the money" is the best choice.

6) Attempt to buy calls on temporary weakness in the stock; and puts, on temporary strength.

7) Usually it is worth the extra cost of the premium to select an option with approximately six months remaining rather than choosing the nearest option.

8) Because the time value of an option declines rapidly as it approaches its expiration date, generally it is wise to either liquidate the option or "roll forward" (sell your option and buy another three to six months forward) when there is two to four weeks remaining before expiration date. And, if you can, the ideal time to take profits is within the first half of the option's life.

4

CYCLES

23

THE MEANING OF CYCLES

Why do market cycles exist? Could it be that subatomic waves or celestial rotations somehow impact economic behavior? Or do they have a more mundane reason relating to yearly tax planning, harvest cycles, short and long-term business cycles, etc.?

Regardless of the underlying forces, our approach here is merely to accept the fact that cycles do exist in markets—for whatever reason—and to use the data empirically to improve our trading results. Cycle frequencies have been found ranging from just a few minutes to thousands of years, with countless cycles within those extremes. The key, therefore, to using cycles is to determine the *frequency* of the most critical cycles, while keeping in mind shorter and longer-term cycles as well. You would use the *critical* cycles for most of your trading decisions. The shorter-term cycles would aid you in refining your timing of entry and exit points; while the longer-term cycles help you determine the overall market trend.

Because one gains perspective from an understanding of long-term cycles, I wish to acquaint you with three very long-term cycles. A 2000-year "cycle of ages" has been identified within which exists the somewhat better-known 510-year "civilization cycle."

510-Year Civilization Cycle

The 510-year cycle was discovered nearly 40 years ago by Dr. Raymond H. Wheeler, Chairman of the Psychology Department at the University of Kansas. Under his direction, more than 200 researchers worked for over twenty years, studying the influences of weather on mankind. Over 3000 years of weather were evaluated along with nearly two million pieces of weather information. Over 20,000 pieces of art were studied, as was literature throughout history. In excess of 18,000 battles were examined. No stone was left unturned.

After this exhaustive research, Dr. Wheeler concluded that the present 510-year cycle would bottom in the 1980s. He expected the "death of the world" to last until the year 2000. It was his conclusion that at the end of the 510-year cycle is when governments break down and nations collapse, and that there is a wave of international wars which are "nation-falling wars." He also expected "the initiative to pass from West to East for the next 510-year period."

170-Year Drought Cycle

Within the 510-year civilization cycle are three 170-year drought cycles, verified by the ring structure of 3000-year-old redwood trees. A number of rings very close together indicates a period of drought; a series of rings further apart indicates a time of good moisture. These have tended to group into both 50-year and 170-year cycles.

At the end of a 170-year cycle, the climate turns cold and there are significant droughts. One man who has done a great deal of study on the 170-year and the 510-year cycles is R. E. McMaster, publisher of *The Reaper* (P. O. Box 39026, Phoenix, AZ 85069). He believes the 170-year cycle is also bottoming. He states: "It looks as if we are just going into one of those cold, dry cycles. The unexpected eruptions of Mt. St. Helens and El Chinchond in Mexico have added to the cooling of the climate by the debris that they have placed in the air. This and other predicted climatic changes could affect our food supply."

Kondratieff Cycle (50-54 Years)

Kondratieff, a Russian economist, based his study primarily on statistical data including wholesale prices, interest rates, wage levels, and indexes of production for the period 1780 to 1920, using the United States, Great Britain, France and Germany as the primary models. His conclusions, presented in a 1925 paper entitled *The Long Waves In Economic Life*, were basically that the existence of a cycle of from 48 to 60 years in the overall economic activity of the Western world was highly probable. These preliminary conclusions have since been reinforced by the more extensive work of Joseph Schumpeter, Edward R. Dewey and others who have concluded the ideal length of the cycle to be 54 years.

Historians tell us that this "half-century" business cycle has actually been in existence thousands of years. In the Old Testament, the land was to lie fallow every seventh year; and after seven groups of these seven years—a total of 49 years—the land was to lie fallow two years in a row. More importantly, it was in this fiftieth year, the Year of Jubilee, that all debts were to be cancelled, all indentured servants set free, and all land reverted back to the original owners—a classical "housecleaning process."

At the beginning of the fifty-year biblical cycle, long-term borrowing would be common, but as the cycle began to draw to a close, money would only be available for a few years, until the forty-ninth year when only one-year loans were available. This also created a real estate cycle. If you bought some land at the very beginning of the cycle, the value was high because you could use it for fifty years; and forty years into the cycle, prices would supposedly be much lower because you could only use it for ten years before the title reverted to the original owner.

The pressing question today is: *Where are we now in the Kondratieff cycle?* Most economists, still hoping for many more years of uninterrupted prosperity, will deny the validity of long waves; but among those analysts that accept it—although there are differences of opinion as to the exact date of the peak—there is near unanimous agreement that it occurred in the 1970s and that we are now in the decline phase. The idealized peaks have been identified as occurring in 1814, 1864, 1920 and 1973.

Richard Zambell, the Director of Economic Research at our firm, Weiss Research, Inc., demonstrates that although the *absolute level* of economic activity has continued to rise, in terms of the *rate* of real GNP growth rates, the approximate peak was indeed in 1973. Moreover, his large-scale econometric model of the economy is unique in that it is probably the first to use this concept as one of its underlying assumptions.

Because cycles are never exact, however, it is more appropriate to look at this cycle in terms of its broad phases, which can be divided roughly into five decades:

First Decade	--	Recovery
Second Decade	--	Boom
Third Decade	--	Peak and Transition
Fourth Decade	--	Collapse
Fifth Decade	--	Trough and Transition

From this perspective, we must also conclude that the 1980s represent the fourth decade in this cycle. One of the leading experts on the Kondratieff Wave is Don Hoppe, publisher of The Donald J. Hoppe Analysis (P. O. Box 977, Crystal Lake, IL 60014). Another newsletter publisher who is deeply committed to this field of research is Jim McKeever, *The McKeever Strategy Letter* (P. O. Box 4130, Medford, OR 97501).

CHAPTER

24

HISTORICAL STOCK-MARKET CYCLES

Just as business cycles have been shown to exist in the economy, so too have cycles been identified in the stock market. But, although their existence is generally agreed upon, the determination of when they will peak or bottom is often the subject of debate. This chapter will introduce you to some of the better research that has been undertaken in the field.

The following work on historical stock-market cycles was taken from Edward R. Dewey's classic *Cycles*. This is known as the bible for anyone interested in cycle behavior and is published by the Foundation for the Study of Cycles in Philadelphia.

THE 9.2-YEAR CYCLE in the stock market is well documented back to the 1830s; and it was calculated that there is only one chance out of 5000 that these occurrences could have been coincidental. Interestingly, this same 9.2-year cycle was documented elsewhere in nature 37 different times. To be completely accurate on the average, the cycle measured exactly 9.225 years. The base year was calculated as 1832.5 and the ideal crests were timed at 3.76753 years after such cycle bottoms.

According to Dewey, the cause of the 9.2-year cycle in stock prices must be sought outside of the market itself because many other completely unrelated phenomena display cycles of this same period with crests or turning points coming at almost exactly the same time. Some such unrelated phenomena which he cited are sunspot activity, the abundance of grasshoppers and tree rings. He felt that there may be one or more environmental forces with periods at or very close to this length, and that these forces may trigger responses on the part of the various phenomena.

137

THE 18.2-YEAR CYCLE in the stock market is well documented but not quite as consistent as the 9.2-year cycle. It was calculated that there is only a one-in-twenty chance that this cycle could be the result of coincidence. Based on data through 1964, the following crests and troughs were found:

TABLE 24-1. 18.2-YEAR CYCLE – ACTUAL

Crest	Trough
1835	1842
1852	1859
1868	1877
1881	1897
1905	1921
1929	1932
1936	1942
1961	

The data of the idealized crests, the actual crests and the differences are shown below:

TABLE 24-2. 18.2-YEAR CYCLE – IDEALIZED

Ideal Crest	Actual Crest	Difference
1833.6	1835.5	+1.9
1851.8	1852.5	+0.7
1870.0	1868.5	-1.5
1882.2	1887.5	+5.3
1906.4	1905.5	-0.9
1924.6	1929.5	+4.9
1942.8	1936.5	-6.3
1961.0	1961.5	+0.5

THE 46-MONTH CYCLE was discovered by Veryl L. Dunbar in 1947 and was later discussed by him in an article called "The Bull Market" which was printed in *Barron's* in June of 1952. The cycle had come true 62 out of 64 times during the past 123 years at the time the article was written, showing an accuracy of 97%. He stated: "In only two instances did the stock index fail to reach a higher level in the year in which the top of the cycle was reached than in the preceding low year of the cycle. Unusually remarkable, however, is the fact that the index was lower in every instance in the year in which the bottom of this cycle was reached than it was in the preceding crest year of the cycle."

Contrary to the usual conception of cycles, the apex does not fall equidistant between two lows, but instead occurs in the year immediately preceding a low. Also, the 46 month cycle seems to be "M" shaped.

The shape might possibly be accounted for by cycles 23 months in length, and perhaps 15 1/3 months in length. Regardless, Dunbar states that the cycle bottom usually occurs one year after the cycle top, suggesting that you should be long three years and short one year.

Dunbar believes that over longer periods of time, the cycles recur at intervals of 3-4-4-4-4-4 years and then repeat with six cycles recurring in a period of approximately 23 years, twelve in 46 years, etc. He also has observed similar rhythms of 23 years and 46 years in other phenomena.

THE 41-MONTH CYCLE is said to have been present in industrial common stock prices from their beginning in 1871. Its average length has been 40.7 months or 3.39 years. The cycle was first observed in 1912 and was secretly used by a group to successfully trade the market during World War I. Some ten years later in 1923, a similar cycle was discovered in commercial paper rates by Professor W. L. Crum of Harvard. At the same time, Professor Joseph Kitchin, also of Harvard, discovered a 40-month cycle existing in six different economic time series.

The original 41-month stock market cycle was later rediscovered in 1935 by Chapin Hoskins of New York, who knew nothing of the earlier work.

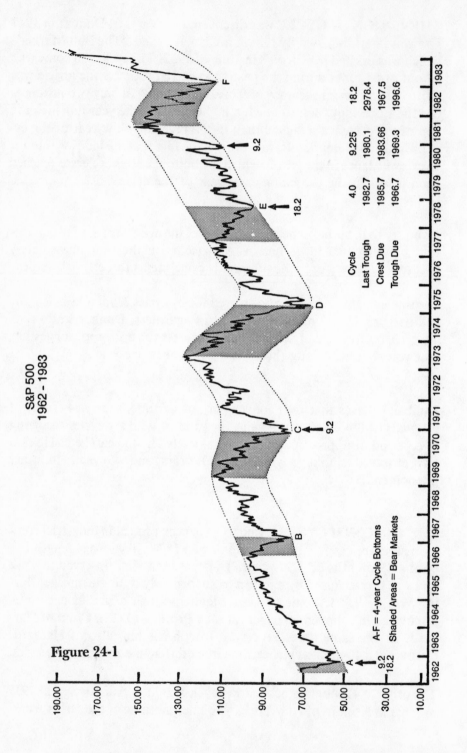

Figure 24-1

S&P 500
1962 - 1983

A-F = 4-year Cycle Bottoms

Shaded Areas = Bear Markets

Cycle	4.0	9.225	18.2
Last Trough	1982.7	1980.1	2978.4
Crest Due	1985.7	1983.66	1967.5
Trough Due	1966.7	1969.3	1996.6

Dewey points out that the existence of these cycles means that important highs followed by important lows tend to succeed each other with a beat and at intervals which average this length. However, it should not be misconstrued that they will succeed each other at the precise length of the cycle, in that some turning points are early and some are late.

In Figure 24-1, I have attempted to update some of this research on historical stock-market cycles. Currently, the three most dominant cycles in the stock market are the 18.2-year cycle, 9.225-year cycle and the 4.0-year cycle (discussed more thoroughly in the next chapter). Other interpretations of the timing of these cycles may be as valid as mine; only time will tell.

JOHN HURST, a pioneer in stock-market cycle work in the late 1960s, identified 12 dominant cycles existing in the stock market. These still exist today, though the duration may have changed slightly (see following table).

TABLE 24-3.   DOMINANT STOCK MARKET CYCLES

Years	Months	Weeks
18		
9		
4.5		
3.0		
1.5	18	
1.0	12	
.75	9	
* .50	6	26
* .25	3	13
	1.5	6.5
	.75	3.25
	.375	1.625

* The 26 and 13-week cycles may also be viewed as combining to form what is, in effect, an 18-week nominal cycle.

JOHN M. COOPER, in later works, identified the low points of the 50-month cycle (Hurst's 4.5 year cycle) and also the 18-month cycle:

TABLE 24-4.   50 MONTH CYCLE

Trough-to-Trough Dates	Duration
<u>1855-1921:</u>	
Jan. 1885 - June 1888	41
June 1888 - Dec. 1890	30
Dec. 1890 - Aug. 1893	32
Aug. 1893 - Aug. 1896	36
Aug. 1896 - Sept. 1900	49
Sept. 1900 - Sept. 1903	36
Sept. 1903 - Nov. 1907	50
Nov. 1907 - July 1910	32
July 1910 - Dec. 1914	53
Dec. 1914 - Dec. 1917	36
Dec. 1917 - Aug. 1921	<u>44</u>
Average	40

NOTE: Between 1885 and 1921, this cycle averaged 40 months in length.

<u>1934 - 1974:</u>	
July 1934 - March 1938	44
March 1938 - April 1942	49
April 1942 - Oct. 1946	54
Oct. 1946 - June 1949	32
June 1949 - Sept. 1953	51
Sept. 1953 - Oct. 1957	49
Oct. 1957 - June 1962	56
June 1962 - Oct. 1966	51
Oct. 1966 - May 1970	44
May 1970 - Dec. 1974	<u>55</u>
Average	50

Thus, we have seen what has been done with cycles in the past. Our next step is to try to apply these same methods to the present.

25

PRACTICAL USE OF CYCLES

A solid knowledge of cycles can keep you on the right side of a major trend and also give you a pretty good idea of when that trend may reverse.

For the "buy-and-hold" stock market investor, a familiarity with long-term cycles—especially the 4-year stock-market cycle—is usually adequate. But the more astute and active stock market traders realize that considerably more money can be made from shorter-term market fluctuations by alternately shifting from the long to the short side of the market. Such an approach, of course, demands more time and effort. What most people don't realize, however, is that the results which can be obtained via short-term trading are potentially phenomenal.

Compare this hypothetical example of *trading versus investing*. Let's say you purchase $10,000 of XYZ stock. The stock does well and by the end of the year, you have a 75% profit of $7,500. Your friend, meanwhile, decides to trade several different stocks, making on average one trade per month, yielding an average profit of 10%, resulting in a total profit of $31,380 or 313% per year. Why the incredible difference? The answer is *compounding*. After each trade, he was able to reinvest the entire proceeds, allowing compounding to work for him. To make it work, however, you have to (1) trade short-term so as to maximize your percent yield per period of time and (2) stay fully invested at all times.

It sounds good in theory, but does it work? The answer is yes—if your *timing and selection* are good. You must select stocks that offer a high probability of moving up or down by a good percentage in a short period of time. After you have selected a stock, you must buy it just as it begins to move. You must also have an objective of what price you expect the stock to reach and in what period of time. Then, when the stock has reached that objective, you must sell it and immediately buy another stock from among the candidates you are tracking that meet your criteria.

Short-term cycles are crucial. By identifying specific cycles for specific stocks, you can learn to predict how prices will be affected – not only in terms of the direction they will move, but also in terms of the speed and the extent of such a move.

Why do stock prices move? It is commonly believed that roughly 75% of stock-price movement occurs as a result of foreseeable, fundamental events influencing investor thinking. This causes the long-term trend. Unforeseen fundamental events add a random element to the market and account for approximately 2% of price movement. *The remaining 23% can be attributed to the influence of cyclic forces*—a large enough influence to allow us to construct short-term trades that take advantage of this movement.

The *duration* or *period* of a cycle is the horizontal measure from trough to trough. The *magnitude* is the vertical measure from peak to trough. Generally, cycles of longer duration exhibit greater magnitude. Cycles may also be summed together to create other cycles.

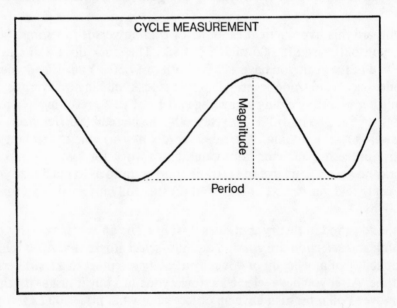

Figure 25-1

A good place to start locating and identifying cycles is in the stock market as a whole. Each stock does have its own cyclicality. But often it is very similar to the overall market. (See previous chapter for examples on how this has been done in the past.)

The next step is to take a chart of the stock market or a particular issue and, moving backwards in time, attempt to identify bottoms. You should find six or seven reasonably distinct bottoms. Measure the distance (in days or weeks) between each one and then simply calculate the average length of your cycle. A typical example might be cycles of 18, 15, 16, 14, 20 and 17 days or an average 100 / 6 = 16.67 days.

In order to project when the cycle will bottom again, we allow for ten percent error in either direction (.10 x 16.67 = 1.67), adding this value to the average or ideal length to find the maximum days in which the cycle can be expected to bottom (16.67 + 1.67 = 18.34), and subtracting it to determine the minimum (16.67 - 1.67 = 15). Thus, we can project—with some degree of certainty—that the price will bottom between 15 and 19 days after our last identified bottom.

By adding this time dimension to our analysis techniques we have now taken a quantum leap forward in market strategy. Suppose we have picked out a stock that we wish to purchase. We believe it is in a strong bull market and have identified a 15 - 19 day cycle. Furthermore, we have determined that the last cycle bottom occurred 12 days ago. Because of our cycle analysis, we can expect the market to move lower until the cycle bottom occurs three to seven days from now. By waiting a few days we will not only be able to buy the stock at a better price but will have reasonable expectations of a swing upwards from then on.

Enveloping

Another technique we can use to help us with cyclic analysis is called "enveloping." The object is to draw a curved channel or envelope around prices, connecting successive lows and successive highs, keeping the channel between them at a constant width. Later, you can then draw a tighter channel within the original channel or a larger channel around it. These envelopes will help you to identify cycle bottoms, to visually see the general direction of the market and to set price objectives by projecting your channels several weeks ahead. Remember, prices are *generally more likely* to remain within the channel boundaries you have projected than to break out of them, but this is no guarantee they will hold in defiance of other indicators:

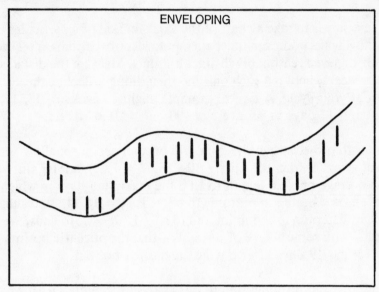

ENVELOPING

Figure 25-2

In earlier chapters we spent a lot of time learning about chart patterns. We learned how to identify the Double Top, Head and Shoulders, Triangle, etc. and how to use them to our advantage. We can tilt the odds in our favor by employing these patterns because they "tend" to resolve themselves in a certain manner. But sometimes the patterns abort, crumble or simply don't work.

Chartists rarely know why a pattern fails or why a pattern is successful. Most don't care to know. But the fact is that, to a large degree, chart patterns are the result of a combination of cyclic forces interacting on the price of a stock. Nearly every chart pattern, when broken down to its basic elements, contains: (1) a trend component; (2) a short-term cycle component; and (3) a longer-term cycle component. Figure 25-3 shows an example of what those components might look like separately, as well as when combined.

Voila! We have created a Head and Shoulders pattern. We have demonstrated how it can be formed as a result of the combination of

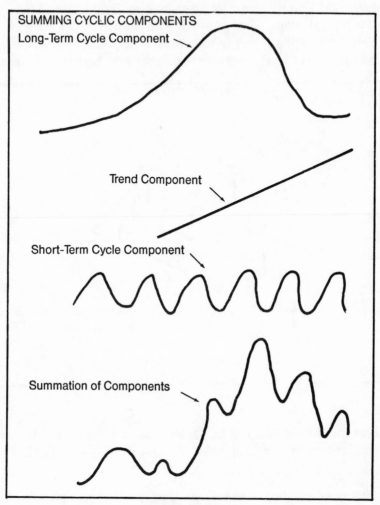

Figure 25-3

cyclic and trend components. The chartist looks for a break of the neckline to confirm that the trend has turned down. The cycle analyst realizes the trend is turning down because the longer-term cycle is topping out and will be moving down for quite some time. They are both looking at the same price pattern and are forming similar conclusions.

The chartist has learned empirically, from examination of hundreds of charts, that a break of the neckline will usually be followed by a major downward move. He must act strictly on probabilities. I feel that the cycle analyst, by understanding the reason behind price movement, has an advantage. You will see why by examining figure 25-4. After an up move, a typical triangle has formed. The chartist, working with probabilities, knows that prices usually break out of triangles in the direction of the trend. Thus, he expects prices to go higher and soon.

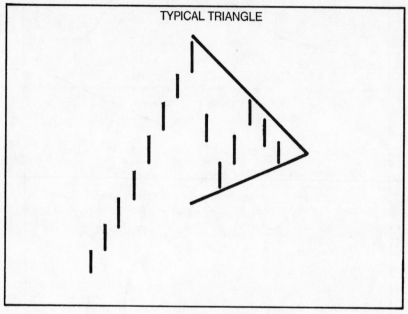

Figure 25-4

But this time the chartist will be fooled. The cycle analyst will realize that a major cycle has just topped and is now moving down as in figure 25-5.

Look at any graph. Can you visually "detrend" the graph—weed out the trend to examine the cycle? Or, can you "decycle" the graph in order to examine just the trend? Probably not. But fortunately your computer can do it for you.

First we will use our computer to find the trends and then to *weed out* those trends, leaving us the cycles.

Finding Trends

Moving averages can help us to view longer-term cycles (which is, in effect, the long-term trend) more clearly by eliminating the presence of shorter-term cycles. For example, a 10-week moving average will

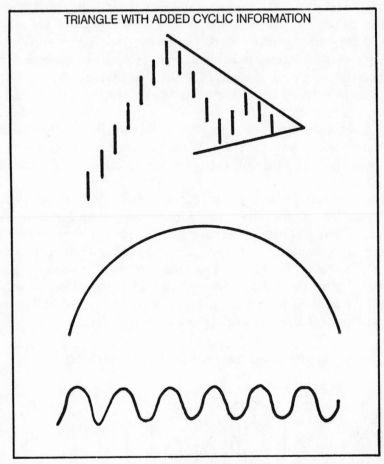

Figure 25-5

eliminate the presence of any cycles 10 weeks or less in duration. By choosing the span of the moving average, you can control which cycles you want to suppress while allowing cycles of longer length to be visible.

Going back to the cycles that we know to exist in the stock market, we can see that a 10-week moving average suppresses the 6.5-week cycle and those smaller, while allowing cycles of 13 weeks or more to come through. A 30-week moving average, commonly used in stock-market forecasting, suppresses the 26-week cycle and those smaller, while allowing the 9-month cycle and those larger to be viewed.

At this time let me alert you to an important caution about moving averages. Many analysts automatically plot the moving average in the slot for the last day of the period. For example, they plot the average for a 10-day period on the 10th day, giving you the impression that the moving average is *lagging* price changes. In cycle work, however, where timing is the main goal, it is best to *center* the moving average, plotting the 10th day between the 5th and 6th day so that stock prices and the average are time coordinated. With this in mind, it might be easier to use an odd number of days so that a stock price can be directly associated with a particular moving average. When you are purchasing a program be sure it allows you the option to plot a "centered" moving average.

A centered moving average also allows you to draw more accurate envelopes. You simply draw in your envelope boundaries at equal distances above and below the moving average line, following the same contour and attempting to find an ideal width that encompasses most tops and bottoms. The centered moving average also makes cycles of smaller duration more visible. As in figure 25-6, they now can be seen to oscillate around the moving average in sympathy with the shortest cycle component that the average does not suppress.

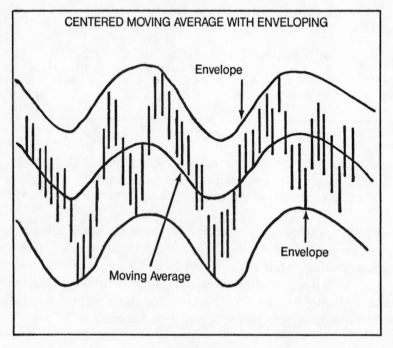

Figure 25-6

Putting the Techniques into Practice

Here are some basic steps you can follow:

Step 1. Browse through a weekly stock or commodity chart book and select those that appear to have good cyclicality.

Step 2. Identify the major bottoms and also draw in your envelope.

Step 3. Build a data file for the issue covering the periods in question.

Step 4. Using a moving average the length of your longest identified cycle, run a centered moving average on the data; and use it to further fine-tune your envelope if necessary.

Step 5. Now try to identify one or two shorter cycles, using one of them to draw in a tighter envelope.

Step 6. Look for *convergence*—a situation in which all three cyclic components will be turning up at nearly the same time. You should get a powerful up move during the time that those cycles are in synch. For example, if you find a 15-week cycle which has just bottomed last week, plus 8-week and 4-week cycles due to bottom in the next week or two, you would have exactly the type of convergence you need to buy a stock.

The technique works equally well in anticipation of a short sale. You identify a market in which the sum of all longer components (in other words, the trend) is down and one or two shorter cycle components are due to top in the near future. A breaking of the uptrend line can help to confirm when those cycles have topped or have started moving down—the ideal time to initiate a short sale.

Figure 25-7 illustrates prices with both a 5-week and 10-week cycle. The square represents your buy zone—the time period when you expect the cycles to bottom and begin moving up. A break in the downtrend line is your signal to buy.

Your transaction is not truly complete until you do one more thing— put in your "stop"—an order which, in this instance, will limit any losses by automatically selling your stocks (or, if you're short, automatically buying it back) should prices start to go against your expectations. Not

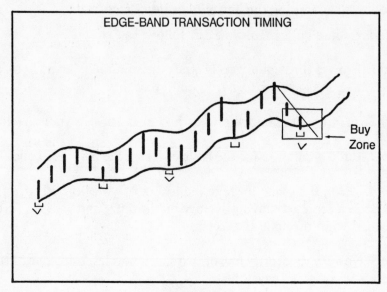

EDGE-BAND TRANSACTION TIMING

Buy
Zone

Figure 25-7

all trades can be winners and it is important that you protect your capital by cutting short any erosion you might suffer on losing trades. A safe place for your stop on this trade would be just below the recent cycle bottoms.

Setting Time & Price Objectives

Assuming the stock does move according to expectations, the next question that arises is: Where do we take profits—when it reaches a predetermined price or after a certain amount of time has elapsed? Determining objectives in advance is a necessary part of the strategy. In order for our plan to work we must be able to evaluate risk versus reward on the amount of funds invested. We must also be able to estimate how long it will take for our objective to be reached in order to maximize our profit per *unit of time* invested.

There are several ways to measure objectives. But first you must consider the time factor. Assuming you are trading based on a 10-week cycle and that the summation of all longer cycles is up, you can expect your 10-week cycle to top approximately six to eight weeks after its last bottom. So, this is the time zone when we can expect to sell the stock.

Another way to get a rough idea of where prices might go is to extend your envelope out into the future. Your price envelope was drawn so as to include nearly all price action in the past. So, it is likely that future price action will be contained within the boundaries of your constant-width envelope projected into the future. When prices reach the top of that envelope they are likely to fall, and when they reach the bottom, are likely to rise.

Moving averages can also be used to predict the extent of a price move. You should construct a one-half span moving average. Thus, if you are trading on a 10-week cycle, you would construct and plot a 5-week "centered" moving average. When the 5-week moving average reverses its direction to up, note the price of the stock and how much it has already moved up. You may expect prices to continue to climb until the stock has moved up this much more.

Another method is to:

(1) Use both a one-half span and full-span moving average (both centered).

(2) Project both moving averages up to current time to fill in the missing few days caused by the lag (because they are centered).

(3) At the point where they cross, note the price of the stock and how much it has moved up from its recent bottom. The stock should continue to move that much higher.

(4) Give your objective a plus or minus ten percent tolerance for errors to set up a *target zone*.

Sometimes, although your cyclic analysis shows that prices still have room to move on the upside in terms of time, prices begin moving up strongly but then fall back somewhat forming either a flag or a triangle. This pause in upward price movement offers a good way to predict the extent of the next price move subsequent to the consolidation period. Referring to figure 25-8 follow these steps:

(1) Measure the diagonal distance from Y to Z.

(2) Find the midpoint and mark it with an M.

(3) Measure the vertical distance from M to X.

(4) Add this same distance to M to get your price objective.

(5) If you're trading in a bear market with short sales, follow exactly the same procedure subtracting the distance to M to determine your target.

(6) Set up your target *zone* as in the previous example.

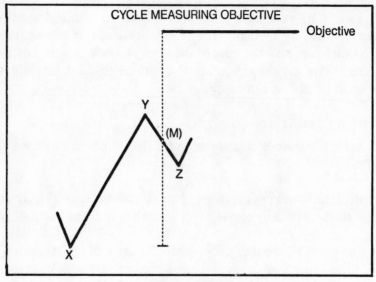

Figure 25-8

Detrending

You have probably been wondering where your computer comes into play in cyclic analysis. We have already covered one area where your computer can save you much time and effort—moving averages. Other techniques such as envelope analysis and projecting objectives can be accomplished via manual, visual and graphic methods. But, when it comes to more sophisticated cyclic analysis such as detrending, use of the computer becomes a must.

Since the price is composed of the summation of a trend component and various cycle components, we can benefit greatly by techniques which separate the two automatically.

In the previous chapter, we found we could better see the trend by eliminating the effect of the shorter term cycles. A moving average of a specific length eliminated the effect of all cycles of that length or less, leaving only the trend and cycles of a longer length present in the data. Conversely if we want to see the cycles more clearly, we can filter out the trend. It is this process which we call "detrending."

It is actually quite simple:

Step 1. Run a moving average on the data. If you select an 11-week moving average, it eliminates the cyclic information of all cycles of eleven weeks or less in length.

Step 2. Subtract the moving average from the actual prices.

Step 3. The result is all price movements *less* the short-term cycles -- ergo the trend. A detrending program can be easily purchased; and Computrac includes one in their package. Figure 25-9 illustrates the process.

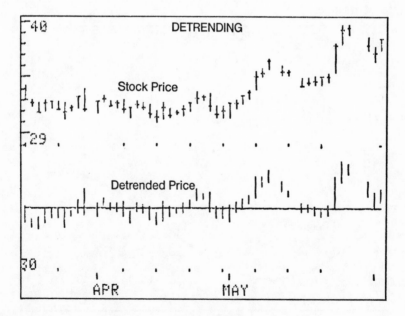

Figure 25-9

FOURIER ANALYSIS is another way to filter out price trends. It refers to various techniques designed to extract as much information as possible from a time series of discrete numbers—including the frequency, amplitude and phase of a series of waves. This method is also called "spectral analysis."

Basically, it separates those fluctuations which have frequencies *below* a certain value from those *above* that value. When we used a moving average to filter out short cycles (high frequencies) and while allowing long cycles (low frequencies) to "pass through" we were using what is called a "lowpass filter." Likewise, when we used the detrending process, allowing only the high frequencies to show through, we were using a "high-pass filter." When a filtering process produces results that lie between two fixed bounds, it is called a "band-pass filter."

Once results have been obtained from spectral analysis, sophisticated curve fitting techniques can be applied to project those results into the future. Explanations of numerical analysis, spectral analysis, filters and curve fitting are beyond the scope of this book. However, because you have a computer, such sophisticated techniques are available to you and are worthy of later investigation. A program to do Fourier analysis is also available on the Computrac system. Figure 25-10 illustrates an example of its use.

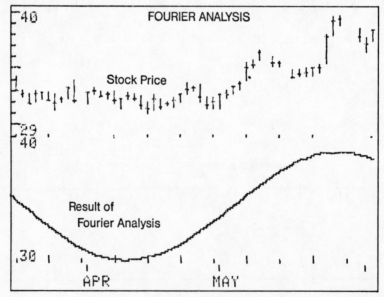

Figure 25-10

Cycle analysis is a massive field in itself. Therefore, in order to help you avoid many hours of time and research on possibly tangential concerns, I have summarized this chapter into 15 basic steps you can follow for limiting losses and maximizing your profits. (Not every step is absolutely necessary for profitable trading. But the more homework you do which produces confirming signals, the greater your margin of certainty.)

1. Begin by trying to identify the presence of cycles in the major averages. For this purpose, you may use the New York Stock Exchange Composite Index, Standard and Poors 500 Index or the Dow Jones Industrial Average.

2. Scan each of the industry groups to determine which are showing relative strength and which are showing relative weakness. (See Program #20.)

3. Keeping in mind the direction of the averages as well as industry groups, scan the charts of individual issues and select about a half dozen that appear to have a well-defined presence of regular cycles.

4. For each stock, project when the cycle you have identified is due to bottom next, (or in a bear market, due to reach a cyclical top.) To do this, measure the distance between each cycle bottom (or top) and average those cycle lengths. Then add the average length to the last cycle bottom allowing for a ten percent error either way.

5. Envelope each of the stocks to better visualize where each is likely to go.

6. If you have one, run a detrending program to better identify your "trading" cycle and any other smaller cycles that might be present.

7. Run a full-span moving average to suppress your cycle and allow you to clearly see the trend.

8. Run a half-span moving average to give you another technique for projecting an objective.

9. Monitor each of the stocks selected. Ideally, for a good "buy" signal,

both the averages and the industry group should be in uptrends. Your stock should be in an uptrend as indicated by an upward rising line on the fullspan moving average. (Or for a good "sell short" signal, all three should be in downtrends.)

10. After the trading cycle has crested and prices begin moving down, a downtrend line should be drawn. Once prices enter the time zone when the trading cycle is due to bottom, the downtrend line should be watched closely. When prices break up through the downtrend line it is time to buy the stock. Favorable volume patterns would show volume decreasing as the stock dropped in price; then increasing as it moved up through its downtrend line. (Likewise, if you're trading on the short side, the time to sell short is when prices break down through your uptrend line while falling from the cycle top.)

11. Place a stop slightly below the recent cycle bottom (or above the recent top, if you are short).

12. Determine an objective of what price the stock might reach and during what time period, corresponding to the crest of your trading cycle. Be sure to take into account the possible effects of any shorter or longer term cycles on the trading cycle. An objective in price can be gained from (a) envelope projection, (b) full and half-span moving average techniques and (c) the measurement technique presented. If you have time, once you've completed this work, for further confirmation refer back to other techniques for projecting objectives via chart patterns (Double Bottoms, Head and Shoulders Bottoms, Triangles, etc.) Also, take into consideration any overhead resistance that might lessen or stall the upmove.

13. As prices move up, making a series of higher bottoms, move your sell stop up accordingly to lock in profits in the event the unexpected should occur. (And if you're short, bring your buy stop down accordingly.)

14. Once prices have reached your objective in time and price, you can either take profits or you can wait for a break of the trend line to stop you out of the trade.

15. As soon as you have taken profits, repeat the process on another

stock which fits your selection criteria.

These same rules work equally well in the commodity markets. But before you move from the relatively tried and tested world of securities traded mostly in New York City to the whirlwind of futures still dominated by the Chicago markets, you should be fully appraised of the potential risks. Unlike most security trading, in commodities you are responsible for, and you could lose, significantly more than the money you put up for margin. Moreover, you could be locked out of the market when it moves by the limit on several consecutive days, not allowing you to exit the market.

Automatic stop-loss orders will help prevent such an occurence, but there is no guarantee they will be executed should prices jump rapidly. (In the last chapter on money management, I lay out some mechanisms for protecting yourself.) The potential for profit, however, is far greater than that in most stock-market situations.

5

COMMODITY MARKETS

26

GETTING STARTED

The terms "commodity markets" and "futures markets" are often used interchangeably, but are not exactly the same.

Futures markets need not be *only commodities*. They refer to all those markets where the actual purchase of physical goods is to take place at a specified future date. Originally, only agricultural commodities such as soybeans or cattle were traded. But now a wide variety of instruments – foreign currencies, T-bonds and T-bills, and precious metals—have been added.

Likewise, commodity markets need not be limited exclusively to "futures." You can buy and sell soybeans for delivery in future months, or you can buy the actual goods ("physicals") in the "spot" or "cash" markets.

For the purpose of this book, however, we use the term commodity markets to refer to "futures" of any kind and we will use the terms interchangeably.

If you have never traded commodities, I would strongly urge you to devote ample time to learning as much as possible about the subject *before* committing your capital. Most major brokerage houses can provide you with free literature. Your local library should also have books on commodity trading. A good comprehensive book for beginners is *Winning in the Commodity Markets* by George Angell, published by Doubleday. I also recommend a subscription to *Futures Magazine*, 219 Parkade, Cedar Falls, IA 50613. Finally, many valuable free publications are available from the Chicago Board of Trade, Marketing Department, LaSalle at Jackson, Chicago, IL 60604.

Many of you who are reading this book have never traded the futures market. You have probably heard fantastic success stories in which a very small investor parlayed a few thousand dollars into millions within a few short years; or you may have heard horror stories of how people have been literally wiped out of house and home.

Both are most likely true; but in the final analysis, it is the losers that outnumber the winners among the speculators in the futures market. It has been estimated that the typical neophyte trader will only survive three to six months before losing his stake. Yet in the same period of time, a handful out of every 100 or so new players entering the market will have turned a $15,000 stake into several hundred thousand dollars. Granted, the luck of the draw played some part in both the winners' and losers' fate.

One reason you may wish to pursue the commodity markets is because it offers more for the money. *The tools of technical analysis that you have learned in this book apply equally well to both stocks and commodities.* So why not avail yourself of the opportunities in the commodity markets?

A futures transaction is no more than a formalized *contract* or promise to buy or sell a commodity or financial instrument on a specific date. It is this contract—and not the physical goods or securities—which is bought and sold; and in practice, only a very small percentage of buyers or sellers actually receive or deliver physical goods.

Futures markets exist primarily to transfer risk—especially from the commercial participant, or hedger, for whom futures markets were designed – to the speculator. The "commercials" are the firms whose business includes the same or similar commodity or financial instrument as that being traded in the futures market—involving agricultural commodities, forest products, precious and other non-ferrous metals, energy, and money market instruments.

The risk seekers, or speculators, can be divided into two categories of traders. The first category—the locals—consists of a group of professional brokers who trade on the floor for the benefit of their own account. Like the specialists in the stock market, they provide a valuable function to the markets because their frequent trading adds "liquidi-ty"—the ability to buy or sell at any time.

Locals, in turn, can be classified according to their frequency of trading as either "position traders," "day traders," or "scalpers." Position traders may hold a position for days or weeks, while day traders close out their position at the end of each day. Scalpers, on the other hand, may get in and out of the market 50 or more times per day. Because they do not pay commissions, they are willing to trade for very small profits. They may initiate and offset trades literally within seconds and may become bullish or bearish on a commodity's prospects in an equally short period of time.

The other category of speculators are usually termed "commission house traders." The term derives from the fact that the orders come into the pit from outside by way of a brokerage house such as Merrill Lynch. This category could be further subdivided into managed funds and in-dividual speculators.

It is important to understand how a commercial producer of a com-modity uses the insurance aspect of the futures market. Suppose a hog breeder expects to bring his animals to market in three months. He knows that at today's price he would have a fair profit. But he has no way of knowing what the price will be three months from now. He may have reason to suspect the possibility that excess supply could lower the price substantially, causing him a loss and possible bankruptcy. Can he af-ford to take that risk? Obviously not. But he can, in effect, sell his hogs *now* at today's high price by selling short the equivalent number of futures contracts in hogs three months out. He will have essentially locked in today's price and transferred the risk to a speculator. If the price of hogs goes down, he loses money when he sells his hogs but he will make up the difference from his profitable short sale in the futures market. Conversely, if the price of hogs rises, he will lose money in the futures market, while obtaining higher prices at market for his own hogs. Thus, regardless of future price movements, he will be insured or "hedged" against loss.

Why are speculators lured to the futures markets? Simply because of the extreme leverage that is available. Since futures positions are taken on low margin, the trader's gains or losses are magnified. With the margin deposit for a future contract often less than five percent of face value, just a small change in price can result in considerable gains or losses relative to the initial deposit.

To protect against catastrophic losses, I would recommend always using stops—the instruction to liquidate your position when a specified price is reached. For example, if you go long (buy) a gold futures contract at $400, you might place a stop at $380 in order to limit your loss in case the market moves down. Conversely, if you sold short a gold futures contract at $500, you might wish to place a protective stop at $520.

Mistakes can be extremely costly in the futures markets. Therefore, it is very important to understand the different types of orders that you can give your broker before you begin trading. Orders can be first classified as either (1) *a day order* which is cancelled if not executed during that day, or (2) *an open order* which remains in effect until cancelled (also referred to as GTC—"good till cancelled"). Orders are assumed to be day orders unless otherwise specified.

In addition, there are four basic trading orders:

(1) *Market order*—one which must be executed by the pit broker as soon as possible after he receives it and at the best obtainable price at that time. Here is an example: "Buy one July silver at the market." In this case, you can be certain to be "filled" (your order executed) at the going price.

(2) *Market-if-touched (MIT) order.* If it's a buy, it becomes a market order as soon as the contract sells or is offered at or *below* the price you have specified; and if it is a sell, it becomes a market order when the contract sells or is bid at or *above* the price you have specified.

(3) *Fixed price order, commonly called a "limit order,"* is an order to buy or sell at a stipulated price. The limit order will be filled as soon as the stipulated price or a price more favorable than the stipulated one can be obtained. Sometimes a limit order can be used to obtain a better fill. In fast moving markets, however, the market may move right past your price, resulting in your order not being executed. Here is an example of a limit order: "Buy one June T-bill at 92.05 or better." In

this case, since you have stated a price, your broker knows that this is a limit order.

(4) *Stop order*. A stop order to buy becomes a market order when the contract sells or is bid at or above the specified level; and if it is a sell order, it becomes a market order when the contract sells or is offered at or below the specified price. A buy stop must always be placed above the current trading level; and a sell stop, below it. Here is how it would work in our previous example on gold: "Buy one April gold at $400. Place an open protective sell stop at $380."

There are other types of fancy orders as well as numerous ways to combine them. A good reference book to have is *Commodity Futures Trading Orders* by J. R. Maxwell, Sr., 234 Main St., Red Bluff, CA 96080.

How To Get Started

A commonly asked question is: "How much money does it take to get started in the futures market?" The answer is that it depends on the brokerage firm with whom you are transacting business. Some brokerage firms will only ask for an initial deposit of $5,000; others may require $25,000 or more.

Once you open an account, a good rule of thumb is to have $4 in your account for every $1 that is margined. As an example, if the margin for copper is $1,200, you should have $4,800 in your account for each contract that you wish to trade. This is a conservative approach to futures trading. It is easy to get carried away and "overtrade" which can often be ruinous. The margin requirements change as the value of the contract increases or decreases in accordance with price or as the volatility of the contract changes.

Commissions

As in the stock market, commissions vary with the services of a brokerage firm. Full service brokerage firms have market research departments and offer fundamental and technical trading advice to their customers. Discount firms generally don't offer such services to their customers and, as a result, are able to reduce their commission rates. A single "round-turn" commission is charged to cover the trades you make to get in and out of each futures position. Unlike the stock market—where commission rates refer to either a buy or sell stock transaction—in the futures market, commissions are quoted on a "round-trip" basis—including both the purchase and sale. To receive a list of major brokerage firms dealing in the futures market, write to The Chicago Board of Trade, Marketing Department, LaSalle at Jackson, Chicago, IL 60604.

27

OPEN INTEREST

In the last chapter, we stated that investors and speculators in the futures market do not buy and sell actual goods or securities. Rather, they deal in *contracts*—an agreement which specifies that the seller will deliver to the buyer a quantity of a commodity or a financial instrument at a specific price on a specific date. *The number of contracts that are in existence at any given time is referred to as the "open interest."*

As a simple illustration, let's say you and I decide to start our own futures market to trade apples; and let's say we set as our standard that 100 bushels will equal one contract.

On the first day of trading, I agree that on December 20, I will deliver to you 500 bushels. You agree that you will buy from me those 500 bushels; and we each put down a small percentage of the total value as a guarantee.

In the parlance of the commodity markets, I have sold short 5 contracts of apples; while you have bought 5 contracts. What is the open interest so far? Very simple: 5 contracts.

Now let's move one step further. On the second day of trading, you get word from your friends in upstate New York that the apple crop is going to be huge this year, depressing the price. So you decide you want to sell out. But I don't know or don't care about that news and want to hold on to my 5 short positions. So, you sell out to a third party who assumes your contracts without affecting my position. The open interest is still five contracts.

However, on the third day of trading, several new buyers and new sellers enter the market, establishing 50 new short positions and 50 new long positions. Open interest increases to a total of 55.

What concerns us here, however, is not so much the absolute level of open interest but the patterns of change. For that purpose, we must define the four types of participants in the markets:

(1) *Old bulls* who have already bought and now hold long positions;

(2) *Old bears* who have already sold, and are now holding short positions;

(3) *New bulls* who are seeking to buy or are in the process of buying now; and

(4) *New bears* who are seeking to sell short or are in the process of selling short.

Try to visualize the market as an arena. Some investors are in the arena and have already made their commitments; while others are on the sidelines seeking to get in. But, remember, in every case, there is invariably one long position for every short position.

Why is it important that we watch open interest? Because by watching the change in open interest, we can often see if the market is strengthening or weakening.

IN A BULL MARKET, when an increase in open interest is accompanied by higher prices, it means that new buyers are continuing to enter the market. They are still willing to keep paying higher prices and, hence, continued strength can be expected.

When prices are still advancing but the open interest begins to go down, it means that new buying has stopped and that the buying being done is primarily by old bears who are exiting the market by covering their short positions. Meanwhile, the old bulls who held long positions are liquidating and taking profits. Therefore, *prices advancing but open in-terest declining is a signal that the price trend may be getting ready to reverse.*

After an uptrend has been under way for some time, open interest must be viewed in a different light. If the absolute level of open interest is extremely high, it indicates that there has been large public participa-tion and that the market could be vulnerable. There probably are few buyers left on the sidelines who have not already bought and, thus, there is little chance open interest will continue to increase. Prices could fall rapidly should adverse news enter the market.

IN A BEAR MARKET, if prices are declining and open interest is in-creasing, it means that new bears are entering the market to sell short and, therefore, should continue to push prices lower.

But when open interest ceases to increase or begins to decline, it is a sign that the new bears are no longer willing to sell short at these lower prices. The selling that is taking place is primarily old bulls who are li-quidating their long positions—an indication that the downward price movement may be coming to an end.

Some of the best work on open interest in commodities has been done by Jim Sibbet who publishes *Let's Talk Silver & Gold,* a market newsletter. Figure 27-1 shows Sibbet's "Eight Rules for Open Interest" which sum-marizes the effects of changing open interest on market conditions. Though these rules are widely accepted, my own research takes some exception to rules 3 and 4. Rather than neutral, when prices are moving sideways and open interest is rising, I interpret this situation as bearish. When prices are moving sideways and open interest is falling, my inter-pretation is bullish.

I would like to add the following considerations:

1. It is best not to try to interpret changes in open interest on a day-to-day basis. It is much more meaningful to watch for changes lasting from several days to a few weeks.

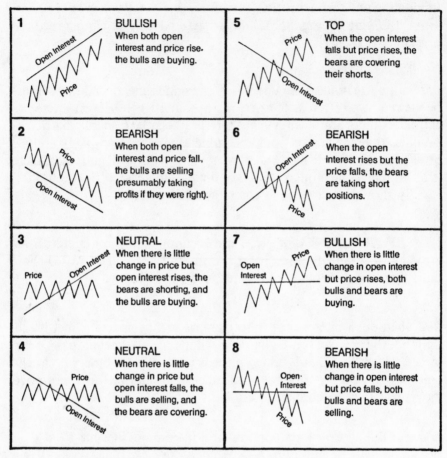

Reprinted from "Contrary Opinion," by R. Earl Hadady

Table 27-1

2. The open interest in many commodities tends to increase and decrease in a more or less fixed seasonal pattern. Therefore, any observed changes in open interest must be compared with the expected seasonal change.

The Commodity Research Bureau (CRB) publishes weekly graphs which display both the average open interest over the past few years and the current open interest, allowing you to detect the seasonal pattern.

Open interest can be plotted using Program #6. Here is an example of open interest graphed with prices on the computer:

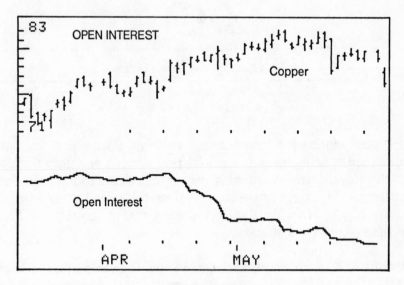

Figure 27-1

28

CONTRARY OPINION

The futures market is a "zero-sum game" in the sense that, for each contract outstanding, there is one long position and one short position and, therefore, there is invariably one losing contract for every winning contract. Due to this mandatory balance between buying and selling, contrary opinion plays an even greater role in future price direction than in the stock market.

Let's say we do a survey of market participants and find that 80% are bullish. How can 80% be bullish when each contract has a winner and a loser? Very simple! In this case, there are many bulls each holding — on the average—a relatively small number of contracts, whereas there are very few bears who must be holding a relatively large number.

The minority in the market, the 20% who are bearish in this instance, will most likely be well financed because they hold a large number of contracts. On the other hand, their opposition is probably lightly financed. Thus, the short positions are said to be in "strong hands" while the longs are in "weak hands" whose decisions are much more influenced by day-to-day price changes. A few adverse days will force them to liquidate their positions and retreat to the sidelines.

Continuing with our example, if 80% of the market participants are bulls, then the average trader who is long (a bull) holds only one-fourth as many contracts as the trader who is short (a bear). If only 10% are bulls, each bear holds on average 9 contracts for every one contract held by a bull.

How is the Bullish Consensus determined? It has been found that the overwhelming majority of commodity speculators follow the advice of various professionals who write market letters for brokerage firms or independent advisory services. Therefore, the trading attitude of the advisors will give us a good estimate of the public's bullishness or bearishness. Results have shown in most cases that if 90 percent of the professional advisors are bullish, then an overwhelming majority of the trading public will, likewise, be bullish.

HADADY PUBLICATIONS, (Imperial Savings Building, Suite 309, 61 South Lake Avenue, Pasadena, CA 91101) conducts a weekly survey of more than 100 of the leading brokerage firms and advisors. Earl Hadady is considered the Grand Master of Contrary Opinion in the commodity markets and has conducted extensive research in the field. You can obtain several years' history of Bullish Consensus readings from him, build a file, and run your own tests on the data (see figure 28-1). Another less ambitious alternative would be to subscribe to his chart service which graphs the Bullish Consensus for each commodity at the bottom of the chart.

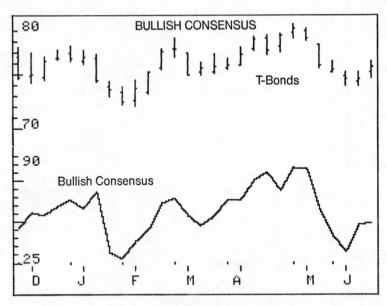

Figure 28-1

To rate the significance of a Bullish Consensus reading, I refer to Hadady's Bullish Consensus Meter: (Figure 28-2).

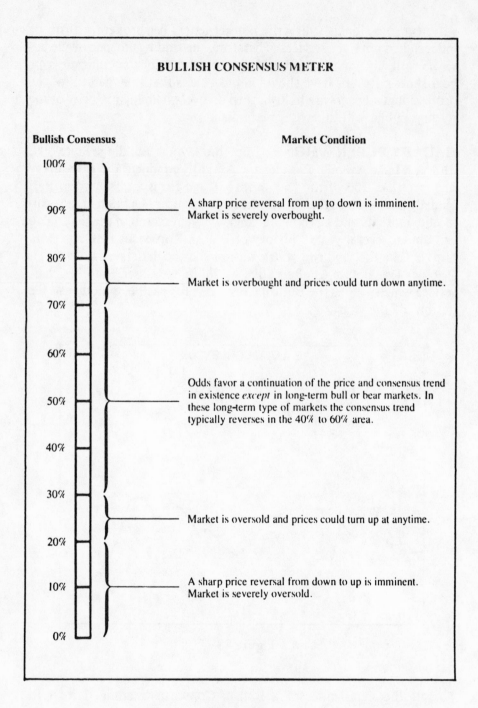

Figure 28-2

An "overbought" condition begins to occur when the Bullish Consensus exceeds 80%; an "oversold" condition when the consensus is less than 30%. A contrarian position should be considered any time the Bullish Consensus is above 80% or below 30%. The probability for a successful contrarian trade increases as the Bullish Consensus approaches the extremes, i.e. 100% and 0%. When the Bullish Consensus percentages are in the ranges of 80 - 90% or 20 - 30%, it is advisable to wait until the trend of the Bullish Consensus reverses direction before entering a position. For a more in-depth study of contrary opinion, I recommend Earl Hadady's *Contrary Opinion*, Hadady Publications, Pasadena, CA 91101.

29

SHORT-TERM TECHNICAL INDICATORS

Because of greater volatility and higher leverage, the futures markets generally require more precise timing of trades than is necessary in the stock market. In the stock market, several days of adverse action can easily be tolerated and may not affect a long-term trade. This, of course, is not the case in the futures markets, where a few days could easily produce a margin call and do catastrophic damage to an account. A good knowledge of Part II will provide the necessary tools to allow you to master short-term timing techniques. The following two short-term indicators are among my favorites. Used properly, they can often identify market tops and bottoms to a day, thus allowing you to enter trades with a limited risk.

Demand Index

THE DEMAND INDEX, developed by Jim Sibbet, (Sibbet Publications, 61 S. Lake Ave., Pasadena, CA 91101), uses a copyrighted formula and, therefore, cannot be reproduced in this book. However, Computrac (with Mr. Sibbet's permission) does offer the indicator as part of their package. The index combines volume and price data in such a way as to become a leading indicator of a price trend change. It is designed so that at the very least it is a coincidental indicator, not a lagging one. This is based on the general observation that volume tends to peak before prices, both in the commodity and stock markets.

The best way to use it is to look for a divergence between the index and prices.

If prices are moving lower or have made a lower bottom while the De-

mand Index is moving higher or has made a higher bottom, this is called bullish divergence and prices should move higher:

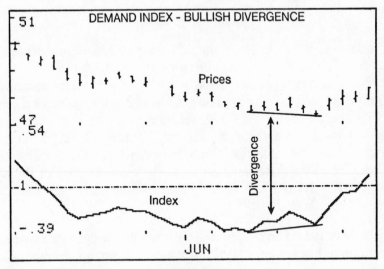

Figure 29-1

If prices are moving higher or have made a higher top while the Demand Index is moving lower or has made a lower top, this is called
bearish divergence and signifies that prices should move lower:

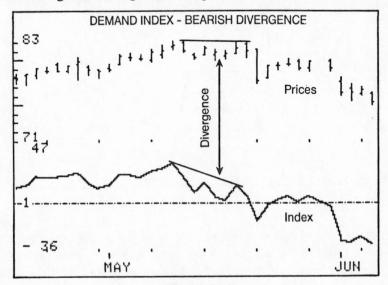

Figure 29-2

Thus, the Demand Index can be used to identify both market tops and market bottoms.

Stochastic Process

This indicator, if run on daily data, is a very short-term oriented but highly accurate method for picking tops and bottoms. I find it can be a great market timing aid and often employ it when making recommendations on the Weiss Financial Futures Hotline which gives specific buy and sell recommendations daily for the interest rate futures, foreign currencies, precious metals markets and other futures markets. The basic principle behind the indicator is this: As prices decrease, the daily closes tend to congregate closer and closer to the extreme lows of the daily range. Conversely, as prices increase, the closes tend to congregate closer to the extreme *highs*.

The indicator generates two lines—an "X" line which is a short-term momentum indicator and a "Y" line which is a moving average of that indicator:

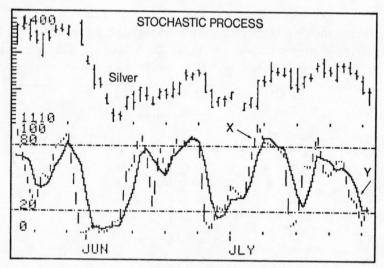

Figure 29-3

The indicator is used much like the Demand Index. The major formation to be looking for is *a divergence between the Y line on the model and the actual price on your chart*. This divergence may take one of two forms: bullish divergence or bearish divergence.

1. *Bullish divergence* occurs when the actual price makes a lower low but the Y line fails to break to new low ground. Your confirmation and signal to buy—immediately—is given on the day that the X line crosses up through the Y line. (Figure 29-4).

2. Referring to figure 29-5, a *bearish divergence* occurs when the actual price makes a higher top yet the Y line has correspondingly failed to do so. Your confirmation and signal to *sell*—immediately—is given on the day that the X line crosses *down* through the Y line.

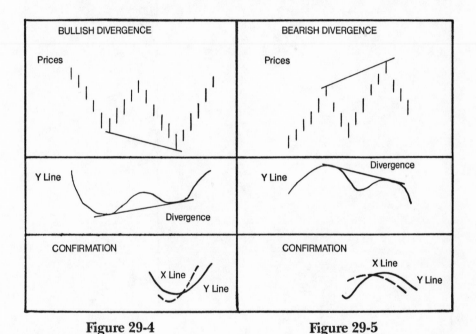

Figure 29-4   **Figure 29-5**

How accurate is the indicator in picking tops and bottoms? In order to judge its ability for yourself, review the Daily Chart on the T-bills extending from October 1981 through June 1982 (figure 29-6). Here are the signals it gave:

(1) The first sell signal was generated on November 30, 1981. Notice that the Y line peaked on November 12 and continued to move lower, while prices moved higher over the next two weeks, setting up our basic divergence. On November 30, the X line crashed down through the lower

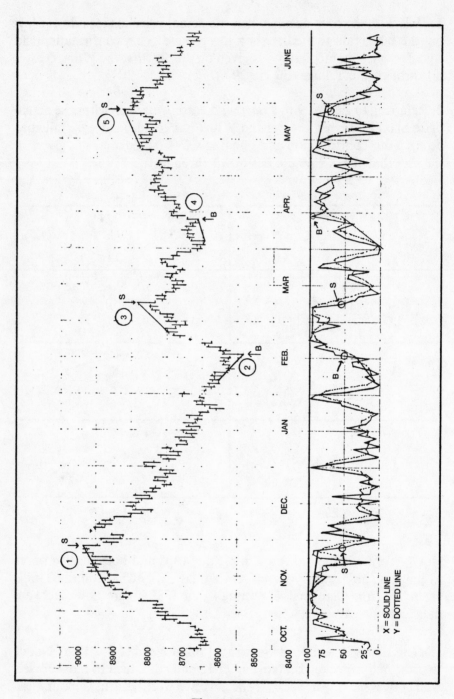

Figure 29-6

top made by the Y line and gave us our signal to sell. Prices fell sharply from that point.

(2) Our first buy signal was generated February 16, 1982—the exact day of the bottom. Notice how the Y line had been rising from February 4, while prices continued to decline, setting up our divergence. On February 16, the X line crossed through the Y line, giving us our buy signal.

(3) The next sell signal was given at the peak of the intermediate top made on March 8, 1982. Prices were moving higher from February 24 to March 8, while the Y line made a slightly lower top on March 5. On March 8, the X line crossed down through the Y line, generating the sell signal.

(4) A good buy signal was again flashed on April 8, 1982. Note that although both prices and the Y line were moving up, the Y line moved much more rapidly, still setting up a divergence.

(5) Another perfect sell signal was given *at the exact top* made on May 21, 1982. Divergence had been set up from higher peaks made in prices on May 21 over May 7, while correspondingly lower peaks were made on the Y line.

The stochastic process is also offered in the Computrac software package. Again, remember to never rely on one indicator alone and to always use stops. When using this indicator to buy, place a stop just below the most recent low. When using the indicator to sell short, place a stop just above the most recent high.

30

MONEY MANAGEMENT

It is only natural when we make an investment or trade that we tend to focus on potential profits rather than dwell on possible losses. We are often so convinced that a particular trade will be profitable that we tend to push to the back of our minds thoughts that something could go awry. But in order to be successful traders, we must face these thoughts head-on. Losing trades are inevitable. It is how we manage and control those losses that eventually determines our success in the markets.

Money management is simply an assortment of techniques that help a trader minimize the risk of loss while still enabling him to participate in major market gains. Ironically, it is very possibly the most critical aspect of futures trading *and* the most overlooked. Whereas stock market investors can sometimes get by without it, in futures markets because of the high leverage available, it is an absolute must! Without the implementation of strict loss-control techniques, sudden catastrophic losses can quickly shrink an account to such an extreme that the possibility of ever attaining profitability becomes remote.

Once a trader fully understands this concept, he has probably learned the most important lesson in trading. Specifically: *The percent gain needed to recover a loss increases geometrically with the loss.* For example, if you lose 15% of your capital, you have to make a 17.6% gain on the balance you have left to get even. If you lose 30% of your capital, it will take a 42.9% gain; and if you lose 50% of your capital, it will take 100%. The following table illustrates this point.

184

TABLE 30-1. RECOVERY TABLE

% Loss Of Initial Capital	% Gain On Balance Required To Recover loss
5	5.3
10	11.1
15	17.6
20	25.0
25	33.3
30	42.9
35	53.8
40	66.7
45	81.8
50	100.0
55	122.0
60	150.0
65	186.0
70	233.0
75	300.0
80	400.0
85	567.0
90	900.0

Hopefully, the table has impressed upon you the fact that preservation of capital is of utmost importance. But exactly how do we go about doing that? A good place to start is to always predetermine an exit point (a stop) *before* you enter a trade.

The stop should meet two requirements. First, it should be "logical" from a technical standpoint. For example, if you are "long," a stop under a previous support area would be logical. Second, and even more important, the stop should be a function of money management—that is, how much you can afford to risk on a particular trade. Certain rules of thumb exist such as limiting your risk to 10% of total capital on any one trade. But such rules are often too general to be of much use. If you employ a trading system, your losses will automatically be limited as a function of the system. Thus, you will not have to define a stop for each trade; the system does it for you. For example, a moving average crossover system will automatically prevent catastrophic losses. Of course, a series of smaller losses could still wipe out your account, but at least you are giving the law of averages an opportunity to work for you.

I. Lee Finberg, a specialist in managed accounts for Prudential-Bache and a frequent public speaker on money management principles, writing in *Money Maker* magazine (December/January 1983) adds the following warning: "Don't stay with unprofitable positions. In futures markets, exiting from unprofitable positions while the loss is relatively small is a must because of the effects of leverage when your position or timing proves wrong."

The proprietary trend-following system that I have designed and employ at Weiss Money Management also pays credence to the old adage: "Cut your losses and let profits run"; and, in practice, it has worked to our advantage. Whenever the market begins moving adversely to the position, the position is automatically exited or reversed.

This is the way most trend-following systems work. By testing the system on several years of past data on each of the markets you intend to trade, you can determine how much back-up money you will need for each contract traded by calculating the "drawdown." This refers to the maximum dollar loss suffered during the test period. Here is a simple example:

TABLE 30-2. DRAWDOWNS

Beginning Balance		$10,000
Trade #1	+ $2,000	$12,000
Trade #2	+ $1,000	$13,000
Trade #3	+ $4,000	$17,000
Trade #4	- $6,000	$11,000
Trade #5	+ $3,000	$14,000
Trade #6	- $8,000	$ 6,000
Trade #7	+ $2,000	$ 8,000
Trade #8	+ $5,000	$13,000
Trade #9	+ $2,000	$15,000
Trade #10	+ $5,000	$20,000

At first glance, this example appears to show a profitable track record. The account went from $10,000 to $20,000 after 10 trades. But what would have occurred if your beginning trade was Trade #4?

TABLE 30-3. DRAWDOWNS

Beginning Balance		$10,000
Trade #4	-$6,000	$ 4,000
Trade #5	+$3,000	$ 7,000
Trade #6	-$8,000	WIPED OUT!

You would never have reached the profit zone—let alone the $20,000 -- because the "drawdown" was too great. Thus, this system is either unworkable or must be capitalized to a greater degree. For instance, had you begun your account with $20,000 rather than $10,000, you would have ended up with a $10,000 or 50% profit and a workable system.

When testing my system one market at a time, I found that approximately four dollars was required for each one dollar margined to assure that the account would not be decimated by drawdowns. For example, a market requiring a $2,000 margin would require an $8,000 beginning account.

However, when I assumed that all nine markets were being traded simultaneously, I found that the maximum drawdown was greatly reduced. The reason is simple: While some markets are losing money, others are profiting, thereby smoothing out the overall performance. In our case, we found that when the Weiss Money Management portfolio was completely diversified, the back-up margin required was reduced from $1 to a ratio of $1.20 to $1. Since far less initial capital was needed, our potential – and actual—yield was greatly multiplied. Needless to say, therefore, *portfolio diversification*, if possible, is highly desirable. It has been proven mathematically and is worth remembering.

The following is a summary of the important points you should keep in mind regarding money management:

1. Avoid large capital losses.

2. Use stops that are "logical" and also a function of money management.

3. Use a trading system if possible.

4. Be adequately capitalized.

5. Be aware of the extent of potential drawdowns.

6. Diversify your portfolio.

Conclusion

Interviews with successful self-made men and women reveal a common theme—a willingness to work hard, and a willingness to take risks. Though these two qualities cannot guarantee success, the lack of either one will more than likely preclude it.

True success stories in the stock and commodity markets, while not unheard of, are at least a rarity. This unfortunate circumstance can be quite easily explained. The vast majority of the investing public, lacking the time and expertise to analyze markets on their own, instead tend to follow what others are doing—the "herd instinct." This usually results in "lemmings into the sea."

Two Wall Street truisms are apropos: "The majority is always wrong" and "if it is obvious, it is obviously wrong."

It is a frustrating fact that a simple survey of price changes in stocks, options and especially the highly leveraged "futures" markets over a period of time reveals to even the casual observer that fortunes could be made if one could make market decisions that were just slightly more right than wrong. Yet the majority of the investing public continues to lose money in the stock and commodity markets.

This occurs because: (1) most investors do not take the time to learn how to analyze markets on their own and thus are forced to rely on others' opinions—tips and rumors, and (2) they allow their emotions to play too much of a role in their decision making. This book will, hopefully, allow you to overcome these problems and make you successful in the stock and commodity markets.

You are now taking control and have taken the first step toward breaking away from the crowd.

APPENDIX

PROGRAMS:

GENERAL INSTRUCTIONS

These programs are intended to help you with market forecasting by allowing your microcomputer to perform many types of analysis presented in this book. Although they are designed for use by persons with no previous computer experience, the procedures described here and on the instruction page of each program must be followed carefully.

HARDWARE. You have two options as follows:

Option #1: Apple II + or Apple IIE microcomputer with a minimum 48K of memory, one disk drive and a video monitor.

Option #2: IBM Personal Computer with 64K of memory, one disk drive, a color/graphics adapter card and a video monitor.

You must own or have access to one of these computer systems to use the programs listed here. (For other purchased software listed in Appendix B, however, various other computers are available).

In addition, three of the programs require a printer. However, if you do not wish to use these three programs, the printer is optional.

With the Apple, you may use any printer that is supported by a Grappler + interface card. (Be sure to purchase the Grappler + interface card that is compatible with the model printer you have purchased.) With the IBM, the IBM Graphics Printer with GRAPHICS.COM software is suggested.

SOFTWARE REQUIREMENTS. Certain programs which usually come with your computer are required to operate the computer and execute your programs. For the Apple you will need Applesoft Basic and DOS 3.3; and for the IBM you will need IBM Personal Computer Advanced Basic and DOS 1.1.

SUGGESTED REFERENCES. Prior to using these programs, it is necessary that you become familiar with the commands and procedures used to control your computer, as described in the manuals provided with your computer. If you did not receive these manuals, or, after reading them, you do not understand them, you should contact your computer dealer for help. These include:

1. *Computer operation manual.* It contains instructions for setting up the hardware and basic procedures for using the machine.

2. *Basic language manual* provided for your version of Basic. This manual will provide information on entering Basic programs into memory, saving those programs for later use, and starting execution of the programs.

3. *Manual for your DOS (disk operating system).* This manual has instructions for handling the disk files that will be used to store the data used by the programs in this book.

GENERAL PROGRAM INSTRUCTIONS. The general program instructions below describe the procedures used to transfer the programs from the listings in the book to the computer, save the programs for later use and execute them. Later, the instruction page for each program will tell you the source of data for that program, explain the format used to store the data on the disk files, show the graph produced by the program and describe how to use it.

Step 1. *Entering the Programs.* The programs in this book are written in two different versions of BASIC—one complete set for the Apple and one for the IBM. Each program step is listed exactly as it should be entered into the computer. If you do not enter the program step exactly, the programs will not execute properly. Since you are not expected to be able to "debug" the program, *you should check each program step against the program listings one by one as you enter them* to insure that no typing error occurs during program entry. (Actual instructions on entering programs into the computer can be found in the Apple II + APPLESOFT Manual and in the IBM BASIC Manual).

Step 2. *Saving the programs.* After you enter the program into the computer, you will want to save it on the disk in order to use it later. The IBM and Apple each provide you with a set of commands that will save a program on disk and later retrieve it for use. You can find these commands in the DOS manual for your Apple or IBM along with instructions on the use of disks. We suggest you name the programs with the letters PROG, followed by the number associated with the program in the book (PROG1, PROG5, etc.). This will allow you to easily retrieve the desired programs from the disk by looking up the number in the program list given on pages iv and v. It would also be a good idea to save all the programs on one single disk and the data for the programs on a different disk or disks. This will allow you to expand the data files as new days and weeks of data are added.

Step 3. *Entering the data.* Before you can actually use a given program you will have to store the data associated with it in the computer. The File Maintenance program (Program #25) is provided to allow easy data entry and updating of files. Since this program is necessary for data entry *it should be one of the first programs entered on the computer.* Information on the data required for each program can be found on the instruction page associated with each program.

Step 4. *Using your programs.* After completing steps 1, 2 and 3 the program is ready for use. The following is a description of the steps necessary to actually use the program with either the IBM or the Apple.

For the Apple:

1. Insert a disk containing the DOS into the disk drive and turn on the computer.

2. Remove the DOS disk and insert the disk containing the desired program into the disk drive.

3. Type LOAD, a space and the program name and hit return. Example: LOAD PROG5

4. Remove the program disk and insert the disk containing the data for this program.

5. Type RUN and hit return.

For the IBM:

1. Insert a disk containing the DOS into the disk drive and turn on the computer.

2. Type BASICA and hit the return key.

3. Remove the DOS disk and insert the disk containing the desired program into the disk drive.

4. Type LOAD" and the program name and hit return. Example: LOAD"PROG5

5. Remove the program disk and insert the disk containing the data for this program.

6. Type RUN and hit return.

Step 5. *Additional data or choices*. The program should then run and produce the desired output in a short period of time. Several of the programs require additional information and these programs will stop to allow you to enter the additional information or to select your choice of output. (These are noted and explained in the instructions provided with the listings).

Step 6. *Print-out*. When the program has produced a graphic display on the screen it will continue to display the graph until you press the return key. During this time you can print the graph if you are using the IBM hardware option with the IBM Graphics Printer. While the graph is being displayed simply hold down the shift key and press the key marked PrtSc. (Additional information about this procedure is available from your IBM computer dealer).

PROGRAM 1

DAILY DATA PLOT

This program allows you to chart the daily open, high, low and close
on any stock or commodity. You have a choice of two chart formats:
A bar chart showing open, high, low, close or a line chart with closing
prices only.

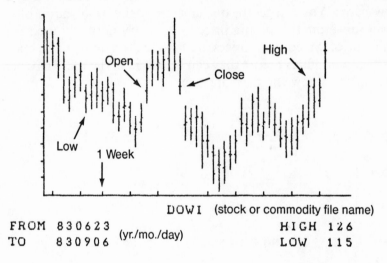

DOWI (stock or commodity file name)

FROM   830623   (yr./mo./day)   HIGH   126
TO   830906   LOW   115

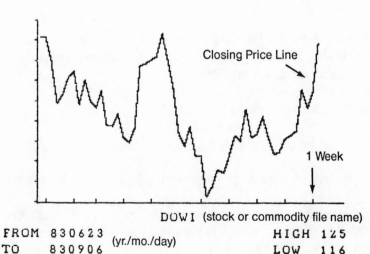

DOWI (stock or commodity file name)

FROM   830623   (yr./mo./day)   HIGH   125
TO   830906   LOW   116

DATA SOURCES. The data for this program are the prices of (1) futures or (2) stock issues or averages as found in the financial section of any newspaper:

(1) *FUTURES*. Use the settlement price for the close. On the T- bonds, Ginnie Maes or T-notes, be sure to convert the numbers from 32nds into decimals. For example 86.16 should be entered as 86.50.

(2) *STOCKS AND OPTIONS*. Usually the opening price is not available in the newspaper. You can get the opening price daily from your broker or you can substitute the closing price in the entry normally used for the opening price. Since stock prices are listed as fractions, these must be converted to decimals before they can be stored in the file. Here are a few examples of how the data appear:

In The Newspaper	After Conversion	In The File
75 1/2	75.50	07550
38 1/8	38.125	03813
91.20	no conversion	09120
156.60	no conversion	15660

Notice that you must enter the data in the file *without decimal points or commas and with all leading zeros.* (For more information on how the data are stored see program #25)

Here are some additional points to remember.

(1) The data must be entered into a type 1 file (see Program #25).

(2) At least 70 days of data must be entered when the file is created.

(3) The file may be given any name which is a legal name for files allowed by your computer. (Consult your DOS manual and BASIC manual for a description of legal file names).

(4) You should keep a separate record of the file name since it will be needed later to use the program.

(5) Any number of stock or commodity files may be created for use with this program. Each stock or commodity must be entered into a different data file with a unique name.

(6) The actual data file used by the program is specified by entering the file name when the program requests it.

PROGRAM USE. Simply follow these four steps:

Step 1. Run the program by following the procedure given in the general program instructions STEP 4.

Step 2. The program will ask you the name of the data file to process. Enter the *name* of any stock or commodity file that was created as a type 1 file (see Program #25).

Step 3. After you type the desired file name press return. The program will load the data into memory, plot the daily prices and then request the type of chart that you wish to see.

Step 4. Press the number that corresponds to the chart that you wish to view. At that time, the graph will be continuously displayed on the screen for you to view until you press return to end the program.

PROGRAM #1   LISTING FOR APPLE II+ OR IIe

```
10   DIM O(70),H(70),L(70),C(70)
20   DIM D1$(70),S(70)
30   TEXT : HOME : VTAB 12: HTAB 8
40   INPUT "ENTER FILE NAME ";A$
50   OP$ =  CHR$ (4) + "OPEN " + A$ + ",L40"
60   RD$ =  CHR$ (4) + "READ " + A$ + ",R"
70   HOME : VTAB 12: HTAB 14
80   FLASH : PRINT "READING FILE":NORMAL
90   PRINT OP$: PRINT RD$;0
100   INPUT X:X = X - 69
110   FOR M = 1 TO 70
```

```
120    PRINT RD$;X: INPUT R$:X = X + 1
130    H(M) =   VAL ( MID$ (R$,13,5))
140    L(M) =   VAL ( MID$ (R$,18,5))
150    O(M) =   VAL ( MID$ (R$,8,5))
160    C(M) =   VAL ( MID$ (R$,23,5))
170    D1$(M) =   LEFT$ (R$,1)
180     IF M < > 20 GOTO 210
190    BD$ =   MID$ (R$,2,6):LP = L(M):HP = H(M)
200    CH = C(M):CL = CH
210     IF (L(M) < LP) THEN LP = L(M)
220     IF (H(M) > HP) THEN HP = H(M)
230     IF (C(M) > CH) THEN CH = C(M)
240     IF (C(M) < CL) THEN CL = C(M)
250     IF M = 70 THEN ED$ =   MID$ (R$,2,6)
260     NEXT M
270     PRINT  CHR$ (4);"CLOSE ";A$
280     TEXT : HOME : VTAB 12: HTAB 13
290     PRINT "CHART SELECTION"
300     VTAB 13: HTAB 16: PRINT "1 - OHLC"
310     VTAB 14: HTAB 16: PRINT "2 - CLOSE"
320     VTAB 16: HTAB 14: PRINT "PLEASE CHOOSE ";
330     GET W: IF (W < 1) OR (W > 2) GOTO 320
340     PRINT  CHR$ (4): GOSUB 450
350     IF W = 1 THEN   GOSUB 540
360     IF W = 2 THEN   GOSUB 660
370    LP = LP / 100
380     VTAB 21: HTAB (20 -   INT ( LEN(A$) / 2)): PRINT A$
390     VTAB 22: PRINT "FROM ";BD$;
400     HTAB 30: PRINT "HIGH ";HP
410     VTAB 23: PRINT "TO   ";ED$;
420     HTAB 30: PRINT "LOW  ";LP
430     VTAB 24: HTAB 12: INPUT "RETURN TO CONTINUE";X$
440     TEXT : HOME : END
450     IF W = 2 THEN HP = CH:LP = CL
460    LP =   INT (LP / 100)
470    HP =   INT (HP / 100 + 1)
480    ST = HP - LP: HGR
490     HPLOT 3,0 TO 3,159 TO 279,159
500     FOR P = 0 TO 158 STEP (158 / ST)
510     HPLOT 1, INT (P) TO 3, INT (P)
520     NEXT P:RA = 158 / (ST * 100)
530    LP = LP * 100: RETURN
540     FOR Q = 20 TO 70
550    HC = 6 + ((Q - 20) * 5)
560    VO =   INT ((O(Q) - LP) * RA)
570     HPLOT HC - 1,158 - VO
580    VH =   INT ((H(Q) - LP) * RA)
590    VL =   INT ((L(Q) - LP) * RA)
600     HPLOT HC,158 - VH TO HC,158 - VL
```

```
610 VC =   INT ((C(Q) - LP) * RA)
620   HPLOT HC + 1,158 - VC
630   HPLOT HC,159
640   IF D1$(Q) = "5" THEN  HPLOT HC,156 TO HC,158
650   NEXT Q: RETURN
660   FOR Q = 20 TO 70
670 HC = 6 + ((Q - 20) * 5)
680 VC = 158 -  INT ((C(Q) - LP) * RA)
690   IF Q = 20 THEN  HPLOT HC,VC:GOTO 710
700   HPLOT  TO HC,VC
710   NEXT Q: FOR Q = 20 TO 70
720   IF D1$(Q) < > "5" GOTO 750
730 HC = 6 + ((Q - 20) * 5)
740   HPLOT HC,156 TO HC,158
750   NEXT Q: RETURN
```

PROGRAM #1   LISTING FOR IBM PC

```
10 DIM O(70), H(70),L(70), C(70)
20 DIM D1$(70), S(70)
30 SCREEN 1: CLS: KEY OFF
40 LOCATE 10,8:INPUT "ENTER FILE NAME ";A$
50 CLS:LOCATE 12,10:PRINT "READING FILE "
60 OPEN A$ AS #1 LEN=39
70 FIELD #1, 1 AS D$, 6 AS DA$
80 FIELD #1,7 AS DD$,5 AS OF$,5 AS HF$,5 AS LF$,5 AS CF$
90 FIELD #1,27 AS DC$,6 AS VO$,6 AS OI$:GET #1,1
100 Z = VAL(OF$)-69:GET #1,Z
110 FOR M = 1 TO 70:H(M) = VAL(HF$)
120 O(M) = VAL(OF$):L(M) = VAL(LF$)
130 C(M) = VAL(CF$):D1$(M) = D$
140 IF M <> 20 GOTO 160
150 BD$ = DA$:LP = L(M):HP = H(M):CH = C(M):CL = C(M)
160 IF M = 70 THEN ED$ = DA$
170 IF L(M) < LP THEN LP = L(M)
180 IF H(M) > HP THEN HP = H(M)
190 IF C(M) > CH THEN CH = C(M)
200 IF C(M) < CL THEN CL = C(M)
210 GET #1:NEXT M:CLOSE #1:CLS
220 LOCATE 12,13:PRINT "CHART SELECTION"
230 LOCATE 13,16:PRINT "1 - OHLC"
240 LOCATE 14,16:PRINT "2 - CLOSE"
250 LOCATE 16,14:PRINT "PLEASE CHOOSE"
260 Y$ = INKEY$:IF (Y$ < "1") OR (Y$ > "2") GOTO 260
270 CLS:GOSUB 560
280 IF Y$ = "1" THEN GOSUB 380
```

```
290 IF Y$ = "2" THEN GOSUB 500
300 LP = LP / 100
310 LOCATE 22,(20 - (LEN(A$)\2)):PRINT A$
320 LOCATE 23,4:PRINT "FROM ";BD$;
330 LOCATE 23,30:PRINT "HIGH ";HP;
340 LOCATE 24,4:PRINT "TO   ";ED$;
350 LOCATE 24,30:PRINT "LOW  ";LP;
360 LOCATE 25,10:INPUT "RETURN TO CONTINUE";X$
370 CLS:RETURN
380 FOR Q = 20 TO 70
390 HC = 26 + ((Q-20) * 5)
400 VO = INT((O(Q) - LP) * RA)
410 PSET (HC - 1,163 - VO)
420 VH = INT((H(Q) - LP) * RA).
430 VL = INT((L(Q) - LP) * RA)
440 LINE (HC,163-VH) - (HC,163-VL)
450 VC = INT((C(Q) - LP) * RA)
460 PSET (HC + 1,163 - VC)
470 PSET (HC,163)
480 IF D1$(Q) = "5" THEN LINE (HC,163) - (HC,165)
490 NEXT Q:RETURN
500 FOR Q = 20 TO 70
510 HC = 26 + ((Q-20) * 5)
520 VC = 163 - INT((C(Q) - LP) * RA)
530 IF Q = 20 THEN PSET (HC,VC) ELSE LINE -(HC,VC)
540 IF D1$(Q)="5" THEN LINE(HC,163)-(HC,165):PSET(HC,VC)
550 NEXT Q:RETURN
560 IF Y$ = "2" THEN HP = CH:LP = CL
570 LP = LP \ 100:HP = HP \ 100 + 1
580 ST = HP - LP:RA = 163 / (ST * 100)
590 LINE (23,0) - (23,163)
600 LINE -(319,163)
610 FOR P = 0 TO 163 STEP (163/ST)
620 LINE (21,INT(P)) - (23,INT(P))
630 NEXT P:LP = LP * 100:RETURN
```

PROGRAM 2

MOVING AVERAGES

This program allows you to generate a moving average line of the daily closing price and view it along with the daily prices. It also lets you select the period of the moving average.

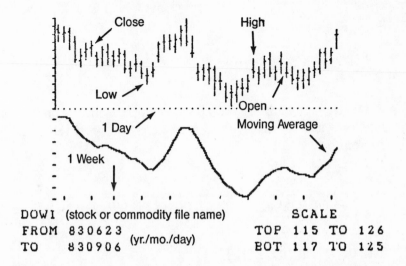

DOWI (stock or commodity file name)   SCALE
FROM 830623   TOP 115 TO 126
TO   830906   (yr./mo./day)   BOT 117 TO 125

DATA SOURCES. The data, data sources and file organization are the same for this program as for Program #1.

PROGRAM USE. Simply follow these eight steps:

Step 1. Run the program by following the procedure given in the general program instructions STEP 4.

Step 2. The program will ask you for the name of the data file to process. You must type the name of any stock or commodity file that you created as a type 1 file (see Program #25).

Step 3. After you type the desired file name, press return. The program will load the data into memory and plot the daily prices.

Step 4. It will then request the number of moving averages that you wish to see. It is suggested that the number be limited to a maximum of three. Type the number and press return.

Step 5. The program will request the period for the first moving average. Enter a number between 1 and 20 and press return. The program will then plot the first moving average.

Step 6. If you selected more than one moving average, it will request the period for the next. Enter a number between 1 and 20, then press return.

Step 7. Repeat step 6 until the desired number of moving averages has been plotted.

Step 8. A graph resembling the above example will be continuously displayed on the screen for you to view until you press return to end the program.

PROGRAM #2   LISTING FOR APPLE II+ OR IIe

```
10   DIM O(70),H(70),L(70),C(70)
20   DIM D1$(70),S(70)
30 C$ = ",R":D$ =  CHR$ (4)
40   TEXT : HOME : VTAB 12: HTAB 8
50   INPUT "ENTER FILE NAME ";A$
60   HOME : VTAB 12: HTAB 14
70   FLASH : PRINT "READING FILE":NORMAL
80   PRINT D$;"OPEN ";A$;",L40"
90   PRINT D$;"READ ";A$
100   INPUT X:X = X - 69
110   FOR M = 1 TO 70
120   PRINT D$;"READ ";A$;C$;X
130   INPUT R$:X = X + 1
140 H(M) =  VAL ( MID$ (R$,13,5))
150 O(M) =  VAL ( MID$ (R$,8,5))
160 L(M) =  VAL ( MID$ (R$,18,5))
170 C(M) =  VAL ( MID$ (R$,23,5))
180 D1$(M) =  LEFT$ (R$,1)
190   IF M < > 20 GOTO 210
200 BD$ =  MID$ (R$,2,6):LP = L(M):HP = H(M)
210   IF M = 70 THEN ED$ =  MID$ (R$,2,6)
220   IF H(M) > HP THEN HP = H(M)
```

```
230   IF L(M) < LP THEN LP = L(M)
240   NEXT M: PRINT D$;"CLOSE ";A$
250   GOSUB 350: GOSUB 540
260   VTAB 21: PRINT A$;
270   HTAB 30: PRINT "SCALE"
280   VTAB 22: PRINT "FROM ";BD$;
290   HTAB 26: PRINT "TOP ";LP;" TO ";HP
300   VTAB 23: PRINT "TO   ";ED$;
310   HTAB 26: PRINT "BOT ";LS;" TO ";HS;
320   VTAB 24: HTAB 12: INPUT "RETURN TO CONTINUE";X$
330   TEXT : HOME : END
350 LP =   INT (LP / 100)
360 HP =   INT (HP / 100 + 1)
370 ST = HP - LP: HGR
380   HPLOT 3,0 TO 3,79
390   FOR P = 0 TO 78 STEP (79 / ST)
400   HPLOT 1, INT (P) TO 3, INT (P)
410   NEXT P:RA = 79 / (ST * 100)
420 LP = LP * 100: FOR Q = 20 TO 70
430 HC = 6 + ((Q - 20) * 5)
440 VO =   INT ((O(Q) - LP) * RA)
450   HPLOT HC - 1,78 - VO
460 VH =   INT ((H(Q) - LP) * RA)
470 VL =   INT ((L(Q) - LP) * RA)
480   HPLOT HC,78 - VH TO HC,78 - VL
490 VC =   INT ((C(Q) - LP) * RA)
500   HPLOT HC + 1,78 - VC
510   HPLOT HC,79
520   IF D1$(Q) = "5" THEN   HPLOT HC,156 TO HC,158
530   NEXT Q:LP = LP / 100: RETURN
540   TEXT : HOME : VTAB 12: HTAB 10
550   INPUT "# OF MOVING AVERAGES ";N
560 Y = 0: FOR B = 1 TO N
570   TEXT : VTAB 14: HTAB 10
580   INPUT "MOVING AVERAGE PERIOD ";Z
590   POKE  - 16300,0: POKE  - 16297,0
600   POKE  - 16301,0: POKE  - 16304,0
610   FOR Q = 20 TO 70:S(Q) = 0
620   IF Q < Z THEN   GOTO 700
630   FOR P = Q - (Z - 1) TO Q
640 S(Q) = S(Q) + C(P)
650   NEXT P:S(Q) = S(Q) / Z
660   IF Y = 1 GOTO 700
670   IF (Q > 19) AND (LS = 0) THEN LS = S(Q)
680   IF S(Q) > HS THEN HS = S(Q)
690   IF S(Q) < LS THEN LS = S(Q)
700   NEXT Q: IF Z < 20 THEN Z = 20
710   IF Y = 1 GOTO 800
720 LS =   INT (LS / 100)
```

```
730 HS =  INT (HS / 100 + 1)
740 TS = HS - LS
750 RA = 79 / (TS * 100)
760  IF Y = 1 GOTO 800
770  FOR K = 79 TO 158 STEP (79 / TS)
780  HPLOT 1, INT (K) TO 3, INT (K)
790  NEXT K
800  FOR Q = Z TO 70
810 HC = 6 + ((Q - 20) * 5)
820 VC = 158 -  INT ((S(Q) - (LS * 100)) * RA)
830  IF Q = Z THEN  HPLOT HC,VC: GOTO 850
840  HPLOT  TO HC,VC
850  NEXT Q:Y = 1
860  NEXT B: RETURN
```

PROGRAM #2   LISTING FOR IBM PC

```
10 DIM O(70), H(70),L(70), C(70)
20 DIM D1$(70), S(70)
30 SCREEN 1: CLS: KEY OFF
40 LOCATE 10,8:INPUT "ENTER FILE NAME ";A$
50 CLS:LOCATE 12,10:PRINT "READING FILE "
60 OPEN A$ AS #1 LEN=39
70 FIELD #1, 1 AS D$, 6 AS DA$
80 FIELD #1,7 AS DD$,5 AS OF$,5 AS HF$,5 AS LF$,5 AS CF$
90 FIELD #1,27 AS DC$,6 AS VO$,6 AS OI$:GET #1,1
100 Z = VAL(OF$)-69:GET #1,Z
110 FOR M = 1 TO 70:H(M) = VAL(HF$)
120 O(M) = VAL(OF$):L(M) = VAL(LF$)
130 C(M) = VAL(CF$):D1$(M) = D$
140 IF M = 20 THEN BD$ = DA$:LP = L(M):HP = H(M)
150 IF M = 70 THEN ED$ = DA$
160 IF L(M) < LP THEN LP = L(M)
170 IF H(M) > HP THEN HP = H(M)
180 GET #1:NEXT M:CLOSE #1
190 CLS:GOSUB 280:GOSUB 450
200 LOCATE 22,2:PRINT A$;
210 LOCATE 22,27:PRINT "SCALE";
220 LOCATE 23,3:PRINT "FROM "BD$;
230 LOCATE 23,21:PRINT "TOP ";LP;" TO ";HP;
240 LOCATE 24,3:PRINT "TO   ";ED$;
250 LOCATE 24,21:PRINT "BOT ";LS;" TO ";HS;
260 LOCATE 25,10:INPUT "RETURN TO CONTINUE";X$
270 CLS:RETURN
280 LP = LP \ 100:HP = HP \ 100 + 1
290 ST = HP - LP:LINE (23,0) - (23,82)
```

```
300 FOR P = 0 TO 81 STEP (82/ST)
310 LINE (21,INT(P)) - (23,INT(P))
320 NEXT P:RA = 82 / (ST * 100)
330 LP = LP * 100:FOR Q = 20 TO 70
340 HC = 26 + ((Q-20) * 5)
350 VO = INT((O(Q) - LP) * RA)
360 PSET (HC - 1,82 - VO)
370 VH = INT((H(Q) - LP) * RA)
380 VL = INT((L(Q) - LP) * RA)
390 LINE (HC, 82-VH) - (HC, 82-VL)
400 VC = INT((C(Q) - LP) * RA)
410 PSET (HC + 1, 82 - VC)
420 PSET (HC,82)
430 IF D1$(Q) = "5" THEN LINE (HC,165) - (HC,163)
440 NEXT Q:LP = LP / 100:RETURN
450 Y = 0:LOCATE 25,1
460 INPUT; "# OF MOVING AVERAGES ";N
470 FOR B = 1 TO N:LOCATE 25,1
480 INPUT; "MOVING AVERAGE PERIOD ";Z
490 LOCATE 25,1:PRINT "                              ";
500 FOR Q = 20 TO 70:S(Q) = 0
510 IF Q < Z GOTO 590
520 FOR P = Q-(Z-1) TO Q
530 S(Q) = S(Q) + C(P)
540 NEXT P:S(Q) = S(Q) / Z
550 IF Y = 1 GOTO 590
560 IF (Q > 19) AND (LS = 0) THEN LS = S(Q)
570 IF S(Q) > HS THEN HS = S(Q)
580 IF S(Q) < LS THEN LS = S(Q)
590 NEXT Q:IF Z < 20 THEN Z = 20
600 IF Y = 1 GOTO 650
610 LS = LS \ 100:HS = HS \ 100 + 1
620 TS = HS - LS:RA = 82 / (TS * 100)
630 FOR K = 82 TO 163 STEP (81/TS)
640 LINE (21,INT(K)) - (23,INT(K)):NEXT K
650 FOR  Q = Z TO 70
660 HC = 26 + (( Q - 20) * 5)
670 VC = 163 - INT((S(Q) - (LS * 100)) * RA)
680 IF Q = Z THEN PSET (HC,VC) ELSE LINE -(HC,VC)
690 NEXT Q:Y = 1:NEXT B:RETURN
```

PROGRAM 3
MOMENTUM

This program allows you to generate a momentum line of the daily closing price and view it along with the daily prices. It also lets you select
the momentum period.

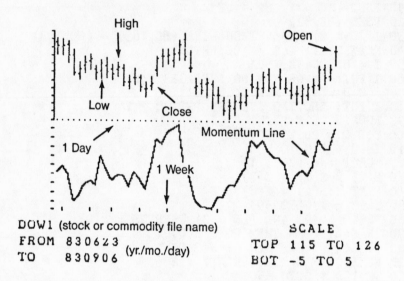

DATA SOURCES. The data, data sources and file organization are the
same for this program as for program #1.

PROGRAM USE. Simply follow these five steps:

Step 1. Run the program by following the procedure given in the general
program instructions STEP 4.

Step 2. The program will ask you for the name of the data file to process. You must type the name of any stock or commodity file that you
created as a type 1 file (see Program #25).

Step 3. After you type the desired file name, press return. The program
will load the data into memory and plot the daily prices.

Step 4. It will then request the period of the momentum that you wish to see. Enter a number between 1 and 20 and press return.

Step 5. The program will then plot the momentum and a graph resembling the example above will be displayed on the screen for you to view until you press return to end the program.

PROGRAM #3   LISTING FOR APPLE II+ OR IIe

```
10    DIM O(70),H(70),L(70),C(70)
20    DIM D1$(70),S(70)
30    C$ = ",R":D$ =  CHR$ (4)
40    TEXT : HOME : VTAB 12: HTAB 8
50    INPUT "ENTER FILE NAME ";A$
60    HOME : VTAB 12: HTAB 14
70    FLASH : PRINT "READING FILE":NORMAL
80    PRINT D$;"OPEN ";A$;",L40"
90    PRINT D$;"READ ";A$
100    INPUT X:X = X - 69
110    FOR M = 1 TO 70
120    PRINT D$;"READ ";A$;C$;X
130    INPUT R$:X = X + 1
140   H(M) =  VAL ( MID$ (R$,13,5))
150   O(M) =  VAL ( MID$ (R$,8,5))
160   L(M) =  VAL ( MID$ (R$,18,5))
170   C(M) =  VAL ( MID$ (R$,23,5))
180   D1$(M) =  LEFT$ (R$,1)
190    IF M < > 20 GOTO 210
200   BD$ =  MID$ (R$,2,6):LP = L(M):HP = H(M)
210    IF M = 70 THEN ED$ =  MID$ (R$,2,6)
220    IF H(M) > HP THEN HP = H(M)
230    IF L(M) < LP THEN LP = L(M)
240    NEXT M: PRINT D$;"CLOSE ";A$
250    GOSUB 350: GOSUB 540
260    VTAB 21: PRINT A$;
270    HTAB 30: PRINT "SCALE"
280    VTAB 22: PRINT "FROM ";BD$;
290    HTAB 26: PRINT "TOP ";LP;" TO ";HP
300    VTAB 23: PRINT "TO   ";ED$;
310    HTAB 26: PRINT "BOT ";LS;" TO ";HS;
320    VTAB 24: HTAB 12: INPUT "RETURN TO CONTINUE";X$
330    TEXT : HOME : END
350   LP =  INT (LP / 100)
360   HP =  INT (HP / 100 + 1)
370   ST = HP - LP: HGR
```

```
380   HPLOT 3,0 TO 3,79
390   FOR P = 0 TO 78 STEP (79 / ST)
400   HPLOT 1, INT (P) TO 3, INT (P)
410   NEXT P:RA = 79 / (ST * 100)
420   LP = LP * 100: FOR Q = 20 TO 70
430   HC = 6 + ((Q - 20) * 5)
440   VO =   INT ((O(Q) - LP) * RA)
450   HPLOT HC - 1,78 - VO
460   VH =   INT ((H(Q) - LP) * RA)
470   VL =   INT ((L(Q) - LP) * RA)
480   HPLOT HC,78 - VH TO HC,78 - VL
490   VC =   INT ((C(Q) - LP) * RA)
500   HPLOT HC + 1,78 - VC
510   HPLOT HC,79
520   IF D1$(Q) = "5" THEN   HPLOT HC,156 TO HC,158
530   NEXT Q:LP = LP / 100: RETURN
540   TEXT : HOME : VTAB 12: HTAB 10
550   INPUT "ENTER MOMENTUM PERIOD ";Z
560   POKE  - 16300,0: POKE  - 16297,0
570   POKE  - 16301,0: POKE  - 16304,0
580   FOR Q = 20 TO 70
590   IF Q < Z + 1 THEN   GOTO 640
600   S(Q) = C(Q) - C(Q - Z)
610   IF Q = Z THEN LS = S(Q):HS = S(Q)
620   IF S(Q) > HS THEN HS = S(Q)
630   IF S(Q) < LS THEN LS = S(Q)
640   NEXT Q: IF Z < 20 THEN Z = 20
650   LS =   INT (LS / 100)
660   HS =   INT (HS / 100 + 1)
670   TS = (HS - LS)
680   RA = 79 / (TS * 100)
690   FOR K = 79 TO 158 STEP (79 / TS)
700   HPLOT 1, INT (K) TO 3, INT (K): NEXT K
710   FOR Q = Z TO 70
720   HC = 6 + ((Q - 20) * 5)
730   VC = 158 -   INT ((S(Q) - (LS * 100)) * RA)
740   IF Q = Z THEN   HPLOT HC,VC: GOTO 760
750   HPLOT   TO HC,VC
760   NEXT Q: RETURN
```

PROGRAM #3   LISTING FOR IBM PC

```
10 DIM O(70), H(70),L(70), C(70)
20 DIM D1$(70), S(70)
30 SCREEN 1:CLS:KEY OFF
40 LOCATE 10,8:INPUT "ENTER FILE NAME ";A$
```

```
50 CLS:LOCATE 12,10:PRINT "READING FILE "
60 OPEN A$ AS #1 LEN=39
70 FIELD #1, 1 AS D$, 6 AS DA$
80 FIELD #1,7 AS DD$,5 AS OF$,5 AS HF$,5 AS LF$,5 AS CF$
90 FIELD #1,27 AS DC$,6 AS VO$,6 AS OI$:GET #1,1
100 Z = VAL(OF$)-69:GET #1,Z
110 FOR M = 1 TO 70:H(M) = VAL(HF$)
120 O(M) = VAL(OF$):L(M) = VAL(LF$)
130 C(M) = VAL(CF$):D1$(M) = D$
140 IF M = 20 THEN BD$ = DA$:LP = L(M):HP = H(M)
150 IF M = 70 THEN ED$ = DA$
160 IF L(M) < LP THEN LP = L(M)
170 IF H(M) > HP THEN HP = H(M)
180 GET #1:NEXT M:CLOSE #1
190 CLS:GOSUB 280:GOSUB 450
200 LOCATE 22,2:PRINT A$;
210 LOCATE 22,27:PRINT "SCALE";
220 LOCATE 23,3:PRINT "FROM ";BD$;
230 LOCATE 23,21:PRINT "TOP ";LP;" TO ";HP;
240 LOCATE 24,3:PRINT "TO   ";ED$;
250 LOCATE 24,21:PRINT "BOT ";LS;" TO ";HS;
260 LOCATE 25,10:INPUT "RETURN TO CONTINUE";X$
270 CLS:RETURN
280 LP = LP \ 100:HP = HP \ 100 + 1
290 ST = HP - LP:LINE (23,0) - (23,82)
300 FOR P = 0 TO 81 STEP (82 / ST)
310 LINE (21,INT(P)) - (23,INT(P))
320 NEXT P:RA = 82 / (ST * 100)
330 LP = LP * 100:FOR Q = 20 TO 70
340 HC = 26 + ((Q-20) * 5)
350 VO = INT((O(Q) - LP) * RA)
360 PSET (HC - 1,82 - VO)
370 VH = INT((H(Q) - LP) * RA)
380 VL = INT((L(Q) - LP) * RA)
390 LINE (HC, 82-VH) - (HC, 82-VL)
400 VC = INT((C(Q) - LP) * RA)
410 PSET (HC + 1, 82 - VC)
420 PSET (HC,82)
430 IF D1$(Q) = "5" THEN LINE (HC,165) - (HC,163)
440 NEXT Q:LP = LP / 100:RETURN
450 LOCATE 25,1
460 INPUT; "ENTER MOMENTUM PERIOD ";Z
470 LOCATE 25,1:PRINT "                          ";
480 FOR Q = 20 TO 70
490 IF Q < Z + 1 GOTO 540
500 S(Q) = C(Q) - C(Q - Z)
510 IF (Q > 19) AND (LS = 0) THEN LS = S(Q)
520 IF (S(Q) > HS) THEN HS = S(Q)
530 IF (S(Q) < LS) THEN LS = S(Q)
540 NEXT Q:IF Z < 20 THEN Z = 20
```

```
550 LS = INT(LS / 100)
560 HS = INT(HS / 100 + 1)
570 TS = HS - LS:RA = 82 / (TS * 100)
580 FOR K = 82 TO 163 STEP (82/TS)
590 LINE (21,INT(K)) - (23,INT(K)):NEXT K
600 FOR  Q = Z TO 70
610 HC = 26 + (( Q - 20) * 5)
620 VC = 163 - INT((S(Q) - (LS * 100)) * RA)
630 IF Q = Z THEN PSET (HC,VC) ELSE LINE -(HC,VC)
640 NEXT Q:RETURN
```

PROGRAM 4
VOLUME

This program allows you to choose a method for displaying the volume and view it along with the daily prices.

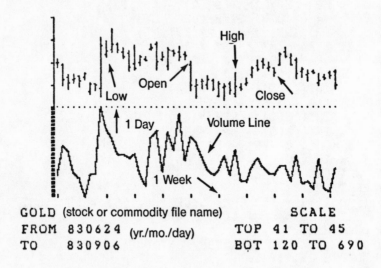

DATA SOURCES. The data, data sources and file organization are the same for this program as for program #1.

PROGRAM USE. Simply follow these four steps:

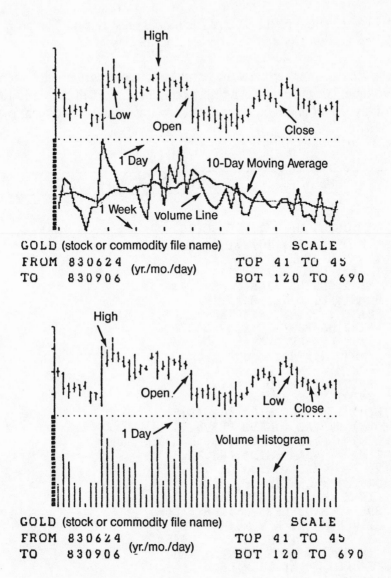

GOLD (stock or commodity file name)   SCALE
FROM 830624   (yr./mo./day)   TOP 41 TO 45
TO   830906   BOT 120 TO 690

GOLD (stock or commodity file name)   SCALE
FROM 830624   (yr./mo./day)   TOP 41 TO 45
TO   830906   BOT 120 TO 690

Step 1. Run the program by following the procedure given in the general program instructions STEP 4.

Step 2. The program will ask you the name of the data file to process. You must type the name of any stock or commodity file that you created as a type 1 file (see Program #25).

Step 3. After you type the desired file name, press return. The program will then present the choices for volume display.

Step 4. Enter a number between 1 and 3 and the program will then plot the volume. Graphs resembling the examples above will be continuously displayed on the screen for you to view until you press return to end the program.

PROGRAM #4   LISTING FOR APPLE II+ OR IIe

```
10    DIM O(70),H(70),L(70),C(70)
20    DIM D1$(70),V(70),S(70)
30 C$ = ",R":D$ =  CHR$ (4)
40    TEXT : HOME : VTAB 12: HTAB 8
50    INPUT "ENTER FILE NAME ";A$
60    HOME : VTAB 12: HTAB 14
70    FLASH : PRINT "READING FILE":NORMAL
80    PRINT D$;"OPEN ";A$;",L40"
90    PRINT D$;"READ ";A$
100   INPUT X:X = X - 69
110   FOR M = 1 TO 70
120   PRINT D$;"READ ";A$;C$;X
130   INPUT R$:X = X + 1
140   H(M) =  VAL ( MID$ (R$,13,5))
150   O(M) =  VAL ( MID$ (R$,8,5))
160   L(M) =  VAL ( MID$ (R$,18,5))
170   C(M) =  VAL ( MID$ (R$,23,5))
180   V(M) =  VAL ( MID$ (R$,28,6))
190   D1$(M) =  LEFT$ (R$,1)
200   IF M <  > 20 GOTO 230
210   BD$ =  MID$ (R$,2,6):LP = L(M)
220   HP = H(M):LV = V(M):HV = LV
230   IF M = 70 THEN ED$ = MID$(R$,2,6)
240   IF H(M) > HP THEN HP = H(M)
250   IF L(M) < LP THEN LP = L(M)
260   IF V(M) > HV THEN HV = V(M)
270   IF V(M) < LV THEN LV = V(M)
280   NEXT M: PRINT D$;"CLOSE ";A$
290   HOME : VTAB 6: HTAB 6
300   PRINT "PLEASE CHOOSE VOLUME DISPLAY METHOD"
310   VTAB 10: HTAB 6: PRINT "1 - VOLUME LINE"
320   VTAB 11: HTAB 6:
      PRINT "2 - LINE & 10-DAY MOVING AVERAGE"
330   VTAB 12: HTAB 6: PRINT "3 - HISTOGRAM"
340   VTAB 14: HTAB 10: PRINT "PLEASE CHOOSE ";
```

```
350   GET C: IF (C < 1) OR (C > 3) GOTO 340
360   PRINT D$: GOSUB 460: GOSUB 650
380   VTAB 21: PRINT A$;
390   HTAB 30: PRINT "SCALE"
400   VTAB 22: PRINT "FROM ";BD$;
410   HTAB 24: PRINT "TOP ";LP;" TO ";HP
420   VTAB 23: PRINT "TO    ";ED$;
430   HTAB 24: PRINT "BOT ";LV;" TO ";HV
440   VTAB 24: HTAB 12: INPUT "RETURN TO CONTINUE";X$
450   TEXT : HOME : END
460 LP =   INT (LP / 100)
470 HP =   INT (HP / 100 + 1)
480 ST = HP - LP: HGR
490   HPLOT 3,0 TO 3,79
500   FOR P = 0 TO 78 STEP (79 / ST)
510   HPLOT 1, INT (P) TO 3, INT (P)
520   NEXT P:RA = 79 / (ST * 100)
530 LP = LP * 100: FOR Q = 20 TO 70
540 HC = 6 + ((Q - 20) * 5)
550 VO =   INT ((O(Q) - LP) * RA)
560   HPLOT HC - 1,78 - VO
570 VH =   INT ((H(Q) - LP) * RA)
580 VL =   INT ((L(Q) - LP) * RA)
590   HPLOT HC,78 - VH TO HC,78 - VL
600 VC =   INT ((C(Q) - LP) * RA)
610   HPLOT HC + 1,78 - VC
620   HPLOT HC,79
630   IF D1$(Q) = "5" THEN   HPLOT HC,156 TO HC,158
640   NEXT Q:LP = LP / 100: RETURN
650 LV =   INT (LV / 1000)
660 HV =   INT (HV / 1000 + 1)
670 TS = (HV - LV)
680 RA = 79 / (TS * 1000)
700   FOR K = 79 TO 158 STEP (79 / TS)
710   HPLOT 1, INT (K) TO 3, INT (K): NEXT K
720   FOR Q = 20 TO 70: IF C < > 2 GOTO 750
730 S(Q) = 0: FOR J = Q - 9 TO Q
740 S(Q) = S(Q) + V(J): NEXT J:S(Q) = S(Q) / 10
750 HC = 6 + ((Q - 20) * 5)
760 VC = 158 -   INT ((V(Q) - (LV * 1000)) * RA)
770   IF C = 3 THEN   GOSUB 870: GOTO 800
780   IF Q = 20 THEN   HPLOT HC,VC:GOTO 800
790   HPLOT  TO HC,VC
800   NEXT Q: IF C < > 2 THEN   RETURN
810   FOR Q = 20 TO 70
820 HC = 6 + ((Q - 20) * 5)
830 VC = 158 -   INT ((S(Q) - (LV * 1000)) * RA)
840   IF Q = 20 THEN   HPLOT HC,VC:GOTO 860
850   HPLOT  TO HC,VC
```

```
860   NEXT Q: RETURN
870   IF Q > 19 THEN  HPLOT HC,158 TO HC,VC
880   RETURN
```

PROGRAM #4   LISTING FOR IBM PC

```
10 DIM O(70), H(70),L(70), C(70)
20 DIM D1$(70), S(70), V(70)
30 SCREEN 1:CLS:KEY OFF
40 LOCATE 10,8:INPUT "ENTER FILE NAME ";A$
50 CLS:LOCATE 12,10:PRINT "READING FILE "
60 OPEN A$ AS #1 LEN=39
70 FIELD #1, 1 AS D$, 6 AS DA$
80 FIELD #1,7 AS DD$,5 AS OF$,5 AS HF$,5 AS LF$,5 AS CF$
90 FIELD #1,27 AS DC$,6 AS VO$,6 AS OI$:GET #1,1
100 Z = VAL(OF$)-69:GET #1,Z
110 FOR M = 1 TO 70:H(M) = VAL(HF$)
120 O(M) = VAL(OF$):L(M) = VAL(LF$)
130 C(M) = VAL(CF$):D1$(M) = D$
140 V(M) = VAL(VO$)
150 IF M <> 20 GOTO 180
160 BD$ = DA$:LP = L(M):HP = H(M)
170 LV = V(M):HV = LV
180 IF M = 70 THEN ED$ = DA$
190 IF V(M) < LV THEN LV = V(M)
200 IF L(M) < LP THEN LP = L(M)
210 IF V(M) > HV THEN HV = V(M)
220 IF H(M) > HP THEN HP = H(M)
230 GET #1:NEXT M:CLOSE #1
240 CLS:LOCATE 6,6
250 PRINT "PLEASE CHOOSE VOLUME DISPLAY METHOD"
260 LOCATE 10,6:PRINT "1 - VOLUME LINE"
270 LOCATE 11,6:PRINT "2 - LINE & 10-DAY MOVING AVERAGE"
280 LOCATE 12,6:PRINT "3 - HISTOGRAM"
290 C$ = INKEY$:IF (C$ < "1") OR (C$ > "3") GOTO 290
300 CLS:GOSUB 400:GOSUB 570
310 HV = HV * 10:LV = LV * 10
320 LOCATE 22,2:PRINT A$;
330 LOCATE 22,27:PRINT "SCALE";
340 LOCATE 23,3:PRINT "FROM ";BD$;
350 LOCATE 23,21:PRINT "TOP ";LP;" TO ";HP;
360 LOCATE 24,3:PRINT "TO   ";ED$;
370 LOCATE 24,21:PRINT "BOT ";STR$(LV);" TO ";STR$(HV);
380 LOCATE 25,10:INPUT "RETURN TO CONTINUE";X$
390 CLS:RETURN
400 LP = LP \ 100:HP = HP \ 100 + 1
```

```
410 ST = HP - LP:LINE (23,0) - (23,82)
420 FOR P = 0 TO 81 STEP (82 / ST)
430 LINE (21,INT(P)) - (23,INT(P))
440 NEXT P:RA = 82 / (ST * 100)
450 LP = LP * 100:FOR Q = 20 TO 70
460 HC = 26 + ((Q-20) * 5)
470 VO = INT((O(Q) - LP) * RA)
480 PSET (HC - 1,82 - VO)
490 VH = INT((H(Q) - LP) * RA)
500 VL = INT((L(Q) - LP) * RA)
510 LINE (HC, 82-VH) - (HC, 82-VL)
520 VC = INT((C(Q) - LP) * RA)
530 PSET (HC + 1, 82 - VC)
540 PSET (HC,82)
550 IF D1$(Q) = "5" THEN LINE (HC,165) - (HC,163)
560 NEXT Q:LP = LP / 100:RETURN
570 LV = INT(LV / 1000):HV = INT(HV / 1000 + 1)
580 TS = HV - LV:RA = 82 / (TS * 1000)
590 FOR K = 82 TO 163 STEP (82/TS)
600 LINE (21,INT(K)) - (23,INT(K)):NEXT K
610 FOR  Q = 20 TO 70:IF C$ <> "2" GOTO 640
620 S(Q) = 0:FOR J = Q - 9 TO Q
630 S(Q) = S(Q) + V(J):NEXT J:S(Q) = S(Q) / 10
640 HC = 26 + ((Q - 20) * 5)
650 VC = 163 - INT((V(Q) - (LV * 1000)) * RA)
660 IF C$ = "3" THEN GOSUB 700:GOTO 680
670 IF Q = 20 THEN PSET (HC,VC) ELSE LINE -(HC,VC)
680 NEXT Q:IF C$ <> "2" THEN RETURN
690 GOSUB 720:RETURN
700 IF Q > 19 THEN LINE (HC,163)-(HC,VC)
710 RETURN
720 FOR  Q = 20 TO 70
730 HC = 26 + ((Q - 20) * 5)
740 VC = 163 - INT((S(Q) - (LV * 1000)) * RA)
750 IF Q = 20 THEN PSET (HC,VC) ELSE LINE -(HC,VC)
760 NEXT Q:RETURN
```

PROGRAM 5
ON-BALANCE VOLUME

This program allows you to generate an on-balance-volume (OBV) line
and view it along with the daily prices.

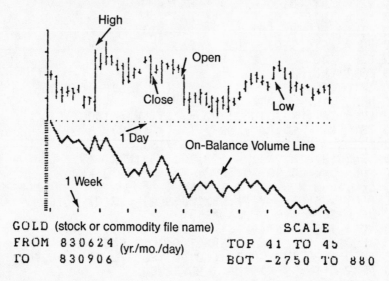

GOLD (stock or commodity file name)   SCALE
FROM 830624 (yr./mo./day)   TOP 41 TO 45
TO   830906   BOT -2750 TO 880

DATA SOURCES. The data, data sources and file organization are the
same for this program as for program #1.

PROGRAM USE. Simply follow these three steps:

Step 1. Run the program by following the procedure given in the general
program instructions STEP 4.

Step 2. The program will ask you the name of the data file to process.
You must type the name of any stock or commodity file that was created
as a type 1 file (see Program #25).

Step 3. After you type the desired file name, press return. The program
will load the data into memory and plot the daily prices, along with the
on-balance-volume line. At that time the graph resembling the example
above will be continuously displayed on the screen for you to view until you press return to end the program.

PROGRAM #5   LISTING FOR APPLE II+ OR IIe

```
10    DIM O(70),H(70),L(70),C(70)
20    DIM D1$(70),V(70)
30    C$ = ",R":D$ =  CHR$ (4)
40    TEXT : HOME : VTAB 12: HTAB 8
50    INPUT "ENTER FILE NAME ";A$
60    HOME : VTAB 12: HTAB 14
70    FLASH : PRINT "READING FILE":NORMAL
80    PRINT D$;"OPEN ";A$;",L40"
90    PRINT D$;"READ ";A$
100    INPUT X:X = X - 69
110    FOR M = 1 TO 70
120    PRINT D$;"READ ";A$;C$;X
130    INPUT R$:X = X + 1
140   H(M) =  VAL ( MID$ (R$,13,5))
150   O(M) =  VAL ( MID$ (R$,8,5))
160   L(M) =  VAL ( MID$ (R$,18,5))
170   C(M) =  VAL ( MID$ (R$,23,5))
180   V(M) =  VAL ( MID$ (R$,28,6))
190   D1$(M) =  LEFT$ (R$,1)
200    IF M = 1 GOTO 230
210    IF C(M) < C(M - 1) THEN V(M) = V(M - 1) - V(M)
220    IF C(M) > C(M - 1) THEN V(M) = V(M - 1) + V(M)
230    IF M <  > 20 GOTO 260
240   BD$ =  MID$ (R$,2,6):LP = L(M)
250   HP = H(M):LV = V(M):HV = LV
260    IF M = 70 THEN ED$ =  MID$ (R$,2,6)
270    IF H(M) > HP THEN HP = H(M)
280    IF L(M) < LP THEN LP = L(M)
290    IF V(M) > HV THEN HV = V(M)
300    IF V(M) < LV THEN LV = V(M)
310    NEXT M: PRINT D$;"CLOSE ";A$
320    GOSUB 420: GOSUB 610
330   HV = HV * 10:LV = LV * 10
340    VTAB 21: PRINT A$;
350    HTAB 30: PRINT "SCALE"
360    VTAB 22: PRINT "FROM ";BD$;
370    HTAB 24: PRINT "TOP ";LP;" TO ";HP
380    VTAB 23: PRINT "TO    ";ED$;
390    HTAB 24: PRINT "BOT ";LV;" TO ";HV
400    VTAB 24: HTAB 12: INPUT "RETURN TO CONTINUE";X$
410    TEXT : HOME : END
420   LP =  INT (LP / 100)
430   HP =  INT (HP / 100 + 1)
440   ST = HP - LP: HGR
450    HPLOT 3,0 TO 3,79
```

```
460   FOR P = 0 TO 78 STEP (79 / ST)
470   HPLOT 1, INT (P) TO 3, INT (P)
480   NEXT P:RA = 79 / (ST * 100)
490   LP = LP * 100: FOR Q = 20 TO 70
500   HC = 6 + ((Q - 20) * 5)
510   VO =   INT ((O(Q) - LP) * RA)
520   HPLOT HC - 1,78 - VO
530   VH =   INT ((H(Q) - LP) * RA)
540   VL =   INT ((L(Q) - LP) * RA)
550   HPLOT HC,78 - VH TO HC,78 - VL
560   VC =   INT ((C(Q) - LP) * RA)
570   HPLOT HC + 1,78 - VC
580   HPLOT HC,79
590   IF D1$(Q) = "5" THEN   HPLOT HC,156 TO HC,158
600   NEXT Q:LP = LP / 100: RETURN
610   LV =   INT (LV / 10000)
620   HV =   INT (HV / 10000 + 1)
630   TS = (HV - LV)
640   RA = 79 / (TS * 10000)
650   IF TS > 30 THEN TS = TS / 10: GOTO 650
660   FOR K = 79 TO 158 STEP (79 / TS)
670   HPLOT 1, INT (K) TO 3, INT (K): NEXT K
680   FOR Q = 20 TO 70
690   HC = 6 + ((Q - 20) * 5)
700   VC = 158 -   INT ((V(Q) - (LV * 10000)) * RA)
710   IF Q = 20 THEN   HPLOT HC,VC:GOTO 730
720   HPLOT   TO HC,VC
730   NEXT Q: RETURN
```

PROGRAM #5   LISTING FOR IBM PC

```
10  DIM O(70), H(70),L(70), C(70)
20  DIM D1$(70), V(70)
30  SCREEN 1:CLS:KEY OFF
40  LOCATE 10,8:INPUT "ENTER FILE NAME ";A$
50  CLS:LOCATE 12,10:PRINT "READING FILE "
60  OPEN A$ AS #1 LEN=39
70  FIELD #1, 1 AS D$, 6 AS DA$
80  FIELD #1,7 AS DD$,5 AS OF$,5 AS HF$,5 AS LF$,5 AS CF$
90  FIELD #1,27 AS DC$,6 AS VO$,6 AS OI$:GET #1,1
100 Z = VAL(OF$)-69:GET #1,Z
110 FOR M = 1 TO 70:H(M) = VAL(HF$)
120 O(M) = VAL(OF$):L(M) = VAL(LF$)
```

```
130 C(M) = VAL(CF$):D1$(M) = D$
140 IF M = 1 THEN V(M) = VAL(VO$):GOTO 170
150 IF C(M) < C(M - 1) THEN V(M) = V(M - 1) - VAL(VO$)
160 IF C(M) > C(M - 1) THEN V(M) = V(M - 1) + VAL(VO$)
170 IF M <> 20 GOTO 200
180 BD$ = DA$:LP = L(M):HP = H(M)
190 LV = V(M):HV = LV
200 IF M = 70 THEN ED$ = DA$
210 IF V(M) < LV THEN LV = V(M)
220 IF L(M) < LP THEN LP = L(M)
230 IF V(M) > HV THEN HV = V(M)
240 IF H(M) > HP THEN HP = H(M)
250 GET #1:NEXT M:CLOSE #1
260 CLS:GOSUB 360:GOSUB 530
270 HV = HV * 10:LV = LV * 10
280 LOCATE 22,2:PRINT A$;
290 LOCATE 22,27:PRINT "SCALE";
300 LOCATE 23,3:PRINT "FROM ";BD$;
310 LOCATE 23,21:PRINT "TOP ";LP;" TO ";HP;
320 LOCATE 24,3:PRINT "TO   ";ED$;
330 LOCATE 24,21:PRINT "BOT ";STR$(LV);" TO ";STR$(HV);
340 LOCATE 25,10:INPUT; "RETURN TO CONTINUE";X$
350 CLS:RETURN
360 LP = LP \ 100:HP = HP \ 100 + 1
370 ST = HP - LP:LINE (23,0) - (23,82)
380 FOR P = 0 TO 81 STEP (82 / ST)
390 LINE (21,INT(P)) - (23,INT(P))
400 NEXT P:RA = 82 / (ST * 100)
410 LP = LP * 100:FOR Q = 20 TO 70
420 HC = 26 + ((Q-20) * 5)
430 VO = INT((O(Q) - LP) * RA)
440 PSET (HC - 1,82 - VO)
450 VH = INT((H(Q) - LP) * RA)
460 VL = INT((L(Q) - LP) * RA)
470 LINE (HC, 82-VH) - (HC, 82-VL)
480 VC = INT((C(Q) - LP) * RA)
490 PSET (HC + 1, 82 - VC)
500 PSET (HC,82)
510 IF D1$(Q) = "5" THEN LINE (HC,165) - (HC,163)
520 NEXT Q:LP = LP / 100:RETURN
530 LV = INT(LV / 1000):HV = INT(HV / 1000 + 1)
540 TS = HV - LV:RA = 82 / (TS * 1000)
550 IF TS > 100 THEN TS = TS / 10
560 FOR K = 82 TO 163 STEP (82/TS)
570 LINE (21,INT(K)) - (23,INT(K)):NEXT K
580 FOR  Q = 20 TO 70
590 HC = 26 + ((Q - 20) * 5)
600 VC = 163 - INT((V(Q) - (LV * 1000)) * RA)
610 IF Q = 20 THEN PSET (HC,VC) ELSE LINE -(HC,VC)
620 NEXT Q:RETURN
```

PROGRAM 6

OPEN INTEREST

This program allows you to generate an open-interest line and view it along with the daily prices.

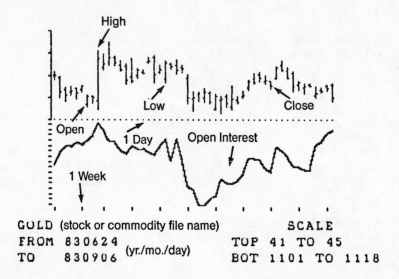

DATA SOURCES. The data, data sources and file organization are the same for this program as for program #1, except that this program cannot be run on stock files. Since stocks do not have open interest you must use a commodity file.

PROGRAM USE. Simply follow these three steps:

Step 1. Run the program by following the procedure given in the general program instructions STEP 4.

Step 2. The program will ask you the name of the data file to process. You must type the name of any commodity file that was created as a type 1 file (see Program #25). A stock file name should not be entered.

Step 3. After you type the desired file name press return. The program will load the data into memory, plot the daily prices, and then the open interest line. At that time the graph resembling the example above will be continuously displayed on the screen for you to view until you press return to end the program.

PROGRAM #6   LISTING FOR APPLE II+ OR IIe

```
10   DIM O(70),H(70),L(70),C(70)
20   DIM D1$(70),I(70)
30   C$ = ",R":D$ =  CHR$ (4)
40   TEXT : HOME : VTAB 12: HTAB 8
50   INPUT "ENTER FILE NAME ";A$
60   HOME : VTAB 12: HTAB 14
70   FLASH : PRINT "READING FILE":NORMAL
80   PRINT D$;"OPEN ";A$;",L40"
90   PRINT D$;"READ ";A$
100   INPUT X:X = X - 69
110   FOR M = 1 TO 70
120    PRINT D$;"READ ";A$;C$;X
130    INPUT R$:X = X + 1
140   H(M) =  VAL ( MID$ (R$,13,5))
150   O(M) =  VAL ( MID$ (R$,8,5))
160   L(M) =  VAL ( MID$ (R$,18,5))
170   C(M) =  VAL ( MID$ (R$,23,5))
180   I(M) =  VAL ( MID$ (R$,34,6))
190   D1$(M) =  LEFT$ (R$,1)
200    IF M < > 20 GOTO 230
210   BD$ =  MID$ (R$,2,6):LP = L(M)
220   HP = H(M):LI = I(M):HI = LI
230    IF M = 70 THEN ED$ =  MID$ (R$,2,6)
240    IF H(M) > HP THEN HP = H(M)
250    IF L(M) < LP THEN LP = L(M)
260    IF I(M) > HI THEN HI = I(M)
270    IF I(M) < LI THEN LI = I(M)
280   NEXT M: PRINT D$;"CLOSE ";A$
290   GOSUB 380: GOSUB 570
300   VTAB 21: PRINT A$;
310   HTAB 30: PRINT "SCALE"
320   VTAB 22: PRINT "FROM ";BD$;
330   HTAB 24: PRINT "TOP ";LP;" TO ";HP
340   VTAB 23: PRINT "TO   ";ED$;
350   HTAB 24: PRINT "BOT ";LI;" TO ";HI
360   VTAB 24: HTAB 12: INPUT "RETURN TO CONTINUE";X$
370   TEXT : HOME : END
380  LP =  INT (LP / 100)
390  HP =  INT (HP / 100 + 1)
400  ST = HP - LP: HGR
```

```
410   HPLOT 3,0 TO 3,79
420   FOR P = 0 TO 78 STEP (79 / ST)
430   HPLOT 1, INT (P) TO 3, INT (P)
440   NEXT P:RA = 79 / (ST * 100)
450   LP = LP * 100: FOR Q = 20 TO 70
460   HC = 6 + ((Q - 20) * 5)
470   VO =  INT ((O(Q) - LP) * RA)
480   HPLOT HC - 1,78 - VO
490   VH =  INT ((H(Q) - LP) * RA)
500   VL =  INT ((L(Q) - LP) * RA)
510   HPLOT HC,78 - VH TO HC,78 - VL
520   VC =  INT ((C(Q) - LP) * RA)
530   HPLOT HC + 1,78 - VC
540   HPLOT HC,79
550   IF D1$(Q) = "5" THEN  HPLOT HC,156 TO HC,158
560   NEXT Q:LP = LP / 100: RETURN
570   LI =  INT (LI / 100)
580   HI =  INT (HI / 100 + 1)
590   TS = (HI - LI)
600   RA = 79 / (TS * 100)
610   FOR K = 79 TO 158 STEP (79 / TS)
620   HPLOT 1, INT (K) TO 3, INT (K): NEXT K
630   FOR Q = 20 TO 70
640   HC = 6 + ((Q - 20) * 5)
650   VC = 158 -  INT ((I(Q) - (LI * 100)) * RA)
660   IF Q = 20 THEN  HPLOT HC,VC:GOTO 680
670   HPLOT  TO HC,VC
680   NEXT Q: RETURN
```

PROGRAM #6   LISTING FOR IBM PC

```
10 DIM O(70), H(70),L(70), C(70)
20 DIM D1$(70), I(70)
30 SCREEN 1:CLS:KEY OFF
40 LOCATE 10,8:INPUT "ENTER FILE NAME ";A$
50 CLS:LOCATE 12,10:PRINT "READING FILE "
60 OPEN A$ AS #1 LEN=39
70 FIELD #1, 1 AS D$, 6 AS DA$
80 FIELD #1,7 AS DD$,5 AS OF$,5 AS HF$,5 AS LF$,5 AS CF$
90 FIELD #1,27 AS DC$,6 AS VO$,6 AS OI$:GET #1,1
100 Z = VAL(OF$)-69:GET #1,Z
110 FOR M = 1 TO 70:H(M) = VAL(HF$)
120 O(M) = VAL(OF$):L(M) = VAL(LF$)
130 C(M) = VAL(CF$):D1$(M) = D$
140 I(M) = VAL(OI$)
```

```
150 IF M <> 20 GOTO 180
160 BD$ = DA$:LP = L(M):HP = H(M)
170 LI = I(M):HI = LI
180 IF M = 70 THEN ED$ = DA$
190 IF I(M) < LI THEN LI = I(M)
200 IF L(M) < LP THEN LP = L(M)
210 IF I(M) > HI THEN HI = I(M)
220 IF H(M) > HP THEN HP = H(M)
230 GET #1:NEXT M:CLOSE #1
240 CLS:GOSUB 330:GOSUB 500
250 LOCATE 22,2:PRINT A$;
260 LOCATE 22,27:PRINT "SCALE";
270 LOCATE 23,3:PRINT "FROM ";BD$;
280 LOCATE 23,21:PRINT "TOP ";LP;" TO ";HP;
290 LOCATE 24,3:PRINT "TO   ";ED$;
300 LOCATE 24,21:PRINT "BOT ";STR$(LI);" TO ";STR$(HI);
310 LOCATE 25,10:INPUT "RETURN TO CONTINUE";X$
320 CLS:RETURN
330 LP = LP \ 100:HP = HP \ 100 + 1
340 ST = HP - LP:LINE (23,0) - (23,82)
350 FOR P = 0 TO 81 STEP (82 / ST)
360 LINE (21,INT(P)) - (23,INT(P))
370 NEXT P:RA = 82 / (ST * 100)
380 LP = LP * 100:FOR Q = 20 TO 70
390 HC = 26 + ((Q-20) * 5)
400 VO = INT((O(Q) - LP) * RA)
410 PSET (HC - 1,82 - VO)
420 VH = INT((H(Q) - LP) * RA)
430 VL = INT((L(Q) - LP) * RA)
440 LINE (HC, 82-VH) - (HC, 82-VL)
450 VC = INT((C(Q) - LP) * RA)
460 PSET (HC + 1, 82 - VC)
470 PSET (HC,82)
480 IF D1$(Q) = "5" THEN LINE (HC,165) - (HC,163)
490 NEXT Q:LP = LP / 100:RETURN
500 LI = INT(LI / 100):HI = INT(HI / 100 + 1)
510 TS = HI - LI:RA = 82 / (TS * 100)
520 FOR K = 82 TO 163 STEP (82/TS)
530 LINE (21,INT(K)) - (23,INT(K)):NEXT K
540 FOR  Q = 20 TO 70
550 HC = 26 + ((Q - 20) * 5)
560 VC = 163 - INT((I(Q) - (LI * 100)) * RA)
570 IF Q = 20 THEN PSET (HC,VC) ELSE LINE -(HC,VC)
580 NEXT Q:RETURN
```

PROGRAM 7
DAILY MOST ACTIVES OSCILLATOR

This program allows you to generate an oscillator of the percentage of stocks in the 15 Daily Most Actives which showed gains for the day.

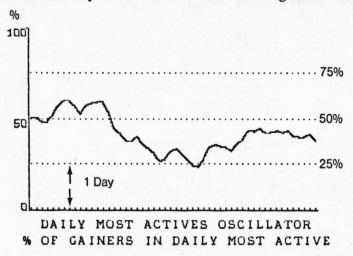

DAILY MOST ACTIVES OSCILLATOR
% OF GAINERS IN DAILY MOST ACTIVE

DATA SOURCE. To build the data file simply follow these seven steps:

Step 1. Find the data for this program in the *Wall Street Journal* on the page entitled "NYSE-Composite Transactions," in the box labeled "Active Stocks." Stocks which were gainers are designated by a "+" in the column marked *chg.*, losers by a "-", and unchanged by a line of dots.

Step 2. Count the number of gainers and write it down.

Step 3. Repeat with the losers and unchanged.

Step 4. Add a "0" in front of any number that is a single digit.

Step 5. You should now have three 2-digit numbers and these should be combined without spaces in the following order: number of gainers, number of losers and number unchanged.

Step 6. You have now converted the data into a 6-digit number which you can enter into the data file for this program.

Example:

Gainers	-	08
Losers	-	06
Unchanged	-	01

The 6-digit number is 080601.

Example:

The 6-digit number is 080601.

Step 7. The data file for this program is a type 3 file (see Program #25). When you create the file, name it ACTIVES and enter at least 65 days of data, updated daily. (See Program #25 for instructions on creating and updating files).

PROGRAM USE. Simply run the program by following the procedure given in the general program instructions STEP 4. It will then produce a graph resembling the example above.

PROGRAM #7   LISTING FOR APPLE II+ OR IIe

```
10 D$ =  CHR$ (4): DIM O(65)
20   TEXT : HOME : VTAB 12: HTAB 14
30   FLASH : PRINT "READING FILE":NORMAL
40   PRINT D$;"OPEN ACTIVES,L8"
50   PRINT D$;"READ ACTIVES,R0"
60   INPUT A:A = A - 61
70   FOR M = 1 TO 61
80   PRINT D$;"READ ACTIVES,R";A + M
90   INPUT R$
100 O(M) =  VAL ( LEFT$ (R$,2))
110  NEXT M: HGR
120  PRINT D$;"CLOSE ACTIVES"
130  HPLOT 20,0 TO 20,159 TO 279,159
```

```
140   FOR P = 22 TO 277 STEP 5
150   HPLOT P,39: HPLOT P,79: HPLOT P,118
160   HPLOT P,157 TO P,158: NEXT P
170   FOR P = 0 TO 158 STEP 15.8
180   HPLOT 17, INT (P) TO 20, INT (P)
190   HPLOT 1,2 TO 3,1 TO 3,7 TO 1,7 TO 4,7
200   HPLOT 10,1 TO 7,1 TO 7,6 TO 8,7 TO 10,7 TO
         11,6 TO 11,2
210   HPLOT 16,1 TO 13,1 TO 13,6 TO 14,7 TO 16,7 TO
         17,6 TO 17,2
220   HPLOT 11,80 TO 7,80 TO 7,83 TO 11,83 TO 10,86
         TO 8,86 TO 7,85
230   HPLOT 16,80 TO 13,80 TO 13,85 TO 14,86 TO 16,86
         TO 17,85 TO 17,81
240   HPLOT 16,153 TO 13,153 TO 13,158 TO 14,159 TO
         16,159 TO 17,158 TO 17,154
250   FOR Q = 10 TO 61:S = 0
260   FOR J = Q - 9 TO Q
270   S = S + (O(J) / 15)
280   NEXT J:S = S / 10
290   VC = 158 - INT (S * 158)
300   HC = 22 + ((Q - 10) * 5)
310   IF Q = 10 THEN   HPLOT HC,VC:GOTO 330
320   HPLOT  TO HC,VC
330   NEXT Q: VTAB 21: HTAB 8
340   PRINT "DAILY MOST ACTIVES OSCILLATOR"
350   VTAB 22: HTAB 6
360   PRINT "% OF GAINERS IN DAILY MOST ACTIVE"
370   VTAB 24: HTAB 12
380   INPUT "RETURN TO CONTINUE";A$
390   TEXT : HOME : END
```

PROGRAM #7   LISTING FOR IBM PC

```
10 DIM O(65):SCREEN 1:KEY OFF:CLS
20 LOCATE 12,14:PRINT "READING FILE"
30 OPEN "ACTIVES" AS #1 LEN=8
40 FIELD #1, 8 AS AC$:GET #1,1
50 Z = VAL(AC$) - 64:GET #1,Z
60 FOR M = 1 TO 65:O(M) = VAL(LEFT$(AC$,2))
70 GET #1:NEXT M:CLOSE #1
80 CLS:LINE (23,0) - (23,163)
90 LINE -(300,163)
100 FOR P = 26 TO 301 STEP 5
110 PSET (P,40): PSET (P,81): PSET (P,121)
120 LINE (P,163) - (P,165):NEXT P
```

```
130 FOR P = 0 TO 163 STEP 16.3
140 LINE (21, INT(P)) - (23, INT(P))
150 NEXT P:LOCATE 1,1:PRINT "100"
160 LOCATE 11,1:PRINT "50"
170 LOCATE 21,2:PRINT "0"
180 FOR Q = 10 TO 65:S = 0
190 FOR J = Q - 9 TO Q
200 S = S + (O(J) / 15)
210 NEXT J:S = S / 10
220 HC = 26 + ((Q - 10) * 5)
230 VC = 163 - INT(S * 163)
240 IF Q = 10 THEN PSET (HC,VC) ELSE LINE -(HC,VC)
250 NEXT Q
260 LOCATE 22,6:PRINT "DAILY MOST ACTIVE OSCILLATOR"
270 LOCATE 23,4:PRINT " % GAINERS IN DAILY MOST ACTIVES"
280 LOCATE 25,10:INPUT "RETURN TO CONTINUE";X$
290 CLS:RETURN
```

PROGRAM 8

NET ADVANCES

This program computes a 30-day cumulative total of the net advances
in the 15 daily most active stocks and plots the totals generated over
the past 55 days.

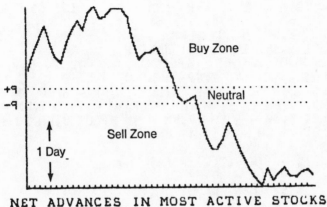

NET ADVANCES IN MOST ACTIVE STOCKS

DATA SOURCE. Use the data file named ACTIVES described in the data source section of Program #7. However, this program requires at least 85 days of data stored in the ACTIVES.

PROGRAM USE. Simply run the program by following the procedure given in the general program instructions STEP 4. It will then produce a graph resembling the example above.

PROGRAM #8   LISTING FOR APPLE II+ OR IIe

```
20 D$ =  CHR$ (4): DIM O(90),T(90)
30   TEXT : HOME : VTAB 12: HTAB 14
40   FLASH : PRINT "READING FILE":NORMAL
50   PRINT D$;"OPEN ACTIVES,L8"
60   PRINT D$;"READ ACTIVES,R0"
70   INPUT A:A = A - 84
80   FOR M = 1 TO 85
90   PRINT D$;"READ ACTIVES,R";A + (M - 1)
100   INPUT R$
110  O(M) =  VAL ( LEFT$ (R$,2)) - VAL ( MID$ (R$,3,2))
120  NEXT M: HGR :X = 0
130   PRINT D$;"CLOSE ACTIVES"
140  HPLOT 20,0 TO 20,159 TO 279,159
150  FOR P = 1 TO 30:X = X + O(P)
160  NEXT P:T(30) = X:HP =  ABS (X)
170  FOR P = 31 TO 81
180  T(P) = T(P - 1) + O(P) - O(P - 30)
190   IF  ABS (T(P)) > HP THEN HP =  ABS (T(P))
200  NEXT P:RA = 158 / (HP * 2)
210 NP = 79 -  INT (9 * RA):NM = 79 +  INT (9 * RA)
220  FOR P = 22 TO 276 STEP 5
230  HPLOT P,NP: HPLOT P,NM
240  HPLOT P,157 TO P,158: NEXT P
250 HPLOT 1,NP TO 5,NP: HPLOT 3, NP - 2 TO 3,NP + 2
260  HPLOT 7,NP-1 TO 7,NP-2: HPLOT 8,NP-3 TO 11,NP-3
265  HPLOT 8,NP TO 11,NP: HPLOT 11,NP - 3 TO 11,NP + 3
270  HPLOT 1,NM TO 5,NM: HPLOT 7,NM - 1 TO 7,NM - 2
280  HPLOT 8,NM - 3 TO 11,NM - 3: HPLOT 8,NM TO 11,NM
285  HPLOT 11,NM - 3 TO 11,NM + 3
290  FOR Q = 30 TO 81
300 VC = 79 -  INT (T(Q) * RA)
310 HC = 22 + ((Q - 30) * 5)
320  IF Q = 30 THEN  HPLOT HC,VC:GOTO 340
330  HPLOT  TO HC,VC
```

```
340  NEXT Q
350  VTAB 21: HTAB 5
360  PRINT "NET ADVANCES IN MOST ACTIVE STOCKS"
370  VTAB 24: HTAB 12
380  INPUT "RETURN TO CONTINUE";A$
390  TEXT : HOME : END
```

PROGRAM #8   LISTING FOR IBM PC

```
10  DIM O(85), T(85):SCREEN 1:CLS
20  LOCATE 12,14:PRINT "READING FILE"
30  OPEN "ACTIVES" AS #1 LEN=8
40  FIELD #1, 8 AS AC$:GET #1,1
50  Z = VAL(AC$) - 84:GET #1,Z
60  FOR M = 1 TO 85
70  O(M) = VAL( LEFT$(AC$,2)) - VAL(MID$(AC$,3,2))
80  GET #1:NEXT M:CLOSE #1
90  CLS:LINE (23,0) - (23,163)
100 LINE -(300,163):X = 0
110 FOR P = 1 TO 30:X = X + O(P)
120 NEXT P:T(30) = X: HP = ABS(X)
130 FOR P = 31 TO 85
140 T(P) = T(P-1) + O(P) - O(P-30)
150 IF ABS(T(P)) > HP THEN HP = ABS(T(P))
160 NEXT P:RA = 163 / (HP*2)
170 NP = 82 - INT(9 * RA): NM = 82 + INT(9 * RA)
180 FOR P = 26 TO 301 STEP 5
190 PSET (P,NP): PSET (P,NM)
200 LINE (P,163) - (P,165):NEXT P
210 LOCATE (NP \ 8) + 1,1:PRINT "+9"
220 LOCATE (NM \ 8) + 1,1:PRINT "-9"
230 FOR Q = 30 TO 85
240 HC = 26 + ((Q - 30) * 5)
250 VC = 81 - INT(T(Q) * RA)
260 IF Q = 30 THEN PSET (HC,VC) ELSE LINE -(HC,VC)
270 NEXT Q
280 LOCATE 22,4:PRINT "NET ADVANCES IN DAILY MOST ACTIVES"
290 LOCATE 25,10:INPUT "RETURN TO CONTINUE";X$
300 CLS:RETURN
```

PROGRAM 9

ADVANCE-DECLINE LINE

This program produces a graph of cumulative daily advancing issues minus daily declining issues over the past 55 days.

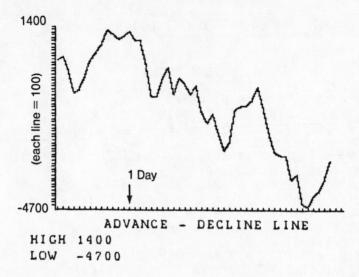

DATA SOURCE. To build the data file, follow these four steps:

Step 1. Find the data for this program in the *Wall Street Journal* in the column beside the charts of the Dow Jones Averages. They are: (1) number of advancing issues, (2) number of declining issues, (3) number of unchanged issues, (4) volume of advancing issues and (5) volume of declining issues.

Step 2. Find the advancing issues, declining issues and unchanged issues in the table "Market Diary" and use the numbers exactly as they are printed.

Step 3. Find the volume figures below the "Market Diary" in the section entitled "Trading Activity." Cross out the two rightmost digits of each figure and enter, without commas, all digits except those two.

Step 4. When you create the file, name it ADVDCL and make sure it contains at least 55 days of data, updated daily. The data file for this program is a TYPE 2 file. (See Program #25 for full instructions on creating and updating the file.)

PROGRAM USE. Simply run the program by following the procedure given in the general program instructions STEP 4. It will then produce a graph resembling the example above.

PROGRAM #9   LISTING FOR APPLE II+ OR IIe

```
10  D$ =  CHR$ (4): DIM TR(65)
20   TEXT : HOME : VTAB 12: HTAB 14
30   FLASH : PRINT "READING FILE":NORMAL
40   PRINT D$;"OPEN  ADVDCL,L28"
50   PRINT D$;"READ ADVDCL,R0"
60   INPUT A:A = A - 54
70   FOR M = 1 TO 55
80   PRINT D$;"READ ADVDCL,R";A + (M - 1)
90   INPUT R$
100 AD =   VAL ( LEFT$ (R$,5))
110 DC =   VAL ( MID$ (R$,6,5))
120 TR(M) = AD - DC
130  IF M = 1 THEN LP = TR(M):HP = LP: GOTO 150
140 TR(M) = TR(M - 1) + TR(M)
150  IF TR(M) > HP THEN HP = TR(M)
160  IF TR(M) < LP THEN LP = TR(M)
170  NEXT M: HGR : PRINT D$;"CLOSE"
180  HPLOT 20,0 TO 20,159 TO 279,159
190  FOR P = 22 TO 277 STEP 5
200  HPLOT P,157 TO P,158: NEXT P
210 HP =   INT (HP / 100 + 1)
220 LP =   INT (LP / 100)
230 ST = HP - LP
240  FOR P = 0 TO 158 STEP (158 / ST)
250  HPLOT 17, INT (P) TO 20, INT (P)
260  NEXT P:RA = 158 / (ST * 100)
270  FOR Q = 1 TO 50
280 VC = 158 -   INT ((TR(Q) - (LP * 100)) * RA)
290 HC = 22 + ((Q - 1) * 5)
300  IF Q = 1 THEN  HPLOT HC,VC: GOTO 320
310  HPLOT  TO HC,VC
320  NEXT Q: VTAB 21: HTAB 12
330  PRINT "ADVANCE - DECLINE LINE"
340  VTAB 22: HTAB 4
```

```
350   PRINT "HIGH ";HP * 100
360   HTAB 4: PRINT "LOW  ";LP * 100
370   VTAB 24: HTAB 12
380   INPUT "RETURN TO CONTINUE";A$
390   TEXT : HOME : END
```

PROGRAM #9   LISTING FOR IBM PC

```
10 DIM TR(65):SCREEN 1:CLS:KEY OFF
20 OPEN "ADVDCL" AS #1 LEN=27
30 FIELD #1,5 AS AD$,5 AS DC$,5 AS UN$,6 AS UV$,6 AS DV$
40 GET #1,1:Z = VAL(AD$) - 54
50 GET #1,Z:FOR M = 1 TO 55
60 AD = VAL(AD$):DC = VAL(DC$)
70 IF M = 1 THEN TR(M)=AD-DC ELSE TR(M)=TR(M-1)+(AD-DC)
80 IF TR(M) > HP THEN HP = TR(M)
90 IF M = 1 THEN LP = TR(M):HP = LP
100 IF TR(M) < LP THEN LP = TR(M)
110 GET #1:NEXT M:CLOSE #1:CLS
120 LINE (23,0)-(23,164):LINE -(300,164)
130 FOR P = 26 TO 301 STEP 5
140 LINE (P,164)-(P,166):NEXT P
150 HP = INT(HP / 100 + 1)
160 LP = INT(LP / 100)
170 ST = HP - LP
180  FOR P = 0 TO 163 STEP (163 / ST)
190 LINE (21, INT(P)) - (23, INT(P)):NEXT P
200 RA = 163 / (ST * 100):FOR Q = 1 TO 55
210 VC = 163 - INT((TR(Q) - (LP * 100)) * RA)
220 HC = 26 + ((Q - 1) * 5)
230 IF Q = 1 THEN PSET (HC,VC) ELSE LINE -(HC,VC)
240 NEXT Q
250 LOCATE 22,9:PRINT "ADVANCE - DECLINE LINE"
260 LOCATE 23,4:PRINT "HIGH ";HP * 100
270 LOCATE 24,4:PRINT "LOW ";LP * 100;
280 LOCATE 25,12:INPUT; "RETURN TO CONTINUE";A$
290 CLS:RETURN
```

PROGRAM 10

UNCHANGED ISSUES INDEX

This program produces a graph of the number of unchanged issues as a percentage of the total issues traded. The percentage over the past 55 days is displayed.

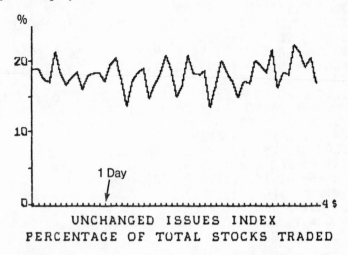

UNCHANGED ISSUES INDEX
PERCENTAGE OF TOTAL STOCKS TRADED

DATA SOURCE. This program uses the data file named ADVDCL as was described in the data source section of Program #9.

PROGRAM USE. Simply run the program by following the procedure given in the general program instructions STEP 4. It will then produce a graph resembling the example above.

PROGRAM #10   LISTING FOR APPLE II+ OR IIe

```
10 D$ =  CHR$ (4): DIM O(65)
20   TEXT : HOME : VTAB 12: HTAB 14
30   FLASH : PRINT "READING FILE":NORMAL
40   PRINT D$;"OPEN ADVDCL,L28"
50   PRINT D$;"READ ADVDCL,R0"
60   INPUT X:X = X - 54
70   PRINT D$;"READ ADVDCL,R";X
```

```
80   FOR M = 1 TO 55: INPUT R$
90   A =   VAL ( LEFT$ (R$,5))
100  D =   VAL ( MID$ (R$,6,5))
110  U =   VAL ( MID$ (R$,11,5))
120  O(M) = U / (A + D + U)
130    PRINT D$;"READ ADVDCL,R";X + M
140    NEXT M: PRINT D$;"CLOSE ACTIVES": HGR
145  RA = 632: IF H > .2 THEN RA = 316
150  HPLOT 20,0 TO 20,159 TO 279,159
160  FOR P = 21 TO 276 STEP 5
170  HPLOT P,157 TO P,158: NEXT P
180  HPLOT 14,153 TO 11,153 TO 11,158 TO 12,159 TO
        14,159 TO 15,158 TO 15,154
190  HPLOT 6,92 TO 7,91 TO 7,97 TO 5,97 TO 9,97
200  HPLOT 14,91 TO 11,91 TO 11,96 TO 12,97 TO 14,97
        TO 15,96 TO 15,92
210  HPLOT 5,29 TO 5,28 TO 9,28 TO 9,29 TO 5,34 TO 9,34
220  HPLOT 14,28 TO 11,28 TO 11,33 TO 12,34 TO 14,34
        TO 15,33 TO 15,29
230  FOR P = 0 TO 158 STEP 31.6
240  HPLOT 17, INT (P) TO 20, INT (P)
250  NEXT P: FOR Q = 1 TO 52
260  VC = 158 -  INT (O(Q) * 632)
270  HC = 21 + ((Q - 1) * 5)
275  IF VC < 0 THEN VC = 0
280  IF Q = 1 THEN  HPLOT HC,VC: GOTO 300
290  HPLOT  TO HC,VC
300  NEXT Q: VTAB 21: HTAB 11
310  PRINT "UNCHANGED ISSUES INDEX"
320  VTAB 22: HTAB 6
330  PRINT "PERCENTAGE OF TOTAL STOCKS TRADED"
340  VTAB 24: HTAB 12
350  INPUT "RETURN TO CONTINUE";A$
360  TEXT : HOME : END
```

PROGRAM #10   LISTING FOR IBM PC

```
10 DIM O(65):SCREEN 1:CLS:KEY OFF
20 LOCATE 12,14:PRINT "READING FILE"
30 OPEN "ADVDCL" AS #1 LEN=27
40 FIELD #1,5 AS AC$,5 AS DC$,5 AS UN$,6 AS UV$,6 AS DV$
50 GET #1,1:Z = VAL(AC$) - 54
60 GET #1,Z:FOR M = 1 TO 55
70 S = VAL(AC$) + VAL(DC$) + VAL(UN$)
80 O(M) = VAL(UN$) / S:GET #1
90 NEXT M:CLOSE #1
```

```
100 CLS:LINE (23,0) - (23,163)
110 LINE -(300,163)
120 FOR P = 26 TO 301 STEP 5
130 LINE (P,163) - (P,165):NEXT P
140 FOR P = 0 TO 163 STEP 32.6
150 LINE (21,INT(P)) - (23,INT(P)):NEXT P
160 FOR Q = 1 TO 55
170 HC = 26 + ((Q - 1) * 5)
180 VC = 163 - INT(O(Q) * 652)
190 IF Q = 1 THEN PSET (HC,VC) ELSE LINE -(HC,VC)
200 NEXT Q:LOCATE 5,1:PRINT "20"
210 LOCATE 13,1:PRINT "10"
220 LOCATE 22,11:PRINT "UNCHANGED ISSUES INDEX"
230 LOCATE 23,6:PRINT "PERCENTAGE OF TOTAL STOCKS TRADED"
240 LOCATE 25,10:INPUT; "RETURN TO CONTINUE";X$
250 CLS:RETURN
```

PROGRAM 11

SHORT SALE RATIOS

This program generates a graph of your choice of three short-sale ratios
over the last 50 weeks.

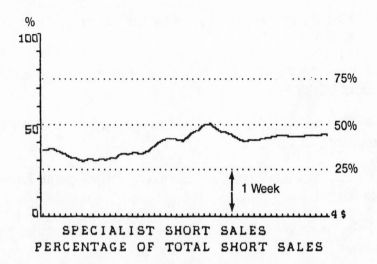

SPECIALIST SHORT SALES
PERCENTAGE OF TOTAL SHORT SALES

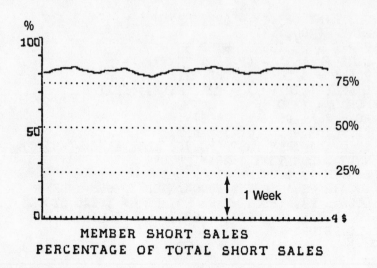

MEMBER SHORT SALES
PERCENTAGE OF TOTAL SHORT SALES

DATA SOURCE. This program uses four kinds of data, all of which are found in *Barron's* Market Laboratory, in the section entitled "Week's Market Statistics" and in the column "Last Week." To build the files, follow these eight steps:

Step 1. Find the *total short sales for the week* in the line labeled "Total Shorts, th sh."

Step 2. Enter this figure (without commas or decimal point) into a file named TSHORTS.

Step 3. Find the *member short sales for the week* in the line labeled "Member shrt, th sh."

Step 4. Enter this figure (without commas or decimal point) into a file named MSHORTS.

Step 5. Find the *specialist short sales for the week* in the line labeled "Speclst shrt, th sh."

Step 6. Enter this figure (without commas or decimal point) into a file named SSHORTS.

Step 7. Find the *odd-lot short sales for the week* in the line labeled "Short sales actual."

Step 8. Enter this figure (without commas or decimal point) into a file named OSHORTS.

All of the files are type 3 (see Program #25) and they must contain at least 56 weeks of data, updated weekly. In addition, each entry in data file TSHORTS must have a corresponding entry in the other files. In other words, the first figure entered into TSHORTS must be from the same week as the first figures entered into the other three files. For each additional figure that you enter into TSHORTS you must enter the figures for the same week into the other three files.

PROGRAM USE. Simply follow these three steps:

Step 1. Run the program by following the procedures given in the general program instructions STEP **4.**

Step 2. The program will ask you for a choice of three short- sale ratios. Enter the number between 1 and 3 that corresponds to the desired short-sale ratio.

Step 3. Press return, and a graph resembling the examples above will be plotted.

PROGRAM #11   LISTING FOR APPLE II+ OR IIe

```
50   TEXT : HOME : VTAB 12: HTAB 8
60   PRINT "ENTER NUMBER OF DESIRED RATIO"
70   VTAB 14: HTAB 6
75   PRINT "1 - MEMBER SHORT SALE RATIO"
80   VTAB 15: HTAB 6
85   PRINT "2 - SPECIALIST SHORT SALE RATIO"
90   VTAB 16: HTAB 6
95   PRINT "3 - ODD LOT SHORT SALE RATIO"
96   VTAB 17: HTAB 12: PRINT "PLEASE CHOOSE";
97   GET Y: IF (Y < 1) OR (Y > 3) GOTO 96
100 D$ = CHR$ (4): PRINT D$: DIM MS(60),TS(60)
120  TEXT : HOME : VTAB 12: HTAB 14
130  FLASH : PRINT "READING FILE": NORMAL
140  PRINT D$;"OPEN TSHORTS,L8"
150  PRINT D$;"READ TSHORTS,R0"
160  INPUT A:A = A - 56
```

```
190   FOR M = 1 TO 56
195   PRINT D$;"READ TSHORTS,R";A + M
200   INPUT R$:TS(M) =  VAL (R$)
203   IF Y = 3 THEN TS(M) = TS(M) * 1000
205   NEXT M
210   IF Y = 1 THEN F$ = "MSHORTS":
        GT$ = "MEMBER SHORT SALES"
220   IF Y = 2 THEN F$ = "SSHORTS":
        GT$ = "SPECIALIST SHORT SALES"
225   IF Y = 3 THEN F$ = "OSHORTS":
        GT$ = "ODD LOT SHORT SALES"
230   PRINT D$;"CLOSE TSHORTS"
240   PRINT D$;"OPEN ";F$;",L8"
250   PRINT D$;"READ ";F$;",R0"
260   INPUT B:B = B - 56
290   FOR M = 1 TO 56
295   PRINT D$;"READ ";F$;",R";B + M
300   INPUT R$:MS(M) =  VAL (R$): NEXT M
330   PRINT D$;"CLOSE ";F$: HGR
430   HPLOT 20,0 TO 20,159 TO 279,159
440   FOR P = 22 TO 277 STEP 5
450   HPLOT P,39: HPLOT P,79: HPLOT P,118
460   HPLOT P,157 TO P,158: NEXT P
480   FOR P = 0 TO 158 STEP 15.8
490   HPLOT 17, INT (P) TO 20, INT (P): NEXT P
502   HPLOT 16,1 TO 13,1 TO 13,6 TO 14,7 TO 16,7 TO
        17,6 TO 17,2
505   HPLOT 16,80 TO 13,80 TO 13,85 TO 14,86 TO 16,86
        TO 17,85 TO 17,81
507   HPLOT 16,153 TO 13,153 TO 13,158 TO 14,159 TO
        16,159 TO 17,158 TO 17,154
509   IF Y = 3 GOTO 560
520   HPLOT 10,1 TO 7,1 TO 7,6 TO 8,7 TO 10,7 TO
        11,6 TO 11,2
540   HPLOT 11,80 TO 7,80 TO 7,83 TO 11,83 TO 10,86
        TO 8,86 TO 7,85
550   HPLOT 1,2 TO 3,1 TO 3,7 TO 1,7 TO 4,7: GOTO 570
560   HPLOT 8,81 TO 9,80 TO 9,86 TO 7,86 TO 11,86
565   HPLOT 7,2 TO 7,1 TO 11,1 TO 11,2 TO 7,7 TO 11,7
570   FOR Q = 5 TO 56:S = 0
573   FOR J = Q - 4 TO Q
576   S = S + (MS(J) / TS(J))
579   NEXT J:S = S / 5
580   IF Y = 3 THEN S = S * 10000
585   VC = 158 -  INT (S * 158)
590   HC = 22 + ((Q - 5) * 5)
600   IF Q = 5 THEN  HPLOT HC,VC: GOTO 620
610   HPLOT  TO HC,VC
620   NEXT Q: VTAB 21: HTAB 20 - (LEN (GT$) / 2)
```

```
640   PRINT GT$: VTAB 22: HTAB 6
660   PRINT "PERCENTAGE OF TOTAL SHORT SALES"
670   VTAB 24: HTAB 12
680   INPUT "RETURN TO CONTINUE";A$
690   TEXT : HOME : END
```

PROGRAM #11   LISTING FOR IBM PC

```
10 DIM MS(60), TS(60):SCREEN 2:KEY OFF:CLS
20 LOCATE 12,10:PRINT "ENTER NUMBER FOR DESIRED RATIO"
30 LOCATE 14,12:PRINT "1 - MEMBER SHORT SALE RATIO"
40 LOCATE 15,12:PRINT "2 - SPECIALIST SHORT SALE RATIO"
50 LOCATE 16,12:PRINT "3 - ODD LOT SHORT SALE RATIO"
60 LOCATE 17,14:PRINT "PLEASE CHOOSE"
70 A$ = INKEY$:IF A$ = "" GOTO 70
80 IF (A$ < "1") OR (A$ > "3") THEN BEEP:GOTO 60
90 SCREEN 1:LOCATE 12,14:PRINT "READING FILE"
100 IF A$ = "1" THEN F$ = "MSHORTS":
       GT$ = "MEMBER SHORT SALES"
110 IF A$ = "2" THEN F$ = "SSHORTS":
       GT$ = "SPECIALIST SHORT SALES"
120 IF A$ = "3" THEN F$ = "OSHORTS":
       GT$ = "ODD LOT SHORT SALES"
130 OPEN "TSHORTS" AS #1 LEN=8
140 FIELD #1, 8 AS TS$:GET #1,1
150 Z = VAL(TS$) - 54:GET #1,Z
160 OPEN F$ AS #2 LEN=8
170 FIELD #2, 8 AS MS$:GET #2,1
180 Z1 = VAL(MS$) - 54:GET #2,Z1
190 FOR M = 1 TO 55:MS(M) = VAL(MS$)
200 TS(M) = VAL(TS$):GET #2
210 GET #1:NEXT M:CLOSE #1:CLOSE #2
220 CLS:LINE (23,0) - (23,163)
230 LINE -(300,163):T$ = "100":M$ = "50"
240 IF A$ = "3" THEN T$ = "20":M$ = "10"
250 FOR P = 26 TO 281 STEP 5
260 PSET (P,40): PSET (P,81): PSET (P,121)
270 LINE (P,163) - (P,165):NEXT P
280 FOR P = 0 TO 163 STEP 16.3
290 LINE (21,INT(P)) - (23,INT(P))
300 NEXT P:LOCATE 1,1:PRINT T$
310 LOCATE 11,1:PRINT M$:LOCATE 21,2:PRINT "0"
320 FOR Q = 5 TO 55:S = 0
330 IF A$ = "3" THEN S = (MS(Q) / TS(Q)) * 5:GOTO 370
340 FOR J = Q - 4 TO Q
350 S = S + (MS(J) / TS(J))
```

```
360 NEXT J:S = S / 5
370 HC = 26 + ((Q - 5) * 5)
380 VC = 163 - INT(S * 163)
390 IF Q = 5 THEN PSET (HC,VC) ELSE LINE -(HC,VC)
400 NEXT Q
410 LOCATE 22,20 - (LEN(GT$)/2):PRINT GT$
420 LOCATE 23,8:PRINT "PERCENTAGE OF TOTAL SHORTS"
430 LOCATE 25,10:INPUT "RETURN TO CONTINUE";X$
440 CLS:RETURN
```

PROGRAM 12

MEMBER TRADING

This program allows you to produce a graph of the exponential moving average of net member trading over the most recent 52 week period.

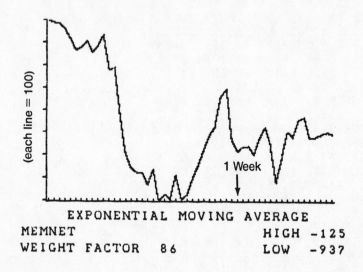

DATA SOURCE. The program uses data found each week in *Barron's* on the page entitled *Barron's* Market Laboratory. The required data is found in the column entitled "Week's Market Statistics" and in the row labeled "Net buy/sell th sh." The single number in this row under the column labeled "Last Week" is used in the file (without commas or decimal point but including a negative sign if present).

The data file used by this program is a type 3 file (see Program #25). It is suggested you name the file MEMNET but any valid file name could be used. It is important, however, to record the name you give to this file since the program will request that information. You must enter at least 52 weeks of data when you create the file and it should be updated weekly. (See Program #25 for full instructions on creating and updating the file).

PROGRAM USE. Simply follow these three steps:

Step 1. Run the program by following the procedure given in the general program instructions STEP 4.

Step 2. The program will then request the name of the file. Enter "MEMNET" or whatever name you chose for the file containing member trading information. Press return.

Step 3. The program will request a weighting factor. Enter .86 and hit return to produce the graph.

NOTE: It is possible to use this program with any type 3 file (see Program #25). Simply enter the name of a data file for which you wish to use an exponential moving average. The weighting factor can be any number between 0 and 1. Experimentation and further reading will show the best weighting factor for your purposes.

PROGRAM #12   LISTING FOR APPLE II+ OR IIe

```
10   DIM S(52),D(52)
20   TEXT : HOME : VTAB 12: HTAB 10
30   INPUT "FILE NAME? ";A$
40   HOME : VTAB 12: HTAB 10
50   INPUT "ENTER WEIGHT FACTOR ";W
60   IF (W > 1) OR (W < 0) GOTO 50
70   TEXT : HOME : VTAB 12: HTAB 10
80   FLASH : PRINT "READING FILE":NORMAL
```

```
90    PRINT  CHR$ (4);"OPEN ";A$;", L8"
100   PRINT  CHR$ (4);"READ ";A$;",RO"
110   INPUT A:A = A - 52
120   FOR M = 1 TO 52
130   PRINT  CHR$ (4);"READ ";A$;",R";A + M
140   INPUT R$:D(M) =  VAL (R$)
150   IF M = 1 THEN HP = D(1):LP = D(1): GOTO 190
160 D(M) = ((1 - W) * D(M)) + (W * D(M - 1))
170   IF D(M) > HP THEN HP = D(M)
180   IF D(M) < LP THEN LP = D(M)
190   NEXT M
200   PRINT  CHR$ (4);"CLOSE ";A$
210 HP =  INT (HP / 100 + 1)
220 LP =  INT (LP / 100)
230 ST% = HP - LP: HGR
240 RA = 158 / (ST% * 100)
250   HPLOT 20,0 TO 20,159 TO 279,159
260   FOR P = 22 TO 277 STEP 5
270   HPLOT P,157 TO P,158
280   NEXT P:PS% = ST%
290   IF PS% > 20 THEN PS% =  INT (PS% / 10): GOTO 290
300   FOR P = 0 TO 158 STEP (158 / PS%)
310   HPLOT 17, INT (P) TO 20, INT (P)
320   NEXT P
330   FOR I = 1 TO 52
340 VC = 158 -  INT ((D(I) - (LP * 100)) * RA)
350 HC = 22 + ((I - 1) * 5)
360   IF I = 1 THEN  HPLOT HC,VC: GOTO 380
370   HPLOT  TO HC,VC
380   NEXT I
390   VTAB 21: HTAB 9
400   PRINT "EXPONENTIAL MOVING AVERAGE"
410   VTAB 22: HTAB 4
420   PRINT A$;
430   HTAB 30: PRINT "HIGH ";HP
440   VTAB 23: HTAB 4
450   PRINT "WEIGHT FACTOR ";W;
460   HTAB 30: PRINT "LOW  ";LP
470   VTAB 24: HTAB 12
480   INPUT "RETURN TO CONTINUE";A$
490   TEXT : HOME : END
```

PROGRAM #12   LISTING FOR IBM PC

```
10 DIM S(52), D(52):SCREEN 1:KEY OFF:CLS
20 LOCATE 12,14:INPUT "FILE NAME ";A$
30 CLS: LOCATE 12,10
40 INPUT "ENTER WEIGHT FACTOR ";W
50 IF (Z > 1) OR (Z < 0) GOTO 40
60 CLS:LOCATE 12,14:PRINT "READING FILE                    "
70 OPEN A$ AS #1 LEN=8:FIELD #1, 8 AS M$
80 GET #1,1:Z = VAL(M$) - 51:GET#1,Z
90 FOR J = 1 TO 52:D(J) = VAL(M$)
100 IF J = 1 THEN HP = D(1):LP = D(1):GOTO 140
110 D(J) = ((1 - W) * D(J)) + (W * D(J - 1))
120 IF D(J) > HP THEN HP = D(J)
130 IF D(J) < LP THEN LP = D(J)
140 GET #1:NEXT J:CLOSE #1
150 HP = INT(HP / 10000 + 1)
160 LP = INT(LP / 10000)
170 ST = HP - LP
180 RA = 163 / (ST * 10000)
190 CLS:LINE (23,0) - (23,164)
200 LINE -(300,164)
210 FOR P = 26 TO 281 STEP 5
220 LINE (P,163) - (P,165)
230 NEXT P:PS = ST
240 IF PS > 20 THEN PS = INT(PS/10): GOTO 240
250 FOR P = 0 TO 163 STEP (163/PS)
260 LINE (21,INT(P)) - (23,INT(P)):NEXT P
270 FOR J = 1 TO 52:HC = 26 + ((J - 1) * 5)
280 VC = 163 - INT((D(J) - (LP * 10000)) * RA)
290 IF J = 1 THEN PSET (HC,VC) ELSE LINE -(HC,VC)
300 NEXT J
310 LOCATE 22,9:PRINT "EXPONENTIAL MOVING AVERAGE";
320 LOCATE 23,1:PRINT A$;:LOCATE 23,29:
    PRINT "HIGH ";HP * 100
330 LOCATE 24,1:PRINT "WEIGHT FACTOR ";W;
340 LOCATE 24,29:PRINT "LOW  ";LP * 100;
350 LOCATE 25,11:INPUT; "RETURN TO CONTINUE ";X$
360 CLS:RETURN
```

PROGRAM 13

FREE RESERVES

This program plots a graph of the levels of net free reserves over the past 52 weeks.

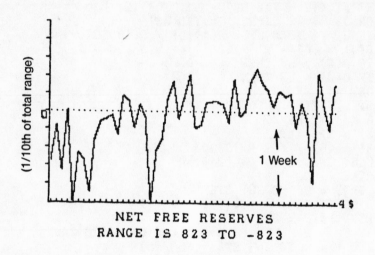

NET FREE RESERVES
RANGE IS 823 TO -823

DATA SOURCE. The data can be found in *Barron's* under the heading "Economic and Financial Indicators," under the columns "Latest Period" and labeled "Free Reserves." The data file used by the program is a type 3 file (see Program #25). When you create the file, name it NETFREE and make sure it contains at least 52 weeks of data, updated weekly. (Complete instructions for creating and updating files can be found with Program #25.)

PROGRAM USE. Simply run the program by following the procedure given in the general program instructions STEP 4, and it will produce a graph resembling the example above.

PROGRAM #13   LISTING FOR APPLE II+ OR IIe

```
10   DIM FR(52):D$ =  CHR$ (4)
20   TEXT : HOME : VTAB 12: HTAB 14
30   FLASH : PRINT "READING FILE":NORMAL
40 HP = 0
50   PRINT D$;"OPEN NETFREE,L8"
60   PRINT D$;"READ NETFREE,R0"
70   INPUT A:A = A - 52
80   FOR M = 1 TO 52
90   PRINT D$;"READ NETFREE,R";A + M
100   INPUT R$:FR(M) =  VAL (R$)
110   IF  ABS (FR(M)) > HP THEN HP =  ABS (FR(M))
120   NEXT M: PRINT D$,"CLOSE NETFREE"
130   HGR
140   HPLOT 20,0 TO 20,159 TO 279,159
150   FOR P = 22 TO 277 STEP 5
160   HPLOT P,157 TO P,158
170   HPLOT P,79: NEXT P
180   FOR P = 0 TO 158 STEP 15.8
190   HPLOT 17, INT (P) TO 20, INT (P)
200   NEXT P:RA = 158 / (HP * 2)
210   HPLOT 16,80 TO 13,80 TO 13,85 TO 14,86 TO 16,86
         TO 17,85 TO 17,81
220   FOR Q = 1 TO 52
230 VC = 79 -  INT (FR(Q) * RA)
240 HC = 22 + ((Q - 1) * 5)
250   IF Q = 1 THEN  HPLOT HC,VC: GOTO 270
260   HPLOT  TO HC,VC
270   NEXT Q
280   VTAB 21: HTAB 14
290   PRINT "NET FREE RESERVES"
300   VTAB 22: HTAB 12
310   PRINT "RANGE IS ";HP" TO -";HP
320   VTAB 24: HTAB 12
330   INPUT "RETURN TO CONTINUE";A$
340   TEXT : HOME : END
```

PROGRAM #13   LISTING FOR IBM PC

```
10 DIM FR(52):SCREEN 1:KEY OFF:CLS
20 LOCATE 12,14:PRINT "READING FILE"
30 OPEN "NETFREE" AS #1 LEN=8
40 FIELD #1, 8 AS FR$:GET #1,1
50 Z = VAL(FR$) - 51:GET #1,Z
60 FOR M = 1 TO 52:FR(M) = VAL(FR$)
70 IF ABS(FR(M)) > HP THEN HP = ABS(FR(M))
80 GET #1:NEXT M:CLOSE #1:CLS
90 LINE (23,0) - (23,164)
100 LINE -(300,164)
110 FOR P = 26 TO 281 STEP 5
120 LINE (P,163) - (P,165)
130 PSET (P,82):NEXT P
140 RA = 163 / (HP * 2)
150 LOCATE 11,2:PRINT "0"
160 FOR Q = 1 TO 52
170 HC = 26 + ((Q-1) * 5)
180 VC = 82 - INT(FR(Q) * RA)
190 IF Q = 1 THEN PSET (HC,VC) ELSE LINE -(HC,VC)
200 NEXT Q
210 LOCATE 22,14:PRINT "NET FREE RESERVES";
220 LOCATE 23,12:PRINT "RANGE IS ";HP;" TO -";HP;
230 LOCATE 25,12:INPUT "RETURN TO CONTINUE";X$
240 CLS:RETURN
```

PROGRAM 14

MONEY GROWTH

This program plots a graph of the percentage growth of M-1 over a 13-week period for the most recent 50 weeks.

DATA SOURCE. Data can be found in *Barron's* under the heading "Economic and Financial Indicators" in the column "Latest Period" and labeled "Money Supply (M1)." The data file used by the program is a type 3 file (see Program #25). When you create the file, name it

SUPPLY and make sure it contains at least 66 weeks of data, updated weekly. (Complete instructions for creating and updating files can be found with Program #25.)

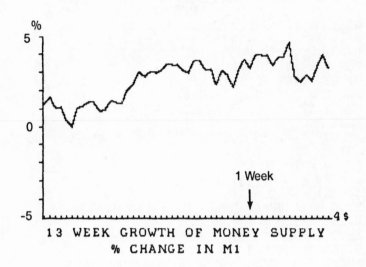

13 WEEK GROWTH OF MONEY SUPPLY
% CHANGE IN M1

PROGRAM USE. Simply run the program by following the procedure given in the general program instructions STEP 4, and it will produce a graph resembling the example above.

PROGRAM #14   LISTING FOR APPLE II+ OR IIe

```
10 D$ =  CHR$ (4): DIM S(65),D(65)
20   TEXT : HOME : VTAB 12: HTAB 14
30   FLASH : PRINT "READING FILE":NORMAL
40   PRINT D$;"OPEN  SUPPLY,L8"
50   PRINT D$;"READ SUPPLY,R0"
```

```
60    INPUT A:A = A - 65
70    FOR M = 1 TO 65
80    PRINT D$;"READ SUPPLY,R";A + M
90    INPUT R$
100   D(M) =  VAL (R$): IF M < 14 GOTO 140
110   S(M) = D(M) - D(M - 13)
120   IF S(M) <  > 0 THEN S(M) = (S(M) / D(M-13)) * 100
130   IF  ABS (S(M)) > HP THEN HP = ABS (S(M))
140   NEXT M: PRINT D$;"CLOSE SUPPLY"
150   PS =  INT (HP + 1):RA = 79 / PS: HGR
160   HPLOT 20,0 TO 20,159 TO 279,159
170   FOR P = 21 TO 276 STEP 5
180   HPLOT P,157 TO P,158: NEXT P
190   FOR P = 0 TO 158 STEP RA
200   HPLOT 17, INT (P) TO 20, INT (P)
210   NEXT P
220   HPLOT 10,77 TO 7,77 TO 7,82 TO 8,83 TO 10,83 TO
         11,82 TO 11,78
230   FOR Q = 14 TO 65
240   VC = 79 -  INT (S(Q) * RA)
250   HC = 21 + ((Q - 14) * 5)
260   IF Q = 14 THEN  HPLOT HC,VC:GOTO 280
270   HPLOT  TO HC,VC
280   NEXT Q
290   VTAB 21: HTAB 7
300   PRINT "13 WEEK GROWTH OF MONEY SUPPLY"
310   VTAB 22: HTAB 14
320   PRINT "% CHANGE IN M1"
330   VTAB 23: HTAB 13
340   PRINT "RANGE IS ";PS;" TO ";- PS;
350   VTAB 24: HTAB 12
360   INPUT "RETURN TO CONTINUE";A$
370   TEXT : HOME : END
```

PROGRAM #14   LISTING FOR IBM PC

```
10 DIM S(65), D(65):SCREEN 1:CLS:KEY OFF
20 LOCATE 12,14:PRINT "READING FILE"
30 OPEN "SUPPLY" AS #1 LEN=8
40 FIELD #1, 8 AS M$
50 GET #1,1:Z = VAL(M$) - 64
```

```
60 GET #1,Z:FOR J = 1 TO 65
70 D(J) = VAL(M$):IF J < 14 GOTO 100
80 S(J) = (D(J) - D(J - 13)) / D(J - 13) * 100
90 IF ABS(S(J)) > HP THEN HP = ABS(S(J))
100 GET #1:NEXT J:CLOSE #1:CLS
110 HP = INT(HP + 1) * 2:RA = 163 / HP
120 CLS:LINE (23,0) - (23,164)
130 LINE -(300,164)
140 FOR P = 26 TO 301 STEP 5
150 LINE (P,162) - (P,164)
160 PSET (P,82):NEXT P
170 FOR P = 0 TO 163 STEP (163/HP)
180 LINE (21,INT(P)) - (23,INT(P)):NEXT P
190 LOCATE 11,2:PRINT "0"
200 FOR J = 14 TO 65
210 HC = 26 + ((J - 14) * 5)
220 VC = 82 - INT(S(J) * RA)
230 IF J = 14 THEN PSET (HC,VC) ELSE LINE -(HC,VC)
240 NEXT J:HP = HP / 2
250 LOCATE 22,7:PRINT "13 WEEK GROWTH OF MONEY SUPPLY";
260 LOCATE 23,14:PRINT " CHANGE IN M1";
270 LOCATE 24,12:PRINT "RANGE IS ";HP;" TO -";HP;
280 LOCATE 25,10:INPUT "RETURN TO CONTINUE";X$
290 CLS:RETURN
```

PROGRAM 15

DISCOUNT RATE

This program plots a graph of the discount rate level for the most recent 50-week period.

DATA SOURCE. Data can be found in *Barron's* under the heading "Money Rates" under the column "Latest Period" and labeled "Discount Rate." If the figure contains a fraction convert it to a decimal before entering it into the file with the decimal point. The data file used by the program is a type 3 file (see Program #25). When you create the file name it DISCOUNT and make sure it contains at least 62 weeks of data, updated weekly. (Complete instructions for creating and updating can be found with Program #25.)

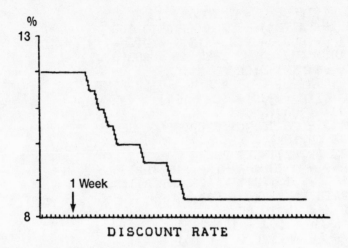

DISCOUNT RATE

PROGRAM USE. Simply run the program by following the procedure given in the general program instructions STEP 4, and it will produce a graph resembling the example above.

PROGRAM #15   LISTING FOR APPLE II+ OR IIe

```
10   DIM S(60):D$ =  CHR$ (4)
20   TEXT : HOME : VTAB 12: HTAB 14
30   FLASH : PRINT "READING FILE":NORMAL
40   PRINT D$;"OPEN DISCOUNT,L8"
50   PRINT D$;"READ DISCOUNT,R0"
60   INPUT X:X = X - 60
70   FOR I = 1 TO 60
80   PRINT D$;"READ DISCOUNT,R";X + I
90   INPUT S(I)
100  IF I = 1 THEN L = S(I):H = L
110  IF S(I) > H THEN H = S(I)
120  IF S(I) < L THEN L = S(I)
130  NEXT I
140   PRINT D$;"CLOSE DISCOUNT"
150 LP =   INT (L)
160 HP =   INT (H + 1)
170 ST = HP - LP: HGR
180  HPLOT 20,0 TO 20,159: HPLOT 20,159 TO 279,159
190  FOR P = 22 TO 277 STEP 4
200  HPLOT P,157 TO P,158: NEXT P
```

```
210   FOR P = 0 TO 158 STEP (158 / ST)
220   HPLOT 17, INT (P) TO 20, INT (P)
230   NEXT P:RA = 158 / ST
240   FOR I = 1 TO 60
250 HC = 22 + (I - 1) * 4
260 VC = 158 -  INT ((S(I) - LP) * RA)
270   IF I = 1 THEN  HPLOT HC,VC: GOTO 290
280   HPLOT  TO HC,VC
290   NEXT : VTAB 21: HTAB 14
300   PRINT "DISCOUNT RATE": VTAB 22: HTAB 12
310   PRINT "RANGE IS ";HP;" TO ";LP
320   VTAB 24: HTAB 12
330   INPUT "RETURN TO CONTINUE";B$
340   TEXT : HOME : END
```

PROGRAM #15   LISTING FOR IBM PC

```
10 DIM DR(60):SCREEN 1:CLS:KEY OFF
20 LOCATE 12,14:PRINT "READING FILE"
30 OPEN "DISCOUNT" AS #1 LEN=8
40 FIELD #1, 8 AS DR$:GET #1,1
50 Z = VAL(DR$) - 59:GET #1,Z
60 FOR K = 1 TO 60
70 DR(K) = VAL(DR$):GET #1
80 IF K = 1 THEN HP = DR(K): LP = DR(K)
90 IF DR(K) > HP THEN HP = DR(K)
100 IF DR(K) < LP THEN LP = DR(K)
110 NEXT K:CLOSE #1
120 HP = INT(HP + 1):LP = INT(LP)
130 ST = HP - LP:RA = 163 / ST
140 CLS:LINE (23,0) - (23,164)
150 LINE -(285,164)
160 FOR P = 26 TO 281 STEP 5
170 LINE (P,163) - (P,165):NEXT P
180 FOR P = 0 TO 163 STEP (163/ST)
190 LINE (21,INT(P)) - (23,INT(P)):NEXT P
200 FOR J = 1 TO 52
210 HC = 26 + ((J - 1) * 5)
220 VC = 163 - INT((DR(J) - LP) * RA)
230 IF J = 1 THEN PSET (HC,VC) ELSE LINE -(HC,VC)
240 NEXT J
250 LOCATE 22,13:PRINT "DISCOUNT RATE";
260 LOCATE 23,10:PRINT "RANGE IS ";HP;" TO ";LP;
270 LOCATE 25,10:INPUT "RETURN TO CONTINUE";X$
280 CLS:RETURN
```

PROGRAM 16
FED FUNDS - DISCOUNT RATE SPREAD

This program plots a graph of the Fed Funds rate minus the discount rate for the most recent 50 week period.

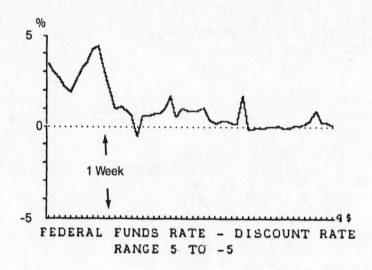

DATA SOURCE. The data can be found in *Barron's* under the heading "Economic and Financial Indicators," under the column "Latest Period" and labeled "Federal Funds" and should be entered with the decimal points. The data file used by the program is a type 3 file (see Program #25). When you create the file, name it FEDFUNDS and make sure it contains at least 52 weeks of data, updated weekly. (Complete instructions for creating and updating can be found with Program #25.) In addition, the file named DISCOUNT described in Program #15 is used.

PROGRAM USE. Simply run the program by following the procedure given in the general program instructions STEP 4, and it will produce a graph resembling the example above.

PROGRAM #16   LISTING FOR APPLE II+ OR IIe

```
10 D$ =  CHR$ (4): DIM S(52)
20   TEXT : HOME : VTAB 12: HTAB 14
30   FLASH : PRINT "READING FILE":NORMAL
40   PRINT D$;"OPEN FEDFUNDS,L8"
50   PRINT D$;"OPEN DISCOUNT,L8"
60   PRINT D$;"READ FEDFUNDS,R0"
70   INPUT A:A = A - 52
80   PRINT D$;"READ DISCOUNT,R0"
90   INPUT B:B = B - 52
100  FOR M = 1 TO 52
110   PRINT D$;"READ FEDFUNDS,R";A + M
120   INPUT R$
130 FF =  VAL (R$)
140   PRINT D$;"READ DISCOUNT,R";B + M
150   INPUT R$:DR =  VAL (R$)
160  S(M) = FF - DR
170   IF  ABS (S(M)) > HP THEN HP = ABS (S(M))
180   NEXT M
190   PRINT D$;"CLOSE FEDFUNDS"
200   PRINT D$;"CLOSE DISCOUNT"
210   HOME : VTAB 12: HTAB 14
220 H =  INT (HP + 1): HGR
230   HPLOT 20,0 TO 20,159 TO 279,159
240   FOR P = 22 TO 277 STEP 5
250   HPLOT P,157 TO P,158
260   HPLOT P,79: NEXT P
270   FOR P = 0 TO 158 STEP (158 / (2 * H))
280   HPLOT 17, INT (P) TO 20, INT (P)
290   NEXT P
300   HPLOT 16,80 TO 13,80 TO 13,85 TO 14,86 TO 16,86
         TO 17,85 TO 17,81
310 RA = 158 / (H * 2)
320   FOR Q = 1 TO 52
330  VC = 79 -  INT (S(Q) * RA)
340 HC = 22 + ((Q - 1) * 5)
350   IF Q = 1 THEN  HPLOT HC,VC: GOTO 370
360   HPLOT  TO HC,VC
370   NEXT Q
380   VTAB 21: HTAB 6
390   PRINT "FEDERAL FUNDS RATE - DISCOUNT RATE"
400   VTAB 22: HTAB 14
410   PRINT "RANGE ";H;" TO -";H
420   VTAB 24: HTAB 12
430   INPUT "RETURN TO CONTINUE";A$
440   TEXT : HOME : END
```

PROGRAM #16   LISTING FOR IBM PC

```
10 DIM S(52):SCREEN 1:KEY OFF:CLS
20 LOCATE 12,14:PRINT "READING FILE"
30 OPEN "FEDFUNDS" AS #1 LEN=8
40 FIELD #1, 8 AS FF$:GET #1,1
50 Z = VAL(FF$) - 51:GET #1,Z
60 OPEN "DISCOUNT" AS #2 LEN=8
70 FIELD #2, 8 AS DR$:GET #2,1
80 Z1 = VAL(DR$) - 51:GET #2,Z1
90 FOR K = 1 TO 52
100 FF = VAL(FF$):GET #1
110 DR = VAL(DR$):GET #2
120 S(K) = FF - DR
130 IF K = 1 THEN HP = ABS(S(1))
140 IF ABS(S(K)) > HP THEN HP = ABS(S(K))
150 NEXT K:CLOSE #1:CLOSE #2:CLS
160 ST = HP * 2:RA = 163 / ST
170 LINE (23,0) - (23,164)
180 LINE -(300,164)
190 FOR P = 26 TO 281 STEP 5
200 LINE (P,163) - (P,165)
210 PSET (P,82):NEXT P:PS = HP * 2
220 IF PS > 20 THEN PS = INT(PS/10): GOTO 220
230 FOR P = 0 TO 163 STEP (163/PS)
240 LINE (21,INT(P)) - (23,INT(P)):NEXT P
250 FOR J = 1 TO 52
260 HC = 26 + ((J - 1) * 5)
270 VC = 82 - INT(S(J) * RA)
280 IF J = 1 THEN PSET (HC,VC) ELSE LINE -(HC,VC)
290 NEXT J
300 LOCATE 22,4:PRINT "FEDERAL FUNDS RATE - DISCOUNT
    RATE";
310 LOCATE 24,10:PRINT "RANGE IS ";HP;" TO -";HP;
320 LOCATE 25,10:INPUT "RETURN TO CONTINUE";X$
330 CLS:RETURN
```

PROGRAM 17

INDUSTRY STOCK GROUP DATA PLOT

This program plots a graph representing the average prices of selected industry stock groups over the most recent 52 week period.

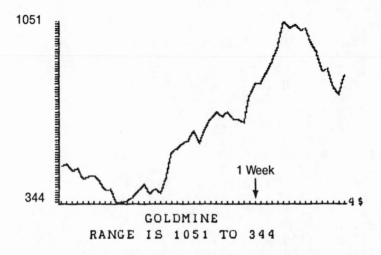

GOLDMINE
RANGE IS 1051 TO 344

DATA SOURCE. The program uses the data files described in the "Data Source" section of Program #20. However, since this program uses only *one* data file at a time, it does not require that you create all 36 files before using it. It also does not require the file NYSECOMP.

PROGRAM USE. Simply follow these two steps:

Step 1. Run the program by following the procedure given in the general program instructions STEP 4.

Step 2. The program will ask you for the name of a stock group you wish to plot. Enter the name of the file and press return. The program will then produce a graph resembling the example above.

PROGRAM #17   LISTING FOR APPLE II+ OR IIe

```
10 D$ =  CHR$ (4): DIM S(52)
20  TEXT : HOME : HTAB 8: VTAB 10
30  INPUT "ENTER FILE NAME ";A$
40  TEXT : HOME : VTAB 12: HTAB 14
50  FLASH : PRINT "READING FILE":NORMAL
60  PRINT D$;"OPEN ";A$;",L8"
70  PRINT D$;"READ ";A$;",R0"
80  INPUT X:X = X - 52
90  FOR I = 1 TO 52
100   PRINT D$;"READ ";A$;",R";X + I
110   INPUT S(I)
120   IF I = 1 THEN L = S(I):H = L
130   IF S(I) > H THEN H = S(I)
140   IF S(I) < L THEN L = S(I)
150   NEXT I:LP =  INT (L / 100)
160   PRINT D$;"CLOSE ";A$
170 HP =  INT (H / 100 + 1)
180 ST = HP - LP: HGR
190 RA = 158 / (ST * 100)
200  HPLOT 20,0 TO 20,159 TO 279,159
210  FOR P = 22 TO 277 STEP 5
220  HPLOT P,157 TO P,158: NEXT P
230 G = 10
240  IF ST < 100 GOTO 280
250 ST =  INT (HP / G + 1) -  INT (LP / G)
260 G = G * 10
270  GOTO 240
280  FOR P = 0 TO 158 STEP (158 / ST)
290  HPLOT 17, INT (P) TO 20, INT (P)
300  NEXT P: FOR I = 1 TO 52
310 HC = 22 + (I - 1) * 5
320 VC = 158 -  INT ((S(I) - (LP * 100)) * RA)
330  IF I = 1 THEN  HPLOT HC,VC: GOTO 350
340  HPLOT  TO HC,VC
350  NEXT I: VTAB 21
360  HTAB (20 -  INT ( LEN (A$) / 2))
370  PRINT A$: VTAB 22: HTAB 10
380  PRINT "RANGE IS ";HP;" TO ";LP
390  VTAB 24: HTAB 12
400  INPUT "RETURN TO CONTINUE";B$
410  TEXT : HOME : END
```

PROGRAM #17   LISTING FOR IBM PC

```
10 SCREEN 1:CLS:KEY OFF:DIM D(52)
20 LOCATE 12,14:INPUT "FILE NAME ";A$
30 CLS:LOCATE 12,14:PRINT "READING FILE"
40 OPEN A$ AS #1 LEN=8
50 FIELD #1, 8 AS M$:GET #1,1
60 Z = VAL(M$) - 51:GET #1,Z
70 FOR J = 1 TO 52:D(J) = VAL(M$):GET #1
80 IF J = 1 THEN HP = D(J): LP = D(J)
90 IF D(J) > HP THEN HP = D(J)
100 IF D(J) < LP THEN LP = D(J)
110 NEXT J:CLOSE #1
120 HP = INT(HP / 100 + 1)
130 LP = INT(LP / 100)
140 ST = HP - LP
150 RA = 163 / (ST * 100)
160 CLS:LINE (23,0) - (23,164)
170 LINE -(300,164)
180 FOR P = 26 TO 281 STEP 5
190 LINE (P,163) - (P,165)
200 NEXT P:PS = ST
210 IF PS > 100 THEN PS = (HP\10+1)-(LP\10): GOTO 210
220 FOR P = 0 TO 163 STEP (163/PS)
230 LINE (21,INT(P)) - (23,INT(P)):NEXT P
240 FOR J = 1 TO 52
250 HC = 26 + ((J - 1) * 5)
260 VC = 163 - INT((D(J) - (LP * 100)) * RA)
270 IF J = 1 THEN PSET (HC,VC) ELSE LINE -(HC,VC)
280 NEXT J
290 LOCATE 22,(20 - INT(LEN(A$) / 2)):PRINT A$;
300 LOCATE 23,9:PRINT "RANGE IS ";HP;" TO ";LP;
310 LOCATE 25,10:INPUT "RETURN TO CONTINUE";X$
320 CLS:RETURN
```

PROGRAM 18

INDUSTRY STOCK GROUP RELATIVE STRENGTH

This program plots a histogram of the relative strength of a selected industry group compared to the NYSE over the past year.

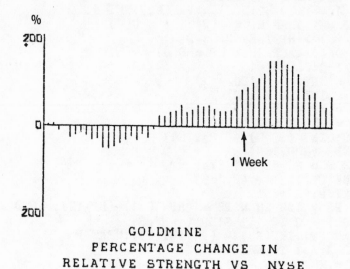

GOLDMINE
PERCENTAGE CHANGE IN
RELATIVE STRENGTH VS   NYSE

DATA SOURCE. The program uses the data files described in the "Data Source" section of Program #20. However, since this program uses only one data file at a time, it does not require that you create all 36 files before using it. In addition, the data file named NYSECOMP, also described in the "Data Source" section of Program #20, is used.

PROGRAM USE. Simply follow these two steps:

Step 1. Run the program by following the procedure given in the general program instructions STEP 4.

Step 2. The program will ask for the name of a stock group data file you wish to plot. Enter the name of the file and press return. The program will then produce a graph resembling the example above.

PROGRAM #18   LISTING FOR APPLE II+ OR IIe

```
10 D$ =  CHR$ (4): DIM S(52)
20   TEXT : HOME : HTAB 8: VTAB 10
30   INPUT "ENTER FILE NAME ";A$
40   TEXT : HOME : VTAB 12: HTAB 14
50   FLASH : PRINT "READING FILE":NORMAL
60   PRINT D$;"OPEN ";A$;",L8"
70   PRINT D$;"READ ";A$;",R0"
80   INPUT X:X = X - 52
90   PRINT D$;"READ ";A$;",R";X
100   INPUT Q1$:Q1 =  VAL (Q1$)
110   PRINT D$;"OPEN NYSECOMP,L8"
120   PRINT D$;"READ NYSECOMP";",R0"
130   INPUT Z:Z = Z - 52
140   PRINT D$;"READ NYSECOMP";",R";Z
150   INPUT N1$:N1 =  VAL (N1$)
160 RF = Q1 / N1
170   FOR I = 1 TO 52
180   PRINT D$;"READ ";A$;",R";X + I
190   INPUT Q1$:Q1 =  VAL (Q1$)
200   PRINT D$;"READ NYSECOMP,R";Z + I
210   INPUT N1$:N1 =  VAL (N1$)
220   S(I) =  INT (((((Q1 / N1) / RF) * 10000) + .5) / 100
230   NEXT I: HGR
240   HPLOT 20,0 TO 20,159: HPLOT 20,79 TO 279,79
250   HPLOT 16,76 TO 13,76 TO 13,81 TO 14,82 TO 17,82
        TO 17,77
260   HPLOT 1,2 TO 2,1 TO 4,1 TO 5,2 TO 1,7 TO 5,7
270   HPLOT 10,1 TO 7,1 TO 7,6 TO 8,7 TO 11,7 TO 11,2
280   HPLOT 16,1 TO 13,1 TO 13,6 TO 14,7 TO 17,7 TO 17,2
290   HPLOT 2,10 TO 4,10: HPLOT 3,9 TO 3,11
300   HPLOT 1,154 TO 2,153 TO 4,153 TO 5,154 TO 1,159
        TO 5,159
310   HPLOT 10,153 TO 7,153 TO 7,158 TO 8,159 TO 11,159
        TO 11,154
320   HPLOT 16,153 TO 13,153 TO 13,158 TO 14,159 TO
        17,159 TO 17,154
330   HPLOT 2,151 TO 4,151
340   FOR I = 1 TO 52
350 K = 24 + (I - 1) * 5
360   HPLOT K,79 TO K,79 - ((S(I) - 100) * .8)
370   NEXT I: PRINT D$;"CLOSE"
380   VTAB 21: HTAB (20 -  INT ( LEN (A$) / 2))
390   PRINT A$: VTAB 22: HTAB 12
400   PRINT "PERCENTAGE CHANGE IN"
410   VTAB 23: HTAB 9
```

```
420    PRINT "RELATIVE STRENGTH VS. NYSE"
430    VTAB 24: HTAB 12
440    INPUT "RETURN TO CONTINUE";B$
450    TEXT : HOME : END
```

PROGRAM #18   LISTING FOR IBM PC

```
10 DIM S(52):SCREEN 1:KEY OFF:CLS
20 LOCATE 12,14:INPUT "FILE NAME ";A$
30 CLS:LOCATE 12,14:PRINT "READING FILE"
40 OPEN A$ AS #1 LEN=8
50 FIELD #1, 8 AS M$
60 GET #1,1:Z = VAL(M$) - 52
70 GET #1,Z:A1 = VAL(M$)
80 OPEN "NYSECOMP" AS #2 LEN=8
90 FIELD #2, 8 AS N$
100 GET #2,1:X = VAL(N$) - 52
110 GET #2,X:N1 = VAL(N$):RF = A1 / N1
120 FOR I = 1 TO 52:GET #1:GET #2
130 S(I) = INT(((((VAL(M$)/VAL(N$))/RF)*10000)+.5)/100
140 NEXT I:CLOSE #1: CLOSE #2:CLS
150 LINE (33,0)-(33,163):LINE (33,82)-(301,82)
160 LOCATE 1,1:PRINT "+200":LOCATE 20,1:PRINT "-200"
170 FOR I = 1 TO 52:HC = 36 + (I - 1) * 5
180 LINE (HC,82) - (HC,82-((S(I) - 100) * .8))
190   NEXT I
200 LOCATE 22,(20 - INT(LEN(A$) / 2)):PRINT A$;
210 LOCATE 23,12:PRINT "PERCENTAGE CHANGE IN"
220 LOCATE 24,9:PRINT "RELATIVE STRENGTH VS. NYSE";
230 LOCATE 25,10:INPUT; "RETURN TO CONTINUE";X$
240 CLS:RETURN
```

PROGRAM 19

RELATIVE STRENGTH TO NYSE (automated)

This program produces the same graphs as Program #18 but if you own a printer it allows you to generate graphs for all of the 36 Industry Stock Groups automatically and print the graphs for later examination. This program requires any printer with a GRAPPLER + interface card for the APPLE II+ option or an IBM GRAPHICS Printer with the Graphics.com program for the IBM PC.

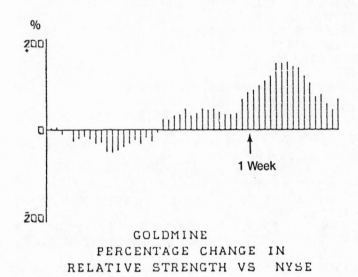

GOLDMINE
PERCENTAGE CHANGE IN
RELATIVE STRENGTH VS NYSE

DATA SOURCE. This program uses the industry stock group files and the files named NYSECOMP and NAMES as described in the ''Data Source'' section of Program #20. All 36 industry stock group files are required for this program.

PROGRAM USE. Simply run the program by following the procedure given in the general program instructions STEP 4, and it will produce a complete series of graphs resembling the example above for each stock group.

PROGRAM #19   LISTING FOR APPLE II+ OR IIe

```
10 D$ =  CHR$ (4): DIM S(52): HOME
20   PRINT D$;"OPEN NYSECOMP,L8"
30   PRINT D$;"READ NYSECOMP,R0"
40   INPUT Z:Z = Z - 52
50   PRINT D$;"OPEN NAMES,L35"
60   FOR J = 1 TO 36
70   PRINT D$;"READ NAMES,R";J
80   INPUT F$,NF$
90   PRINT D$;"READ NYSECOMP,R";Z
100   INPUT N1$:N1 =  VAL (N1$)
110   PRINT D$;"OPEN ";F$;",L8"
120   PRINT D$;"READ ";F$;",R0"
130   INPUT X:X = X - 52
140   PRINT D$;"READ ";F$;",R";X
150   INPUT F1$:F1 =  VAL (F1$)
160 RF = F1 / N1
170   FOR M = 1 TO 52
180   PRINT D$;"READ ";F$;",R";X + M
190   INPUT F1$:F1 =  VAL (F1$)
200   PRINT D$;"READ NYSECOMP,R";Z + M
210   INPUT N1$:N1 =  VAL (N1$)
220 S(M) =  INT ((((F1 / N1) / RF) * 10000) + .5) / 100
230   NEXT M: PRINT D$;"CLOSE ";F$
240   HGR : HPLOT 20,0 TO 20,159
250   HPLOT 20,79 TO 279,79
260   HPLOT 16,153 TO 13,153 TO 13,158 TO 14,159 TO
         17,159 TO 17,154
270   HPLOT 1,2 TO 2,1 TO 4,1 TO 5,2 TO 1,7 TO 5,7
280   HPLOT 1,154 TO 2,153 TO 4,153 TO 5,154 TO 1,159
         TO 5,159
290   HPLOT 10,1 TO 7,1 TO 7,6 TO 8,7 TO 11,7 TO 11,2
300   HPLOT 10,153 TO 7,153 TO 7,158 TO 8,159 TO 11,159
         TO 11,154
310   HPLOT 16,1 TO 13,1 TO 13,6 TO 14,7 TO 17,7 TO 17,2
320   HPLOT 16,76 TO 13,76 TO 13,81 TO 14,82 TO 17,82
         TO 17,77
330   FOR I = 1 TO 52
340 K = 24 + (I - 1) * 5
350   HPLOT K,79 TO K,79 - ((S(I) - 100) * .8)
360   NEXT I: VTAB 21
370   HTAB (20 -  INT ( LEN (NF$) / 2))
380   PRINT NF$: VTAB 22: HTAB 10
390   PRINT "PERCENTAGE CHANGE IN"
400   VTAB 23: HTAB 7
```

```
410   PRINT "RELATIVE STRENGTH VS. NYSE"
420   PRINT D$;"PR#1": PRINT  CHR$ (9);"GM"
430   PRINT  CHR$ (3); CHR$ (2): PRINT D$;"PR#0"
440   PRINT D$: HOME : NEXT J: PRINT D$;"CLOSE"
450   TEXT : HOME : END
```

PROGRAM #19   LISTING FOR IBM PC

```
10 DIM S(52):SCREEN 1:KEY OFF:CLS
20 OPEN "NYSECOMP" AS #2 LEN=8
30 FIELD #2, 8 AS N$
40 OPEN "NAMES" AS #3 LEN=35
50 FIELD 3,8 AS F$,27 AS NF$
60 FOR R = 1 TO 36:GET #3,R
70 A$ = F$:OPEN A$ AS #1 LEN=8
80 FIELD #1, 8 AS M$
90 GET #1,1:Z = VAL(M$) - 52
100 GET #1,Z:A1 = VAL(M$)
110 GET #2,1:X = VAL(N$) - 52
120 GET #2,X:N1 = VAL(N$):RF = A1 / N1
130 FOR I = 1 TO 52:GET #1:GET #2
140 S(I) = INT(((((VAL(M$)/VAL(N$))/RF)#10000)+.5)/100
150 NEXT I:CLOSE #1:CLS
160 LINE (33,0)-(33,163):LINE (33,82)-(301,82)
170 LOCATE 1,1:PRINT "+200":LOCATE 20,1:PRINT "-200"
180 FOR I = 1 TO 52:HC = 36 + (I - 1) # 5
190 LINE (HC,82) - (HC,82-((S(I) - 100) # .8))
200  NEXT I:Y = INSTR(NF$," ") - 1
210 IF Y > 0 THEN Y$ = LEFT$(NF$,Y) ELSE Y$ = NF$
220 LOCATE 22,(20 - INT(LEN(Y$) / 2)):PRINT Y$;
230 LOCATE 23,10:PRINT "PERCENTAGE CHANGE IN"
240 LOCATE 24,7:PRINT "RELATIVE STRENGTH VS. NYSE";
250 CALL PRTSCR
260 NEXT R:CLOSE #2:CLOSE #3:CLS:RETURN
```

PROGRAM 20
RELATIVE STRENGTH RANKINGS

This program produces a table which shows the industry stock group strength relative to the NYSE. (For example if the stock group is up 10% over the previous year vs. 20% for the NYSE, the relative strength will be 50%). The table also provides information on the percentage change strength over the previous week. (This program requires any printer with a GRAPPLER + interface card for the APPLE II + option or an IBM GRAPHICS Printer with the Graphics.com program for the IBM PC.)

DATA SOURCE. Three different classes of data are used:

(1) *NYSE composite weekly closing price.* This figure can be found in *Barron's* on the "Market Laboratory" page. It is the rightmost number on the row labeled "NYSE Comp.," in the section "Other Market Indicators." Enter the data without the decimal point in a type 3 file and name it NYSECOMP. At least 52 weeks of data must be entered, updated weekly.

(2) *The names of the 36 industry stock groups.* These are found in *Barron's.* Enter each stock group name *and* the file name listed below that it is associated with into a type 4 file named NAMES (see Program #25).

INDUSTRY STOCK GROUP NAME	FILE NAME
AIRCRAFT MANUFACTURING	AIRCRAFT
AIR TRANSPORTATION	AIRTRANS
AUTOMOBILES	AUTOS
AUTOMOBILE EQUIPMENT	AUTOEQP
BANKS	BANKS
BLDG MATERIALS & EQUIPMENT	BLDGM&E
CHEMICALS	CHEMICAL
CLOSED-END INVESTMENTS	INVEST
DRUGS	DRUGS
ELECTRICAL EQUIPMENT	ELEEQUIP
FOODS AND BEVERAGES	FOOD&BEV

FARM EQUIPMENT	FARMEQP
GOLD MINING	GOLDMINE
GROCERY CHAINS	GROCERY
INSTALLMENT FINANCING	INSTFIN
INSURANCE	INSURE
LIQUOR	LIQUOR
MACHINE TOOLS	MACHINET
MACHINERY (HEAVY)	MACHINE
MOTION PICTURES	MOVIES
NON-FERROUS METALS	NOTIRON
OFFICE EQUIPMENT	OFFEQUIP
OIL	OIL
PACKING	PACKING
PAPER	PAPER
RAILROAD EQUIPMENT	RAILEQP
RETAIL MERCHANDISE	RETAIL
RUBBER	RUBBER
STEEL AND IRON	STEEL
TELEVISION	TELE
TEXTILES	TEXTILES
TOBACCO	TOBACCO
DOW-JONES INDUSTRIALS	DJINDUS
DOW-JONES TRANSPORTATION	DJTRANS
DOW-JONES UTILITIES	DJUTIL
DOW-JONES COMPOSITE	DJCOMP

(3) *The weekly price level of the 36 Industry Stock Groups.* Each price level is found in the column with the most recent date of the *"Barron's* Stock Group Averages." Enter the data (without the decimal points) into 36 separate Type 3 files (see Program #25). When you create each file make sure you name it with the file name from the list above. The files must contain at least 52 weeks of data and each entry must have a corresponding entry in the file named NYSECOMP described above. In other words, the first entry into each stock group file must come from the same week as the first entry in NYSECOMP and all succeeding entries must have the same relationship to each other. These files should be updated weekly. (See Program #25 for full details on creating and updating files).

PROGRAM USE. Simply follow these three steps:

Step 1. Run the program by following the procedure given in the general program instructions STEP 4.

Step 2. It will ask you to choose from 3 possible comparison periods (1 year, 6 months, and 3 months).

Step 3. Press the number (1-3) that corresponds to the desired comparison period, and the program will produce a table listing all 36 stock groups in order by relative strength for each group as shown in the example in chapter 21.

PROGRAM #20   LISTING FOR APPLE II+ OR IIe

```
10   DIM S(36),R(36),V(36)
20 D$ =  CHR$ (4)
30   FOR K = 1 TO 36:S(K) = K: NEXT
40   HOME : HTAB 8: VTAB 10
50   PRINT "CHOOSE COMPARISON PERIOD"
60   HTAB 12: PRINT "1 - 1 YEAR"
70   HTAB 12: PRINT "2 - 6 MONTHS"
80   HTAB 12: PRINT "3 - 3 MONTHS"
90   VTAB 15: HTAB 10: PRINT "ENTER PERIOD ";
100   GET B: IF (B < 1) OR (B > 3) GOTO 100
110   PRINT D$
120   PRINT D$;"OPEN NYSECOMP,L8"
130   PRINT D$;"READ NYSECOMP,R0"
140   INPUT Z
150   IF B = 1 THEN B = 51:T$ = "1 YEAR"
160   IF B = 2 THEN B = 25:T$ = "6 MONTHS"
170   IF B = 3 THEN B = 12:T$ = "3 MONTHS"
180   PRINT D$;"READ NYSECOMP,R";Z - B
190   INPUT N1$:N1 =  VAL (N1$)
200   PRINT D$;"READ NYSECOMP,R";Z - 1
210   INPUT N3$:N3 =  VAL (N3$)
220   PRINT D$;"READ NYSECOMP,R";Z
230   INPUT N2$:N2 =  VAL (N2$)
240   PRINT D$;"CLOSE NYSECOMP"
250   PRINT D$;"OPEN NAMES,L35"
260   FOR I = 1 TO 36
270   PRINT D$"READ NAMES,R";I
```

```
280   INPUT A$,Q$
290   PRINT D$;"OPEN ";A$;",L8"
300   PRINT D$;"READ";A$;",R0"
310   INPUT X
320   PRINT D$;"READ ";A$;",R";X - B
330   INPUT Q1
340   PRINT D$;"READ ";A$;",R";X - 1
350   INPUT Q3
360   PRINT D$;"READ ";A$;",R";X
370   INPUT Q2
380   R(I) =  INT(((Q2/N2) / (Q1/N1) * 10000) + .5)/100
390   E =  INT(((Q3/N3) / (Q1/N1) * 10000) + .5)/100
400   V(I) =  INT((R(I) - E) * 100 + .5) / 100
410   F = I
420   FOR M = 1 TO I
430   IF R(F) > R(S(M)) THEN L = S(M):S(M) = F:F = L
440   NEXT M:S(M - 1) = F
450   PRINT D$;"CLOSE ";A$
460   NEXT I
470   HOME : PRINT D$;"PR#1"
480   PRINT D$;"PR#1"
490   HTAB 13: PRINT "GROUP RELATIVE STRENGTH"
500   VTAB 2: HTAB 17: PRINT "PERIOD ";T$: VTAB 4
510   HTAB 9: PRINT "STOCK";: HTAB 30: PRINT "RELATIVE";
515   HTAB 40: PRINT "NET": HTAB 9: PRINT "GROUP";
520   HTAB 30: PRINT "STRENGTH";: HTAB 40:
         PRINT "CHANGE": VTAB 7
530   PRINT D$;"PR#0"
540   FOR I = 1 TO 36
550   PRINT D$;"READ NAMES,R";S(I)
560   INPUT A$,Q$
570   PRINT D$;"PR#1"
580   PRINT Q$;: HTAB 30: PRINT R(S(I));: HTAB 40:
         PRINT V(S(I))
590   NEXT I: PRINT D$;"PR#0"
600   PRINT D$;"CLOSE NAMES"
610   TEXT : HOME : END
```

PROGRAM #20   LISTING FOR IBM PC

```
10 DIM S(36), R(36), V(36)
20 FOR K = 1 TO 36: S(K) = K: NEXT
30 SCREEN 1:KEY OFF:CLS:LOCATE 8,10
40 PRINT "CHOOSE COMPARISON PERIOD"
50 LOCATE 10,12:PRINT "1 -  1 YEAR  "
60 LOCATE 11,12:PRINT "2 -  6 MONTHS"
```

```
70 LOCATE 12,12:PRINT "3 -  3 MONTHS"
80 B$ = INKEY$:IF (B$ < "1") OR (B$ > "3") GOTO 80
90 CLS:LOCATE 12,14:PRINT "READING FILE"
100 OPEN "NAMES" AS #1 LEN=35:FIELD 1,8 AS F$,27 AS NF$
110 OPEN "NYSECOMP" AS #2 LEN=8:FIELD 2,8 AS N$
120 GET #2,1:Z = VAL(N$)
130 IF B$ = "1" THEN X = 51: T$ = "1 YEAR"
140 IF B$ = "2" THEN X = 25: T$ = "6 MONTHS"
150 IF B$ = "3" THEN X = 12: T$ = "3 MONTHS"
160 GET #2,Z - X:N1 = VAL(N$)
170 GET #2,Z - 1: N3 = VAL(N$)
180 GET #2,Z: N2 = VAL(N$)
190 CLOSE #2
200 FOR I = 1 TO 36:GET #1,I
210 OPEN F$ AS #3 LEN=8:FIELD 3,8 AS G$
220 GET #3,1:F1 = VAL(G$)
230 GET #3,F1 - X:Q1 = VAL(G$)
240 GET #3,F1 - 1:Q3 = VAL(G$)
250 GET #3,F1:Q2 = VAL(G$)
260 R(I) = INT(((Q2/N2) / (Q1/N1) * 10000) + .5) / 100
270 E = INT(((Q3/N3) / (Q1/N1) * 10000) + .5) / 100
280 V(I) = INT(((R(I) - E) * 100 + .5) / 100
290 F = I:FOR M = 1 TO I
300 IF R(F) > R(S(M)) THEN SWAP S(M),F
310 NEXT M:S(M - 1) = F:CLOSE #3:NEXT I
320 OPEN "LPT1:" AS #2
330 PRINT #2,STRING$(13," ");
        "GROUP RELATIVE STRENGTH VS. NYSE"
340 PRINT #2," ":PRINT #2,STRING$(17," ");"PERIOD ";T$
350 PRINT #2," ":PRINT #2," ":PRINT #2,STRING$(9," ");
        "STOCK";
360 PRINT #2,STRING$(15," ");"RELATIVE";STRING$(10," ");
        "NET"
370 PRINT #2,STRING$(9," ");"GROUP";
380 PRINT #2,STRING$(15," ");"STRENGTH";STRING$(10," ");
        "CHANGE"
390 PRINT #2," ":PRINT #2," "
400 FOR I = 1 TO 36:GET #1,S(I)
410 PRINT #2,NF$;STRING$(3," ");R(S(I));STRING$(6," ");
        V(S(I))
420 NEXT I: CLOSE #1:CLOSE #2:RETURN
```

PROGRAM 21

STOCK MARKET CREDIT

This program allows you to produce a graph of your choice of two different monthly figures of stock-market credit. The graph covers the past two years and includes a 12-month moving average line.

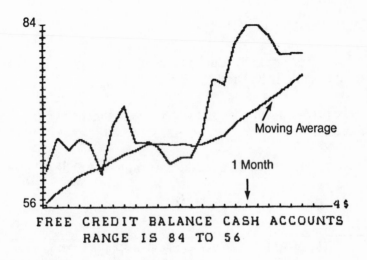

FREE CREDIT BALANCE CASH ACCOUNTS
RANGE IS 84 TO 56

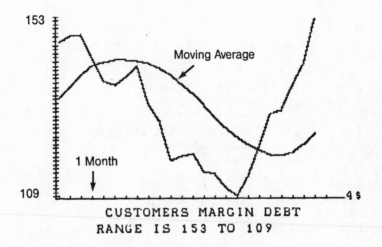

CUSTOMERS MARGIN DEBT
RANGE IS 153 TO 109

DATA SOURCE. Data for this program can be found in *Barron's* in the section labeled "New York Stock Exchange Monthly Figures," under the column marked "Latest Period." Two figures are used - "Customers Margin Debt," and "Free Credit Balance Cash Acct's." Enter Customer Margin Debt figures, without decimal points, into a type 3 file (see Program #25) named MARGDEBT. Enter free Credit Balance Cash Account figures, also without decimal points, into a type 3 file named FREECRED. Create both files with at least 36 months of data updated monthly. (See Program #25 for a full explanation of procedures for creating and updating files.)

PROGRAM USE. Simply follow these four steps:

Step 1. Run the program by following the procedure given in the general program instructions STEP 4.

Step 2. The program will ask you to choose between the two series. Enter your choice, 1 or 2.

Step 3. The program will then produce a graph resembling the example above.

PROGRAM #21   LISTING FOR APPLE II+ OR IIe

```
10 D$ =  CHR$ (4): TEXT : HOME
20   DIM O(36),X(36): VTAB 12: HTAB 4
30   PRINT "SELECT 1 FOR FREE CREDIT CASH"
40   VTAB 13: HTAB 4: PRINT "SELECT 2 FOR MARGIN DEBT"
50   VTAB 15: HTAB 7: PRINT "PLEASE SELECT";
60   GET Z: IF (Z < 1) OR (Z > 2) GOTO 60
70   IF Z = 1 THEN T$ = "FREECRED"
80   IF Z = 2 THEN T$ = "MARGDEBT"
90   TEXT : HOME : VTAB 12: HTAB 14
100   FLASH : PRINT "READING FILE": NORMAL
110   PRINT D$;"OPEN ";T$;",L8"
120   PRINT D$;"READ ";T$;",R0"
130   INPUT A:A = A - 36
140   FOR M = 1 TO 36
150   PRINT D$;"READ ";T$;",R";A + M
160   INPUT R$
170 O(M) =  VAL (R$)
```

```
180   IF M = 13 THEN LP = O(M):HP = LP
190   IF O(M) < LP THEN LP = O(M)
200   IF O(M) > HP THEN HP = O(M)
210   IF M < 13 GOTO 270
220   X(M) = 0: FOR J = M - 11 TO M
230   X(M) = X(M) + O(J): NEXT J
240   X(M) = X(M) / 12
250   IF X(M) > HP THEN HP = X(M)
260   IF X(M) < LP THEN LP = X(M)
270   NEXT M: PRINT D$;"CLOSE ";T$
280   LP =   INT (LP / 100)
290   HP =   INT (HP / 100 + 1)
300   ST = HP - LP: HGR
310   HPLOT 20,0 TO 20,159 TO 279,159
320   FOR J = 23 TO 263 STEP 10
330   HPLOT J,157 TO J,158: NEXT J
340   FOR J = 0 TO 158 STEP (158 / ST)
350   HPLOT 18, INT (J) TO 22, INT (J)
360   NEXT J:RA = 158 / (ST * 100)
370   FOR Q = 13 TO 36
380   VC = 158 -  INT ((O(Q) - (LP * 100)) * RA)
390   HC = 23 + ((Q - 13) * 10)
400   IF Q = 13 THEN  HPLOT HC,VC:GOTO 420
410   HPLOT  TO HC,VC
420   NEXT Q
430   FOR Q = 13 TO 36
440   VC = 158 -  INT ((X(Q) - (LP * 100)) * RA)
450   HC = 23 + ((Q - 13) * 10)
460   IF Q = 13 THEN  HPLOT HC,VC:GOTO 480
470   HPLOT  TO HC,VC
480   NEXT Q: VTAB 21: HTAB 6
490   IF Z=1 THEN PRINT
         "FREE CREDIT BALANCE CASH ACCOUNTS"
500   IF Z=2 THEN PRINT "CUSTOMERS MARGIN DEBT"
510   VTAB 22: HTAB 11
520   PRINT "RANGE IS ";HP;" TO ";LP
530   VTAB 24: HTAB 12
540   INPUT "RETURN TO CONTINUE";A$
550   TEXT : HOME : END
```

PROGRAM #21   LISTING FOR IBM PC

```
10 DIM O(36),X(36):SCREEN 1:CLS:KEY OFF
20 LOCATE 12,1:PRINT"SELECT 1 FOR FREE CREDIT BALANCE"
30 LOCATE 13,1:PRINT"SELECT 2 FOR CUSTOMERS MARGIN DEBT"
40 PRINT "PLEASE CHOOSE ";
```

```
 50 Z$ = INKEY$:IF (Z$ < "1") OR (Z$ > "2") GOTO 50
 60 IF Z$="1" THEN F$="FREECRED":T$="FREE CREDIT BALANCE"
 70 IF Z$="2" THEN F$="MARGDEBT":T$="CUSTOMERS MARGIN DEBT"
 80 CLS:LOCATE 12,14:PRINT "READING FILE"
 90 OPEN F$ AS #1 LEN=8:FIELD #1, 8 AS F1$
100 GET #1,1:Z = VAL(F1$) - 35
110 GET #1,Z:FOR M = 1 TO 36
120 O(M) = VAL(F1$)
130 IF M = 13 THEN LP = O(M):HP = O(M)
140 IF O(M) > HP THEN HP = O(M)
150 IF O(M) < LP THEN LP = O(M)
160 IF M < 13 GOTO 220
170 X(M) = 0:FOR J = M - 11 TO M
180 X(M) = X(M) + O(J):NEXT J
190 X(M) = X(M) / 12
200 IF X(M) > HP THEN HP = X(M)
210 IF X(M) < LP THEN LP = X(M)
220 GET #1:NEXT M:CLS:CLOSE #1
230 HP = (HP \ 100 + 1):LP = (LP \ 100)
240 ST = HP - LP:RA = 163 / (ST * 100)
250 LINE (23,0) - (23,163)
260 LINE -(270,163)
270 FOR P = 26 TO 266 STEP 10
280 LINE (P,163) - (P,165):NEXT P
290 FOR P = 0 TO 163 STEP (163 / ST)
300 LINE (21,INT(P)) - (23,INT(P))
310 NEXT P:FOR Q = 13 TO 36
320 VC = 163 - INT((O(Q) - (LP * 100)) * RA)
330 HC = 26 + ((Q - 13) * 10)
340 IF Q = 13 THEN PSET (HC,VC) ELSE LINE -(HC,VC)
350 NEXT Q:FOR Q = 13 TO 36
360 VC = 163 - INT((X(Q) - (LP * 100)) * RA)
370 HC = 26 + ((Q - 13) * 10)
380 IF Q = 13 THEN PSET (HC,VC) ELSE LINE -(HC,VC)
390 NEXT Q:LOCATE 22,(20 - (LEN(T$) / 2))
400 PRINT T$;:LOCATE 23,9
410 PRINT "RANGE IS ";HP * 100;" TO ";LP * 100;
420 LOCATE 25,10:INPUT; "RETURN TO CONTINUE";X$
430 CLS:RETURN
```

PROGRAM 22

DOW JONES UTILITY AVERAGE

This program produces a graph which represents the Dow-Jones utilities average over the past 50 weeks overlaid by a 15-week moving average of the Dow-Jones Utilities average.

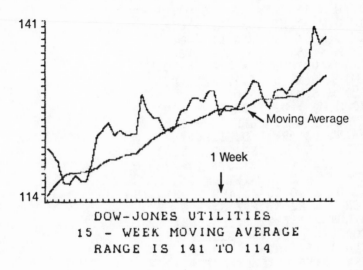

```
            DOW-JONES UTILITIES
       15 - WEEK MOVING AVERAGE
         RANGE IS 141 TO 114
```

DATA SOURCE. This program uses one of the industry stock group files described in Program #20. The required data file is named DJUTIL and contains the weekly Dow-Jones Utilities figure from "*Barron's* Stock Group Averages." (See the data section of Program #20 for a full description of the data file.) This program requires at least 65 weeks of data in the file.

PROGRAM USE. Simply run the program by following the procedure given in the general program instructions STEP 4, and it will produce a graph resembling the example above.

PROGRAM #22   LISTING FOR APPLE II+ OR IIe

```
30   DIM O(66),S(66):D$ =  CHR$ (4)
40   TEXT : HOME : VTAB 12: HTAB 14
50   FLASH : PRINT "READING FILE":NORMAL
60   PRINT D$;"OPEN DJUTIL,L8"
70   PRINT D$;"READ DJUTIL,RO"
80   INPUT A:A = A - 64
90   PRINT D$;"READ DJUTIL,R";A
100   FOR M = 1 TO 65: INPUT R$
110  O(M) =  VAL (R$)
120   IF M = 15 THEN HP = O(M):LP = HP
130   IF O(M) > HP THEN HP = O(M)
140   IF O(M) < LP THEN LP = O(M)
150   IF M < 15 THEN  GOTO 210
160  S(M) = 0: FOR J = M - 14 TO M
170  S(M) = S(M) + O(J): NEXT J
180  S(M) = S(M) / 15
190   IF S(M) > HP THEN HP = S(M)
200   IF S(M) < LP THEN LP = S(M)
210   PRINT D$;"READ DJUTIL,R";A + M
220   NEXT M:LP =  INT (LP / 100)
230  HP =  INT (HP / 100 + 1): HGR
240  ST = HP - LP: PRINT D$;"CLOSE"
250   HPLOT 20,0 TO 20,159 TO 279,159
260   FOR P = 22 TO 277 STEP 5
270   HPLOT P,157 TO P,158: NEXT P
280   FOR P = 0 TO 158 STEP (158 / ST)
290   HPLOT 17, INT (P) TO 20, INT (P)
300   NEXT P:RA = 158 / (ST * 100)
310   FOR Q = 15 TO 65
320  VC = 158 -  INT ((O(Q) - (LP * 100)) * RA)
330  HC = 22 + ((Q - 15) * 5)
340   IF Q = 15 THEN  HPLOT HC,VC:GOTO 360
350  HPLOT  TO HC,VC
360   NEXT Q: FOR Q = 15 TO 65
370  VC = 158 - INT((O(Q) - (L * 100)) * RA)
380  HC = 22 + ((Q - 15) * 5)
390   IF Q = 15 THEN  HPLOT HC,VC:GOTO 410
400  HPLOT  TO HC,VC
410   NEXT Q: VTAB 21: HTAB 12
420   PRINT "DOW-JONES UTILITIES"
430   VTAB 22: HTAB 10
440   PRINT "15 - WEEK MOVING AVERAGE"
```

```
450   VTAB 23: HTAB 12
460   PRINT "RANGE IS ";HP;" TO ";LP
470   VTAB 24: HTAB 12
480   INPUT "RETURN TO CONTINUE";A$
490   TEXT : HOME : END
```

PROGRAM #22   LISTING FOR IBM PC

```
10 DIM D(66), S(66):SCREEN 1:CLS:KEY OFF
20 OPEN "DJUTIL" AS #1 LEN=8
30 FIELD #1, 8 AS D$:GET #1,1:A = VAL(D$)
40 A = A - 64:GET #1,A:FOR M = 1 TO 65
50 D(M) = VAL(D$):IF M = 1 THEN HP = D(M):LP = HP
60 IF D(M) > HP THEN HP = D(M)
70 IF D(M) < LP THEN LP = D(M)
80 IF M < 15 GOTO 140
90 S(M) = 0:FOR J = M - 14 TO M
100 S(M) = S(M) + D(J):NEXT J
110 S(M) = S(M) / 15
120 IF S(M) > HP THEN HP = S(M)
130 IF S(M) < LP THEN LP = S(M)
140 GET #1:NEXT M:CLOSE #1
150 LP = LP \ 100:HP = HP \ 100 + 1
160 ST = HP - LP:RA = 163 / (ST * 100)
170 LINE (23,0) - (23,163):LINE -(301,163)
180 FOR P = 26 TO 301 STEP 5
190 LINE (P,165) - (P,163):NEXT P
200 FOR P = 0 TO 163 STEP (163 / ST)
210 LINE (20,INT(P)) - (23,INT(P)):NEXT P
220 FOR Q = 15 TO 65
230 VC = 163 - INT((D(Q) - (LP * 100)) * RA)
240 HC = 26 + ((Q - 15) * 5)
250 IF Q = 15 THEN PSET (HC,VC) ELSE LINE -(HC,VC)
260 NEXT Q:FOR Q = 15 TO 65
270 VC = 163 - INT((S(Q) - (LP * 100)) * RA)
280 HC = 26 + ((Q - 15) * 5)
290 IF Q = 15 THEN PSET (HC,VC) ELSE LINE -(HC,VC)
300 NEXT Q:LOCATE 22,12
310 PRINT "DOW-JONES UTILITIES":LOCATE 23,10
320 PRINT "15 - WEEK MOVING AVERAGE":LOCATE 24,11
330 PRINT "RANGE IS ";HP;" TO ";LP;:LOCATE 25,12
340 INPUT; "RETURN TO CONTINUE ";A$:CLS:RETURN
```

PROGRAM 23
TRIN

This program plots a graph of the 10-day moving average of TRIN for the past 55 days.

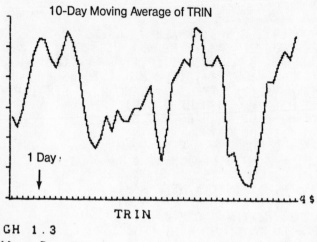

10-Day Moving Average of TRIN

DATA SOURCE. Program #23 uses the data file ADVDCL described in Program #9. Please refer to the "Data Source" section of that program for full details.

PROGRAM USE. Simply run the program by following the procedure given in the general program instructions STEP 4, and it will produce a graph resembling the example above.

PROGRAM #23   LISTING FOR APPLE II+ OR IIe

```
10 D$ =  CHR$ (4): DIM TR(65),S(65)
20  TEXT : HOME : VTAB 12: HTAB 14
30  FLASH : PRINT "READING FILE":NORMAL
40  PRINT D$;"OPEN  ADVDCL,L28"
50  PRINT D$;"READ ADVDCL,R0"
```

```
60    INPUT A:A = A - 61
70    FOR M = 1 TO 61
80    PRINT D$;"READ ADVDCL,R";A + M
90    INPUT R$
100   AD =   VAL ( LEFT$ (R$,5))
110   DC =   VAL ( MID$ (R$,6,5))
120   UV =   VAL ( MID$ (R$,16,6))
130   DV =   VAL ( RIGHT$ (R$,6))
140   TR(M) = (AD / DC) / (UV / DV)
150    IF M < 10 GOTO 220
160   S(M) = 0: FOR K = M - 9 TO M
170   S(M) = S(M) + TR(K)
180    NEXT K:S(M) = S(M) / 10
190    IF S(M) > HP THEN HP = S(M)
200    IF M = 10 THEN LP = S(M):HP = LP
210    IF S(M) < LP THEN LP = S(M)
220    NEXT M: HGR : PRINT D$;"CLOSE"
230   HPLOT 20,0 TO 20,159 TO 279,159
240   FOR P = 22 TO 277 STEP 5
250   HPLOT P,157 TO P,158: NEXT P
260   HP =   INT (HP * 10 + 1)
270   LP =   INT (LP * 10)
280   ST = HP - LP
290    FOR P = 0 TO 158 STEP (158 / ST)
300   HPLOT 17, INT (P) TO 20, INT (P)
310    NEXT P:HP = HP / 10:LP = LP / 10
320   RA = 158 / (HP - LP)
330    FOR Q = 10 TO 61
340   VC = 158 -   INT ((S(Q) - LP) * RA)
350   HC = 22 + ((Q - 10) * 5)
360    IF Q = 10 THEN  HPLOT HC,VC:GOTO 380
370   HPLOT  TO HC,VC
380    NEXT Q: VTAB 21: HTAB 7
390   PRINT "TRIN 10-DAY MOVING AVERAGE"
400   VTAB 22: HTAB 4: PRINT "HIGH";HP
410   HTAB 4: PRINT "LOW  ";LP
420   VTAB 24: HTAB 12
430   INPUT "RETURN TO CONTINUE";A$
440   TEXT : HOME : END
```

PROGRAM #23   LISTING FOR IBM PC

```
10 DIM TR(65),S(65):SCREEN 1:CLS
20 OPEN "ADVDCL" AS #1 LEN=27
30 FIELD #1,5 AS AD$,5 AS DC$,5 AS UN$,6 AS UV$,6 AS DV$
40 GET #1,1:Z = VAL(AD$) - 64
50 GET #1,Z:FOR M = 1 TO 65
60 AD = VAL(AD$):DC = VAL(DC$)
70 UV = VAL(UV$):DV = VAL(DV$)
80 TR(M) = (AD / DC) / (UV / DV)
90 IF M < 10 GOTO 160
100 FOR K = M - 9 TO M
110 S(M) = S(M) + TR(K)
120 NEXT K:S(M) = S(M) / 10
130 IF S(M) > HP THEN HP = S(M)
140 IF M = 10 THEN LP = S(M):HP = LP
150 IF S(M) < LP THEN LP = S(M)
160 GET #1:NEXT M:CLOSE #1:CLS
170 LINE (23,0)-(23,164):LINE -(300,164)
180 FOR P = 26 TO 301 STEP 5
190 LINE (P,164)-(P,166):NEXT P
200 HP = INT(HP * 10 + 1)
210 LP = INT(LP * 10)
220 ST = HP - LP
230  FOR P = 0 TO 163 STEP (163 / ST)
240 LINE (21, INT(P)) - (23, INT(P)):NEXT P
250 HP = HP / 10:LP = LP / 10
260 RA = 163 / (HP - LP)
270 FOR Q = 10 TO 65
280 VC = 163 - INT((S(Q) - LP) * RA)
290 HC = 26 + ((Q - 10) * 5)
300 IF Q = 10 THEN PSET (HC,VC) ELSE LINE -(HC,VC)
310 NEXT Q
320 LOCATE 22,7:PRINT "TRIN 10-DAY MOVING AVERAGE"
330 LOCATE 23,4:PRINT "HIGH ";HP
340 LOCATE 24,4:PRINT "LOW ";LP;
350 LOCATE 25,12:INPUT; "RETURN TO CONTINUE";A$
360 CLS:RETURN
```

PROGRAM 24
RETRACE

This program produces a list of retracement levels in terms of a percentage rise (or decline) from a specified high or (low) along with the corresponding prices.

DATA SOURCE. Program #24 requires no data files. It does, however, require a printer.

PROGRAM USE. Simply follow these four steps:

Step 1. Run the program by following the procedure given in the general program instructions STEP 4. Make sure that your printer is ready for use.

Step 2. The program will ask you if this is a downward or upward retracement. Choose one.

Step 3. The program will request the price at the top of the move. Enter that price and press return.

Step 4. It will then request the price at the bottom of the move. Enter that price and press return. The program will then produce the list.

PROGRAM #24   LISTING FOR APPLE II+ OR IIe

```
10   HOME : PRINT "ENTER 1 FOR DOWNWARD RETRACEMENT"
12   PRINT "      2 FOR UPWARD RETRACEMENT"
13   PRINT "   PLEASE CHOOSE ";
14   GET Z: IF (Z < 1) OR (Z > 2) GOTO 14
16   PRINT  CHR$ (4)
20   INPUT "ENTER PRICE OF TOP ";T
30   INPUT "ENTER PRICE OF BOTTOM ";B
40   PRINT  CHR$ (4);"PR#1"
50   PRINT  CHR$ (9);"80N"
60   PRINT "PRICE","RETRACE %","PRICE","RETRACE %"
70 R =  ABS (T - B)
```

```
80   FOR J = 2 TO 100 STEP 2
85   IF Z = 1 GOTO 107
90 NL = B + J * (R / 100)
100 RL = B + (J - 1) * (R / 100)
105   GOTO 110
107 NL = T - J * (R / 100)
109 RL = T - (J - 1) * (R / 100)
110 NL =  INT (NL * 100 + .55) / 100
120 RL =  INT (RL * 100 + .55) / 100
130   PRINT RL,J - 1,NL,J
140   NEXT J: PRINT  CHR$ (4);"PR#0":END
```

PROGRAM #24   LISTING FOR IBM PC

```
10 SCREEN 2:CLS
20 PRINT "ENTER 1 FOR DOWNWARD RETRACEMENT"
30 PRINT "         2 FOR UPWARD RETRACEMENT"
40 Z$ = INKEY$: IF (Z$ < "1") OR (Z$ > "2") GOTO 40
50 INPUT "ENTER PRICE AT TOP ";T
60 INPUT "ENTER PRICE AT BOTTOM ";B
70 OPEN "LPT1:" AS #1
80 PRINT #1,"PRICE","RETRACE %","PRICE","RETRACE %"
90 R = ABS(T - B)
100 FOR K = 2 TO 100 STEP 2
110 IF Z$ = "1" GOTO 150  .
120 NL = B + (K * R)/100
130 RL = B + ((K - 1) * R)/100
140 GOTO 170
150 NL = T - K * (R / 100)
160 RL = T - (K - 1) * (R / 100)
170 NL = INT(NL * 100 + .55) / 100
180 RL = INT(RL * 100 + .55) / 100
190 PRINT #1,RL,K-1,NL,K
200 NEXT K:RETURN
```

PROGRAM 25

FILE MAINTENANCE

This program allows you to create and maintain the files which are required by Programs #1 - #23 by giving you a choice of three operations
as follows:

(1) Enter data into a new file (create a new file).

(2) Add data to an old file (update the data file).

(3) Change data in an old file (edit a data file).

DATA SOURCE. The "Data Source" section of each program describes
the numbers used as data, suggested file names, and file types for that
program. Please refer to the program whose files you are dealing with
for that information. Most of the programs give mandatory file names
and the minimum number of data points necessary to run the program.
You should be familiar with these requirements before you attempt to
create data files for a given program.

PROGRAM USE. Simply follow these three steps:

Step 1. Run the program by following the procedure given in the general
program instructions STEP 4.

Step 2. Enter the name of the file that you wish to create or change.
(Mandatory and suggested file names can be found in the "Data Source"
section of each individual program description.)

Step 3. Specify the file type as specified in the "Data Source" section
which describes the file. File type 3 requires one number for each entry, while the other file types require several numbers or words to be
entered. The program will ask you for entry of the required data. (See
below for full description of file types.)

CREATING NEW DATA FILES. *File creation* must be done before
you run any program that uses a given data file and you must enter a

minimum number of data points as specified in the "Data Source" section of each individual program. Be sure to read the information concerning file names and the mandatory number of data points given on the instruction page of each program before you create a data file for that program.

Step 1. Follow the procedure for using programs given in the general program instructions.

Step 2. The program will ask you for your choice of operation. Press 1.

Step 3. The program will then ask you for a file name. Type the name of the file that you wish to create and press return.

Step 4. The program will ask you for the file type. Press the number that corresponds to the file type specified in the "Data Source" section of where the file was described.

Step 5. The program will now ask you to begin entering data.

Step 6. After you make each entry and press return the program will ask you if the entry is correct. If it is, press Y; if not, press N and the program will allow you to re-enter the data.

Step 7. If the entry is correct, the program will ask if there are more entries to be made. If there are, press Y and continue entering. If there are no data points left to enter, press N and the file will be saved on the disk in the disk drive.

UPDATING DATA FILES. *File updating* allows you to add new data to your file as it becomes available. To use this option, follow the steps above for file creation but in step 2 press the choice #2 instead of #1. File updating can only be performed on files which have already been created.

MAKING CHANGES IN DATA FILES. *File editing* allows you to change previously entered data which are incorrect. In order to use this option you must keep a list of the entries numbered in sequence from oldest to newest. This will allow you to identify the entry that will be edited by entering the number associated with that entry when the program requests it. Simply follow these steps:

Steps 1 and 2. (Same as file creation above).

Step 3. Select #3. This can only be performed on a file which has already been created and there is no limit to the number of data points which may be edited.

Step 4. (Same as file creation above).

Step 5. The program will now request the number of the entry to be corrected.

Steps 6 - 7. (Same as file creation above). In addition if you wish to view the data that is currently in the file simply press return when you are prompted for an entry. The current value for that entry will be displayed and the program will proceed to the next entry. If you wish to modify an entry displayed in this manner press N when asked if the entry is correct. Pressing return alone does not modify an entry value but it can be used to skip over correct entries to the get to incorrect entry which you do wish to edit.

There are four specific types of files used by the programs in this book. The text below presents an overview of the organization of these files. (For additional information on random files consult the DOS manual for your hardware option.)

Type 1. File Type 1 is used to store daily information on stocks or commodities. Each data point contains all of the information for a single day and it is stored in the file as a line of 39 digits. The line of digits is organized as follows:

Information	Digit Number
Day of week	1
Monday - 1	
Tuesday - 2	

Wednesday - 3

Thursday - 4

Friday - 5

Date - (yymmdd)   2 - 7

Opening price   8 - 12

(closing price if stock)

High price   13 - 17

Low price   18 - 22

Closing price   23 - 27

Volume   28 - 33

Open interest   34 - 39

Example: DECEMBER GOLD   Tuesday, August 30, 1983

OPEN	HIGH	LOW	CLOSE	VOLUME	OPEN INTEREST
427.50	430.20	425.50	428.50	23,000	45,609

The information given above would appear in the file as the following 39 digit number:
283083042750430204255042850023000045609.

Type 2. File Type 2 is used to store daily advance/ decline information with each entry containing all of the information for a single day. The entry is stored in the file as a line of 27 digits, organized as follows:

Information	Digit Number
Number of Advancing Issues	1 - 5

Number of Declining Issues	6 - 10
Number of Unchanged Issues	11 - 15
Volume of Advancing Issues	16 - 21
Volume of Declining Issues	22 - 27

Example: Friday, September 16, 1983

Advancing Issues	Declining Issues	Unchanged Issues	Volume of Advancing Issues	Volume of Declining Issues
1,008	551	394	55,569,600	12,926,800

The information given above would appear in the file as the following 27 digit number:

010080055100394555696129268.

Type 3. File Type 3 is used to store many different kinds of data. Each entry is a single eight-digit number and may represent daily, weekly, or monthly data.

Type 4. File Type 4 is used only for the file NAMES described in Program #20. Each entry is a string of 35 characters representing an industry stock group name and the suggested file name associated with it, and is organized as follows:

Information	Digit Number
File Name	1 - 8
Stock Group Name	9 - 35

Example:

INDUSTRY GROUP NAME	SUGGESTED FILE NAME
Foods and Beverages	FOOD&BEV

The information given above would appear in the file as the following 35 character string: FOOD&BEVFOODS AND BEVERAGES.

PROGRAM #25   LISTING FOR APPLE II+ OR IIe

```
10    TEXT : HOME : VTAB 2: HTAB 4
20    PRINT "ACTION TO PERFORM": VTAB 4
30    HTAB 7: PRINT "1 - ENTER DATA IN A NEW FILE"
40    VTAB 5: HTAB 7
50    PRINT "2 - ADD DATA TO AN OLD FILE"
60    VTAB 6: HTAB 7
70    PRINT "3 - CHANGE DATA IN AN OLD FILE"
80    VTAB 8: HTAB 9: PRINT "PLEASE CHOOSE";
90    GET A: IF (A < 1) OR (A > 3) GOTO 90
100   VTAB 12: HTAB 6: PRINT D$
110   INPUT "ENTER NAME OF FILE ";F$: HOME
120   VTAB 2: HTAB 4: PRINT "TYPE OF FILE"
130   VTAB 4: HTAB 7
140   PRINT "1 - STOCK OR COMMODITY FILE"
150   VTAB 5: HTAB 7
160   PRINT "2 - ADVANCE - DECLINE FILE"
170   VTAB 6: HTAB 7
180   PRINT "3 - OTHER FILES"
190   VTAB 7: HTAB 7
200   PRINT "4 - NAMES FILE"
210   VTAB 9: HTAB 9: PRINT "PLEASE CHOOSE";
220   GET T: IF (T < 1) OR (T > 4) GOTO 220
225   HOME : VTAB 10: HTAB 7: PRINT "WORKING . ."
230   D$ =  CHR$ (4): IF T = 1 THEN P = 40
240   PRINT D$: IF T = 2 THEN P = 28
250   IF T = 3 THEN P = 8
260   IF T = 4 THEN P = 35
270   PRINT D$;"OPEN ";F$;",L";P
280   IF A = 1 THEN X = 1: GOTO 400
290   IF A < > 2 GOTO 320
300   PRINT D$;"READ ";F$;",R0"
310   INPUT X:X = X + 1: PRINT D$
320   IF A < > 3 GOTO 400
330   VTAB 20: HTAB 4
340   INPUT "ENTER DATA POINT NUMBER ";X
350   PRINT D$;"READ ";F$;",R";X
360   INPUT R$: PRINT D$
400   IF T = 1 THEN  GOSUB 600
410   IF T = 2 THEN  GOSUB 1100
420   IF T = 3 THEN  GOSUB 1500
430   IF T = 4 THEN  GOSUB 1600
440   PRINT D$;"WRITE ";F$;",R";X
442   IF T = 1 THEN R$ = R1$ + R2$ + R3$ + R4$ + R5$
      + R6$ + R7$ + R8$
444   IF T = 2 THEN R$ = R1$ + R2$ + R3$ + R4$ + R5$
```

```
446   IF T = 4 THEN R$ = R1$ + R2$
448   PRINT R$: PRINT D$
450   VTAB 22: HTAB 4: PRINT "MORE DATA POINTS ?";
460   GET MR$: IF (MR$ <> "Y") AND (MR$ <> "N") GOTO 460
470   PRINT D$:HOME:IF MR$ = "Y" THEN X = X + 1:GOTO 320
480   IF A = 3 GOTO 500
490   PRINT D$;"WRITE ";F$;",RO": PRINT X
500   PRINT D$;"CLOSE ";F$: HOME :END
600   HOME : VTAB 2: HTAB 4
610   INPUT "ENTER DAY OF WEEK (1-5) ";Z$
620   IF A < > 3 GOTO 660
625 R1$ =   LEFT$ (R$,1)
630   IF Z$ = "" THEN Z$ = R1$
640   VTAB 3: HTAB 2: PRINT "FIGURE WAS ";
650   PRINT R1$;" FIGURE IS NOW ";Z$
660 R1$ =   LEFT$ (Z$,1):Z$ = "": VTAB 4
670   HTAB 4: INPUT "ENTER DATE (YYMMDD) ";Z$
680   IF A < > 3 GOTO 720
685 R2$ =   MID$ (R$,2,6)
690   IF Z$ = "" THEN Z$ = R2$
700   VTAB 5: HTAB 2: PRINT "FIGURE WAS ";
710   PRINT R2$;" FIGURE IS NOW ";Z$
720 R2$ =   LEFT$ (Z$,6):Z$ = "": VTAB 6
730   HTAB 4: INPUT "ENTER OPENING PRICE ";Z$
740   IF A < > 3 GOTO 780
745 R3$ =   MID$ (R$,8,5)
750   IF Z$ = "" THEN Z$ = R3$
760   VTAB 7: HTAB 2: PRINT "FIGURE WAS ";
770   PRINT R3$;" FIGURE IS NOW ";Z$
780 R3$ =   RIGHT$ ("     " + Z$,5):Z$ = "": VTAB 8
790   HTAB 4: INPUT "ENTER HIGHEST PRICE ";Z$
800   IF A < > 3 GOTO 840
805 R4$ =   MID$ (R$,13,5)
810   IF Z$ = "" THEN Z$ = R4$
820   VTAB 9: HTAB 2: PRINT "FIGURE WAS ";
830   PRINT R4$;" FIGURE IS NOW ";Z$
840 R4$ =   RIGHT$ ("     " + Z$,5):Z$ = "": VTAB 10
850   HTAB 4: INPUT "ENTER LOWEST PRICE ";Z$
860   IF A < > 3 GOTO 900
865 R5$ =   MID$ (R$,18,5)
870   IF Z$ = "" THEN Z$ = R5$
880   VTAB 11: HTAB 2: PRINT "FIGURE WAS ";
890   PRINT R5$;" FIGURE IS NOW ";Z$
900 R5$ =   RIGHT$ ("     " + Z$,5):Z$ = "": VTAB 12
910   HTAB 4: INPUT "ENTER CLOSING PRICE ";Z$
920   IF A < > 3 GOTO 960
925 R6$ =   MID$ (R$,23,5)
930   IF Z$ = "" THEN Z$ = R6$
940   VTAB 13: HTAB 2: PRINT "FIGURE WAS ";
```

```
950    PRINT R6$;" FIGURE IS NOW ";Z$
960  R6$ =  RIGHT$ ("     " + Z$,5):Z$ = "": VTAB 14
970    HTAB 4: INPUT "ENTER VOLUME ";Z$
980    IF A <  > 3 GOTO 1020
985  R7$ =  MID$ (R$,28,6)
990    IF Z$ = "" THEN Z$ = R7$
1000   VTAB 15: HTAB 2: PRINT "FIGURE WAS ";
1010    PRINT R7$;" FIGURE IS NOW ";Z$
1020  R7$ =  RIGHT$ ("      " + Z$,6):Z$ = "": VTAB 16
1030   HTAB 4: INPUT "ENTER OPEN INTEREST ";Z$
1040   IF A <  > 3 GOTO 1080
1045  R8$ =  MID$ (R$,34,6)
1050   IF Z$ = "" THEN Z$ = R8$
1060   VTAB 17: HTAB 2: PRINT "FIGURE WAS ";
1070    PRINT R8$;" FIGURE IS NOW ";Z$
1080  R8$ =  RIGHT$ ("      " + Z$,6):Z$ = "": VTAB 20
1090   HTAB 2: PRINT "ARE ALL THE FIGURES CORRECT ?";
1092    GET KG$: IF (KG$ <> "Y")AND(KG$ <> "N") GOTO 1092
1094    PRINT D$: IF KG$ = "N" GOTO 600
1096   HOME : RETURN
1100   HOME : VTAB 2: HTAB 3
1110   INPUT "NUMBER OF ADVANCING ISSUES ";Z$
1120   IF A <  > 3 GOTO 1160
1125  R1$ =  LEFT$ (R$,5)
1130   IF Z$ = "" THEN Z$ = R1$
1140   VTAB 3: HTAB 2: PRINT "FIGURE WAS ";
1150    PRINT R1$;" FIGURE IS NOW ";Z$
1160  R1$ =  RIGHT$ ("0000" + Z$,5):Z$ = "": VTAB 4
1170   HTAB 3: INPUT "NUMBER OF DECLINING ISSUES ";Z$
1180   IF A <  > 3 GOTO 1220
1185  R2$ =  MID$ (R$,6,5)
1190   IF Z$ = "" THEN Z$ = R2$
1200   VTAB 5: HTAB 2: PRINT "FIGURE WAS ";
1210    PRINT R2$;" FIGURE IS NOW ";Z$
1220  R2$ =  RIGHT$ ("0000" + Z$,5):Z$ = "": VTAB 6
1230   HTAB 3: INPUT "NUMBER OF UNCHANGED ISSUES ";Z$
1240   IF A <  > 3 GOTO 1280
1245  R3$ =  MID$ (R$,11,5)
1250   IF Z$ = "" THEN Z$ = R3$
1260   VTAB 7: HTAB 2: PRINT "FIGURE WAS ";
1270    PRINT R3$;" FIGURE IS NOW ";Z$
1280  R3$ =  RIGHT$ ("0000" + Z$,5):Z$ = "": VTAB 8
1290   HTAB 3: INPUT "VOLUME OF ADVANCING ISSUES ";Z$
1300   IF A <  > 3 GOTO 1340
1305  R4$ =  MID$ (R$,16,6)
1310   IF Z$ = "" THEN Z$ = R4$
1320   VTAB 9: HTAB 2: PRINT "FIGURE WAS ";
1330    PRINT R4$;" FIGURE IS NOW ";Z$
1340  R4$ =  RIGHT$ ("00000" + Z$,6):Z$ = "": VTAB 10
```

```
1350   HTAB 3: INPUT "VOLUME OF DECLINING ISSUES ";Z$
1360   IF A <  > 3 GOTO 1400
1365 R5$ =   MID$ (R$,22,6)
1370   IF Z$ = "" THEN Z$ = R5$
1380   VTAB 11: HTAB 2: PRINT "FIGURE WAS ";
1390   PRINT R5$;" FIGURE IS NOW ";Z$
1400 R5$ =   RIGHT$ ("00000" + Z$,6):Z$ = "": VTAB 20
1410   HTAB 2: PRINT "ARE ALL THE FIGURES CORRECT ?";
1420   GET KG$: IF (KG$ <> "Y")AND(KG$ <> "N") GOTO 1420
1430   PRINT D$: IF KG$ = "N" GOTO 1100
1440   HOME : RETURN
1500   HOME : VTAB 2: HTAB 4
1510   INPUT "ENTER DATA POINT ";Z$
1520   IF A <  > 3 GOTO 1560
1530   IF Z$ = "" THEN Z$ = R$
1540   VTAB 3: HTAB 2: PRINT "FIGURE WAS ";
1550   PRINT R$;" FIGURE IS NOW ";Z$
1560 R$ =   RIGHT$ ("        " + Z$,8):Z$ = "": VTAB 20
1570   HTAB 2: PRINT "IS THE FIGURE CORRECT ?";
1580   GET KG$: IF (KG$ <> "Y")AND(KG$ <> "N") GOTO 1580
1590   PRINT D$: IF KG$ = "N" GOTO 1500
1595   HOME : RETURN
1600   HOME : VTAB 2: HTAB 4
1610   INPUT "ENTER STOCK GROUP NAME ";Z$
1620   IF A <  > 3 GOTO 1660
1625 R1$ =   LEFT$ (R$,8)
1630   IF Z$ = "" THEN Z$ = R1$
1640   VTAB 3: HTAB 2: PRINT "FIGURE WAS ";
1650   PRINT R1$;" FIGURE IS NOW ";Z$
1660 R1$ = Z$:Z$ = "": VTAB 4
1670   HTAB 4: INPUT "ENTER SUGGESTED FILE NAME ";Z$
1680   IF A <  > 3 GOTO 1720
1685 R2$ =   RIGHT$ (R$,27)
1690   IF Z$ = "" THEN Z$ = R2$
1700   VTAB 5: HTAB 2: PRINT "FIGURE WAS ";
1710   PRINT R2$;" FIGURE IS NOW ";Z$
1720 R2$ = Z$:Z$ = "": VTAB 20
1730   HTAB 2: PRINT "ARE BOTH NAMES CORRECT ?";
1740   GET KG$: IF (KG$ <  > "Y") AND (KG$ <  > "N") GOTO 174
1750   PRINT D$: IF KG$ = "N" GOTO 1600
1760   HOME : RETURN
```

PROGRAM #25   LISTING FOR IBM PC

```
10 SCREEN 2:CLS:KEY OFF
20 LOCATE 8,8:PRINT "ACTION TO PERFORM"
30 LOCATE 10,10:PRINT "1 - ENTER DATA IN A NEW FILE"
```

```
40 LOCATE 11,10:PRINT "2 - ADD DATA TO AN OLD FILE"
50 LOCATE 12,10:PRINT "3 - CHANGE DATA IN AN OLD FILE"
60 LOCATE 14,12:PRINT "PLEASE CHOOSE ";
70 A$ = INKEY$:IF (A$ < "1") OR (A$ > "3") GOTO 70
80 LOCATE 20,10:INPUT; "ENTER NAME OF THE FILE";F$
90 CLS:LOCATE 8,8:PRINT "TYPE OF FILE"
100 LOCATE 10,10:PRINT "1 - STOCK OR COMMODITY FILE"
110 LOCATE 11,10:PRINT "2 - ADVANCE - DECLINE FILE"
120 LOCATE 12,10:PRINT "3 - OTHER FILES"
130 LOCATE 13,10:PRINT "4 - NAMES FILE"
140 LOCATE 15,12:PRINT "PLEASE CHOOSE ";
150 T$ = INKEY$:IF (T$ < "1") OR (T$ > "4") GOTO 150
160 CLS:LOCATE 12,15:PRINT "WORKING . . ."
170 IF T$ <> "1" GOTO 220
180 OPEN F$ AS #1 LEN=39
190 FIELD 1,1 AS D$,6 AS DA$,5 AS OF$,5 AS HF$,5 AS LF$
200 FIELD 1,22 AS ZZ$,5 AS CF$,6 AS VO$,6 AS OI$
210 FIELD 1,39 AS FL$
220 IF T$ <> "2" GOTO 260
230 OPEN F$ AS #1 LEN=28
240 FIELD 1,5 AS AD$,5 AS DC$,5 AS UN$,6 AS UV$,6 AS DV$
250 FIELD #1,28 AS FL$
260 IF T$ <> "3" GOTO 290
270 OPEN F$ AS #1 LEN=8:FIELD 1,8 AS F1$
280 FIELD #1,8 AS FL$
290 IF T$ <> "4" GOTO 320
300 OPEN F$ AS #1 LEN=35:FIELD #1,8 AS FT$,27 AS NF$
310 FIELD #1,35 AS FL$
320 IF A$ = "1" THEN X = 1
330 IF A$ = "2" THEN GET#1,1:X = VAL(FL$)
340 CLS:MR$ = "Y":WHILE MR$ = "Y":LOCATE 8,10
350 IF A$ = "3" THEN INPUT "ENTER DATA POINT NUMBER ";X
360 X = X + 1:KG$ = "N":IF A$ = "3" THEN GET #1,X
370 IF T$ = "1" THEN GOSUB 510
380 IF T$ = "2" THEN GOSUB 840
390 IF T$ = "3" THEN GOSUB 1070
400 IF T$ = "4" THEN GOSUB 1140
410 PUT #1,X
420 LOCATE 25,8:PRINT"MORE DATA POINTS TO ENTER (Y/N) ?"
430 MR$=INKEY$:IF (MR$ <> "Y")AND(MR$ <> "N") GOTO 430
440 CLS:WEND:LSET FL$ = "":IF A$ = "3" GOTO 500
450 IF T$ = "1" THEN LSET OF$ = STR$(X)
460 IF T$ = "2" THEN LSET AD$ = STR$(X)
470 IF T$ = "3" THEN LSET F1$ = STR$(X)
480 IF T$ = "4" THEN LSET FT$ = STR$(X)
490 PUT #1,1
500 CLS:LOCATE 1,1:CLOSE #1:RETURN
510 WHILE KG$="N":CLS:LOCATE 5,10:
    PRINT "ENTER DAY OF WEEK (1-5) ";
```

```
520 Z$ = INKEY$:IF (Z$ < "1") OR (Z$ > "5") GOTO 520
530 LSET D$ = Z$:Z$ = "":LOCATE 7,10
540 INPUT "ENTER DATE (YYMMDD) ";Z$
550 IF A$ <> "3" GOTO 570 ELSE IF Z$ = "" THEN Z$ = DA$
560 LOCATE 7,35:PRINT "FIGURE WAS ";DA$;
        " FIGURE IS NOW ";Z$
570 LSET DA$ = Z$:Z$ = ""
580 LOCATE 9,10:INPUT "ENTER OPENING PRICE ";Z$
590 IF A$ <> "3" GOTO 610 ELSE IF Z$ = "" THEN Z$ = OF$
600 LOCATE 9,35:PRINT "FIGURE WAS ";OF$;
        " FIGURE IS NOW ";Z$
610 LSET OF$ = Z$:Z$ = ""
620 LOCATE 11,10:INPUT "ENTER HIGHEST PRICE ";Z$
630 IF A$ <> "3" GOTO 650 ELSE IF Z$ = "" THEN Z$ = HF$
640 LOCATE 11,35:PRINT "FIGURE WAS ";HF$;
        " FIGURE IS NOW ";Z$
650 LSET HF$ = Z$:Z$ = ""
660 LOCATE 13,10:INPUT "ENTER LOWEST  PRICE ";Z$
670 IF A$ <> "3" GOTO 690 ELSE IF Z$ = "" THEN Z$ = LF$
680 LOCATE 13,35:PRINT "FIGURE WAS ";LF$;
        " FIGURE IS NOW ";Z$
690 LSET LF$ = Z$:Z$ = ""
700 LOCATE 15,10:INPUT "ENTER CLOSING PRICE ";Z$
710 IF A$ <> "3" GOTO 730 ELSE IF Z$ = "" THEN Z$ = CF$
720 LOCATE 15,35:PRINT "FIGURE WAS ";CF$;
        " FIGURE IS NOW ";Z$
730 LSET CF$ = Z$:Z$ = ""
740 LOCATE 17,10:INPUT "ENTER VOLUME   ";Z$
750 IF A$ <> "3" GOTO 770 ELSE IF Z$ = "" THEN Z$ = VO$
760 LOCATE 17,35:PRINT "FIGURE WAS ";VO$;
        " FIGURE IS NOW ";Z$
770 LSET VO$ = LEFT$(Z$,6):Z$ = ""
780 LOCATE 19,10:INPUT "ENTER OPEN INTEREST ";Z$
790 IF A$ <> "3" GOTO 810 ELSE IF Z$ = "" THEN Z$ = OI$
800 LOCATE 19,35:PRINT "FIGURE WAS ";OI$;
        " FIGURE IS NOW ";Z$
810 LSET OI$ = LEFT$(Z$,6):LOCATE 25,8:
        PRINT "ARE ALL THE FIGURES CORRECT (Y/N) ?";
820 KG$=INKEY$:IF (KG$ <> "Y")AND(KG$ <> "N") GOTO 820
830 Z$ = "":WEND:RETURN
840 WHILE KG$ = "N":CLS:Z$ = ""
850 LOCATE 9,10:INPUT"ENTER NUMBER OF ADVANCING ISSUES "
        ;Z$
860 IF A$ <> "3" GOTO 880 ELSE IF Z$ = "" THEN Z$ = AD$
870 LOCATE 10,40:PRINT "FIGURE WAS ";AD$;
        " FIGURE IS NOW ";Z$
880 LSET AD$ = Z$:Z$ = ""
890 LOCATE 11,10:INPUT"ENTER NUMBER OF DECLINING ISSUES "
        ;Z$
```

```
900 IF A$ <> "3" GOTO 920 ELSE IF Z$ = "" THEN Z$ = DC$
910 LOCATE 12,40:PRINT "FIGURE WAS ";DC$;
        " FIGURE IS NOW ";Z$
920 LSET DC$ = Z$:Z$ = ""
930 LOCATE 13,10:INPUT"ENTER NUMBER OF UNCHANGED ISSUES "
        ;Z$
940 IF A$ <> "3" GOTO 960 ELSE IF Z$ = "" THEN Z$ = UN$
950 LOCATE 14,40:PRINT "FIGURE WAS ";UN$;
        " FIGURE IS NOW ";Z$
960 LSET UN$ = Z$:Z$ = ""
970 LOCATE 15,10:INPUT"ENTER VOLUME OF ADVANCING ISSUES "
        ;Z$
980 IF A$ <> "3" GOTO 1000 ELSE IF Z$ = "" THEN Z$ = UV$
990 LOCATE 16,40:PRINT "FIGURE WAS ";UV$;
        " FIGURE IS NOW ";Z$
1000 LSET UV$ = Z$:Z$ = ""
1010 LOCATE 17,10:INPUT"ENTER VOLUME OF DECLINING ISSUES "
        ;Z$
1020 IF A$ <> "3" GOTO 1040 ELSE IF Z$ = "" THEN Z$=DV$
1030 LOCATE 18,40:PRINT "FIGURE WAS ";DV$;
        " FIGURE IS NOW ";Z$
1040 LSET DV$ = LEFT$(Z$,6):LOCATE 25,8:
        PRINT "ARE ALL THE FIGURES CORRECT (Y/N) ?";
1050 KG$=INKEY$:IF (KG$ <> "Y")AND(KG$ <> "N") GOTO 1050
1060 WEND:RETURN
1070 WHILE KG$ = "N":CLS:Z$ = ""
1080 LOCATE 5,10:INPUT "ENTER DATA POINT ";Z$
1090 IF A$ <> "3" GOTO 1110 ELSE IF Z$ = "" THEN Z$=F1$
1100 LOCATE 5,40:PRINT "FIGURE WAS ";F1$;
        " FIGURE IS NOW ";Z$
1110 LSET F1$ = Z$:LOCATE 25,8:
        PRINT "IS THE FIGURE CORRECT (Y/N) ?";
1120 KG$=INKEY$:IF (KG$ <> "Y")AND(KG$ <> "N") GOTO 1120
1130 WEND:RETURN
1140 WHILE KG$ = "N":CLS:Z$ = ""
1150 LOCATE 5,10:INPUT "ENTER STOCK GROUP NAME ";Z$
1160 IF A$ <> "3" GOTO 1180 ELSE IF Z$ = "" THEN Z$=NF$
1170 LOCATE 6,20:PRINT "NAME WAS ";NF$;
        " NAME IS NOW ";Z$
1180 LSET NF$ = Z$:Z$ = "":LOCATE 7,10:
        INPUT "ENTER SUGGESTED FILE NAME ";Z$
1190 IF A$ <> "3" GOTO 1210 ELSE IF Z$ = "" THEN Z$=FT$
1200 LOCATE 8,20:PRINT "FILE NAME WAS ";FT$;
        " FILE NAME IS NOW ";Z$
1210 LSET FT$ = Z$:LOCATE 25,8:
        PRINT "ARE BOTH NAMES CORRECT (Y/N) ?";
1220 KG$=INKEY$:IF (KG$ <> "Y")AND(KG$ <> "N") GOTO 1220
1230 Z$ = "":WEND:RETURN
```

APPENDIX

B

DATABASE AND SOFTWARE SOURCES

DATABASES

Commodity Systems, Inc.
200 W. Palmetto Park Road
Boca Raton, FL 33432

Cost varies with priority (time
  accessed) and number of
  contracts accessed.
Complete commodity data base
  including "perpetual" contracts.

CompuService Info. Ctr.
H & R Block
5000 Arlington Center Blvd.
Columbus, Ohio 43220

$30 one-time fee, plus $5
  per-hour user fee and 3 cents+
  per item.
Oldest database, with prices,
  volume and dividend data on
  40,000 stocks, bonds and
  options issued since 1974. It
  also includes Standard &
  Poor's and Value Line
  corporate files.

Interactive Data Corp.
486 Jotten Pond Road
Waltham, MA 02154

$50 per month basic fee +$.05
  per packet purchased in
  excess of 500 per month
Provides stock & option price
  information as well as various
  market indices.

News/Retrieval
Dow Jones & Co.
P.O. Box 300
Princeton, NJ 08540

$50 basic fee plus $75 annual
  charge & 10 cents and up
  per-minute user fee.
Market prices, news and

earnings estimates on 2,400 companies. Wall Street Week transcripts and 10-K extracts.

Remote Computing Corp.
1044 Northern Boulevard
Roslyn, NY 15576

Time-shared databases of options, commodities and securities featuring customized programming options. For the Apple.

Source Telecomputing
Readers Digest Assn.
1616 Anderson Rd.

$100 subscription fee, plus $7.75 per-hour user fee.
Price, volume, sales, earnings and 51 other financial benchmarks for 3,100 companies be grouped and ranked for screening.

SOFTWARE SOURCES

Apple Analyst
Intermountain Technical Services
P.O. Box 6062
Bellevue, WA 98007

Features 20 programs for technical analysis of the stock and commodities markets including a trading simulation option.
For the Apple.

Commodity Integrated Systems
David Anddman
505 N. Lake Shore Dr., #2203
Chicago, IL 60611

$1,500
Features range finder day-trading method of support and resistance points, based on smoothed moving averages.
For the TRS-80 I & III and Apple.

CompuTrac
Technical Analysis Group
1021 - 9th Street
New Orleans, VA 70115

$1,800, plus $200 annual
   fee
Advanced technical analy-
   sis programs including
   such mathematical exotica
   as regression analysis,
   momentum charting and
   demand aggregates. It
   combines price, volume
   and open interest figures
   into one indicator.

Crawford Data Systems
Optionx, Version 1.0
P.O. Box 705
Somis, CA 93066

$95
Calculates the correct
   theoretical value of an
   option by using the Black-
   Scholes and Cleeton
   mathematical models.
For the Apple.

Fashion International
Ivan Holt
2467 Fashion Avenue
Long Beach, CA 90810

$450
Researches all moving average crossover systems to
   find currently profitable
   systems.
For the Apple and TRS-80.

Hop Research
H. J. Wilson
P.O. Box 5784
Pasadena, TX 77505

Contains 18 programs on
   market analysis based on
   the book "Advanced
   Commodity Trading Techniques."
For Apple II and TRS-80.

Intraday Analyst
Technical Analysis Group
1021 9th Street
New Orleans, VA 70115

$1,500
Calculates up-to-the-
   minute quotes and emits
   an "audible alarm" when
   any of up to 20 commodity contracts exceeds a stop
   point.

Investors' Micro Messenger
George Arndt
P. O. Box 319
Harvard, MA 01451

Provides stock and com-
modity software - many
different systems.

Investpak
McGraw Hill Publ. Co.
1221 Avenue of the Americas
New York, YN 10020

$200
Computes, among other
things, transaction
costs, stock and portfo-
lio valuations and upside
breakeven points for a
strip or straddle on
several options.

Kate's Komputers (Advisor)
Box 1675
Sausalito, CA 94965

$600
Provides instant analysis
of portfolio value and
tracks options approach-
ing parity, gains or
losses and stop points.

Kate's Komputers (Analyst)
Box 1675
Sausalito, CA 94965

$600
Graphics system for technical analysis of the stock
and commodities markets.
Produces bar charts, point
and figure, and
logarithms.
Also can generate and display any technical
formula. For the Apple.

Macro-Trend
Steven Bollt
7420 Westlake Ter., Ste. 1509
Bethesda, MD 20817

$2,000 for 1-year lease
Commodity trading program
For the Apple.

Magnum System
Management Services
2901 Clendenen Lane

$350
Program allows testing of
stock or commodity

Longview, TX 75601

trading systems to determine profit potential and allow for refinements.
For the TRS-80, I, II & III

Mar-tec Stock Market Software
Technical Analysis Package
33794 Copper Lantern
Dana Point, Ca 92629

$490
Uses cyclic timing techniques using two moving averages. (These techniques were demonstrated in this book.)
For TRS-80, Models I & III.

Market Analyzer
Dow Jones News Retrival
P.O. Box 300
Princeton, NJ 08540

$350
Is an assortment of basic and intermediate technical analysis procedures like oscillators of moving averages and cumulative volume indicators.

Market Analyzer
N-Squared Computing
P.O. Box 264
Silverton, OR 97381

$295
Technical analysis software includes exponential smoothing, arithmetic averaging, ratios, sums, differences, transforms, detrends and time-lag analyses.
Also advance-decline line indicators.
For the IBM-PC.

Market Illustrator
N-Squared Computing
P.O. Box 264
Silverton, OR 97381

$195
Program plots, smooths and displays ratios and differences for the nontechnical investor. Program features include a split screen for comparing data

with program-generated indicators.
Also includes a weekly historical data base made up of over 130 statistics compiled from *Barron's*.
For the IBM-PC.

Market Micropscope
Dow Jones & Co.
P.O. Box 300
Princeton, NJ 08540

$700
Simultaneously analyzes up to 20 of 68 financial variables on 3,200 stocks and can rank securities based on estimated earnings.

Market Technical Analysis
Ampero Software Products
5230 Clark Ave., Suite 12-A
Lakewood, CA 90712

$39.95
Programs include cycle analysis, moving averages, OBV, momentum and strength indicators.
For the TRS-80.

Market Tracker
H & H Trading Company
P.O. Box 549
Clayton, Ca 94517

$190
Stock market timing program designed to catch intermediate-term swings in the Dow Jones Industrial Average.
Provides an intermediate composite market index via six technical indicators.
For Apples and TRS-80

Micro/Scan
ISYS Corp.
50 Chuch Street

$3,600
Price includes monthly updates of prices and

Cambridge, MA 02238

corporate financial data
for a fundamental
analysis of 1,400 stocks;
26 variables can be
selected and companies
ranked by stock
market price multiple,
discount to book value
and other combinations.

The Monitor
First Flight Data Systems
P.O. Box 555
Kitty Hawk, NC 27949

$2,300
Real time ticker and portfolio monitoring program
that allows user to log on
to the New York Stock
Exchange ticker consolida-
ted "A" tape without the
15-minute delay.
Program computes A/D
line, upticks and down-
ticks, and a data file on
up to 4,000 stocks.
For the Apple.

On-balance Volume Charting
Stock Market Software
44 Front Street
Ashland, MA 01721

$1,500 plus $300 annual fee
Program charts the on-
balance volume, price and
moving averages for user-
selected stocks.
For the Apple.

Optioncalc
Savant Software
P.O. Box 440278
Houston, TX 77042

$65
Calculates theoretical
values of put and call
options.
For the IBM and Apple.

Options-80
Box 471
Concord, MA 01742

$125
Stock options investing
program.

Options Analysis
Rocky Mountain Computer
System
4427 Dalhart Road, N.W.
Calgary, Alberta,
CANADA T3A 1B8

For the Apple II and TRS-80 I & III.

$995
Analyzes calls, puts, combinations, ratio writes and more
For the TRS-80.

Portware
15724 Tucker Lane
Edina, MN 55436

$440; Trial $49.50
A system for option trading
For the Apple.

ProfitTaker
Investment Growth Corporation
3601 Swann Avenue, Suite 205
Tampa, FL 33609

$1495
Commodity Trading System Software generates precise buy-sell trading signals. Forecasts signals for next day's close. All system parameter values are user selectable. Includes ProfitAnalyst history tester. CSI compatible. Available on floppy or hard disk for Apple and IBM.

Smart
Software Resources, Inc.
186 Alewife Brook Parkway
Cambridge, MA 02138

$1,750 plus $400 license fee
Provides the capability to graph and analyze stocks, bonds, commodities, options and related economic indices. Data is available from their own data service.
Advanced statistical features such as descriptive statistics and regression analysis are also available.
Price varies with options.
For the Apple.

SMAS
Spiral Enterprises
P.O. Box 5219
Fort Worth, TX 76986

$169.95
Combines fundamental and
technical analysis to
select and track stocks
as well as the general
market.
For TRS-80, Models I & III.

Stock and Options Analysis
Creative Computing Software
P.O. Box 789-M
Morristown, NJ 07960

$99.95
How to hedge listed options
against common stocks.
For the TRS-80.

Stock Market Monitor
Galactic Software Ltd.
11520 N. Port Washington Road
Mequon, WI 53092

$89.00
Tells if stock is outper-
forming or underperform-
ing the general market.
For the TRS-80.

Stock and Options Strategy Sys.
Creative Logic Systems
P.O. Box 8320
Waco, TX 76710

$149
A portfolio system that
allows you to track all
types of investments.
Includes a weekly news-
letter detailing stock
selection strategy.
For TRS-80 Model II & III.

Stock Option Evaluator
Sported Microsoftware, Inc.
355 California Drive, Suite 121
Burlingame, CA 94010

$50/month licensing fee.
Program enables the
investor to determine the
theoretical values of
stock price, volatility
and interest rates.
For the Apple.

Stock Tracker
H & H Trading Company
P.O. Box 549
Clayton, Ca 94517

Cost varies.
Program provides buy/sell/
hold signals including
pyramiding. Compatible

with Dow Jones
Database.
For Apple I, II & III; TRS-
80 I & II.

Stockcalc
RLJ Software Applications
306 West Wolcott Street
Hillsdale, MI 49242

Stock analysis system for
the IBM-PC.

Stockchart II
Micro-Investment Software
9621 Bowie Way
Stockton, Ca 95209

$350
Uses Granville's "On
Balance Volume" analysis
for identifying volume
breakout and volume field
trend of stocks.
For IBM-PC.

Stockcraft
Decision Economics, Inc.
14 Old Farm Road
Cedar Knolls, NJ 07927

$148
Program contains portfolio
management feature as
well as technical analysis
and plotting.
For the Apple.

Stockpak
Standard & Poors Corp.
25 Broadway
New York, NY 10004

$50 plus $200 annual update
fee
A beginner's fundamental
analysis kit, containing
30 financial categories on
900 companies, runs on
only Radio Shack
personal computers.

Stockplot
Cook Compusystems
309 Lincolnshire
Irving, TX 75061

$99
Provides storage of stock or
commodity data. Plots
bar charts, point and
figure charts, and moving
averages. Requires 64K.

Stop Options Tracking
Finsoft
16-06 Quail Ridge Drive
Plainsboro, NJ 08536

$49
Analyzes put/call options, spreads, hedges, strategies and covered or uncoverd writing. Also identifies undervalued options.
For the IBM-PC.

Strohl Stock System
Strohl Systems Group
Plymouth Meeting, PA 19462

$495
Analyzes trends of selected stocks indicating buy, sell and stop recommendations.
For the IBM-PC.

Technical Trader
Memory Systems
5212 Hoffman
Skokie, IL 60077

$350
Provides commodity software.

Wall Street Plotter
Dickens Data Systems, Inc.
3050 Holcomb Bridge Rd., Ste. A
Norcross, GA 30071

$125
Program provides technical analysis of stocks, commodities and market averages.
For the Apple.

Wall Street Tap
Software, Inc.
810 West Broadway
Vancouver, BC,
CANADA V52 4C9

$149.95
Three programs provide moving averages, point and figure, OBV and other technical studies.
For the Apple I, II and TRS-80 I and III.

INDEX